Liliane
FRIEDRICH
A Psychological Appro

Liliane Frey-Rohn

# FRIEDRICH NIETZSCHE

## A Psychological Approach
## to his Life and Work

**DAIMON**
VERLAG

Title of the original German edition:
*Jenseits der Werte seiner Zeit:*
*Friedrich Nietzsche im Spiegel seiner Werke,*
by Liliane Frey-Rohn;
edited by Lela Fischli and Robert Hinshaw.
ISBN 3-85630-016-3
Copyright © 1984 by Daimon Verlag, Zürich.

*Friedrich Nietzsche: A Psychological Approach to his Life and Work,*
by Liliane Frey-Rohn;
edited by Robert Hinshaw and Lela Fischli;
translated from the German by Gary Massey.

First edition copyright © 1988 by Daimon Verlag,
Am Klosterplatz, CH-8840 Einsiedeln, Switzerland

ISBN 3-85630-507-6

Original cover design and illustration by Joel T. Miskin,
adapted for this English edition by Adrienne Pearson.

In grateful memory
of my honored teacher
C.G. Jung

# CONTENTS

## TRANSLATOR'S NOTE

The footnote reference to primary sources in this book are to the standard German-language editions, where appropriate followed by references to the standard English translations (in brackets). In the case of Nietzsche, no standard translation of his collected works appears to be available, and so I have omitted from the footnotes the various translations that have been consulted, listing them here, instead. Excellent translations of Nietzsche exist by Walter Kaufmann and R.J. Hollingdale, and these, by and large, have been directly employed in this work. At times, however, I have adapted these translations to the particular requirements of the text or replaced them with my own, especially where shorter phrases have been interpolated within Dr. Frey-Rohn's text. Furthermore, most of Nietzsche's bequest remains untranslated (apart from the passages included in *The Will to Power*): here, too, I have used my translations. The following translations of Nietzsche's works proved indispensable: *Basic Writings of Nietzsche,* translated and edited, with commentaries, by Walter Kaufmann, New York: Modern Library, 1968; *The Viking Portable Nietzsche,* edited and translated by Walter Kaufmann, Harmondsworth: Penguin Books, 1976; Friedrich Nietzsche, *The Gay Science,* translated, with a commentary, by Walter Kaufmann, New York: Vintage Books, 1974; Friedrich Nietzsche, *The Will to Power,* translated by Walter Kaufmann and R.J. Hollingdale, ed. Walter Kaufmann, New York: Vintage Books, 1968;

Friedrich Nietzsche, *Untimely Meditations,* trans. R.J. Hollingdale, Cambridge: Cambridge University Press, 1983; Friedrich Nietzsche, *Daybreak,* trans. R.J. Hollingdale, Cambridge: Cambridge University Press, 1982; Friedrich Nietzsche, *Dithyrambs of Dionysus,* trans. R.J. Hollingdale, Connecticut: Black Swan, 1984; Friedrich Nietzsche, *Human All-Too-Human,* trans. Marion Faber, with Stephen Lehmann, Lincoln: University of Nebraska Press, 1984. In addition, passages by C.G. Jung have been taken from the English translation of his *Collected Works,* Princeton: Princeton University Press, and London: Routledge and Kegan Paul, 1953-71 (indicated by 'C.W.'), whilst those by Freud are quoted from the Standard Edition of the *Complete Psychological Works of Sigmund Freud,* London: The Hogarth Press, and Toronto: Clark, Irwin and Co., 1953-74 (indicated by 'S.E.'). The translations of all other sources are my own.

G.M.

## EDITORS' FOREWORD

Many books have been written on the life and work of Friedrich Nietzsche, and it would be justifiable to ask what prompts yet another publication on this extraordinary figure.

In reading the first draft of this book, it was clear to us that the writer was providing not merely one more biographical sketch of Nietzsche. On the basis of the inexorable development of this particular individual, Liliane Frey-Rohn debates several questions central to life itself, questions that are of relevance to us all. One essential problem concerns the nature of good and evil, another, the notion of truth, and a third question discussed is the problem of nihilism as a direct consequence of losing the value of truth and of the death of God. Finally, the author examines, in the context of Nietzsche's great visions, the dangers arising from an identification of the personality with the numinosity of existence.

The life of Friedrich Nietzsche, with its incessant searching, its inner struggle, its critical debate with a world he saw as mendacious, and its many other deceptions and disorders, thus becomes exemplary for the striving of all humanity towards truth and meaning. Liliane Frey-Rohn has succeeded in using one individual's confrontation with the problems of good and evil to directly address the reader, and in such a way as to allow a clearer appreciation of our own life. She demonstrates various facets of this question with the subtle and discriminating insight of a psychologist who has herself experienced the depth of this issue in long years of work with her own analytical cases. As a result, the discussion goes well beyond a presentation of one man's fate: it addresses and brings understanding of an existential problem that faces us all and continues to pose ever new challenges to humankind.

Of further psychological and philosophical interest is the debate on the question of how we recognize truth, which was a quest fundamentally important to Nietzsche all his life. After first having sought an absolute truth, Nietzsche came to realize, in the course of his life, how fragile this ideal was in the light of the subjective impulses that emanate from the instincts. This ultimately led him to refute the possibility of true knowledge. His life is an illustration of how close the annulment of truth lay to nihilism. Although Nietzsche attempted to overcome his own nihilistic impulses, it provides an important insight into his own failure.

A third essential issue discussed by Liliane Frey in this book is that of the danger which can result from experiencing the eternal or the divine. Using the example of Nietzsche's own experiences, she displays the often unconscious tendencies of persons so affected to acquire notions of their own heroic and superior natures, and to fall prey to delusions of grandeur and fantasies of divinity. This psychic phenomenon of inflation is a particularly portentous stage in the development initiated by the identification of the ego with an externally projected, godlike image. If, in a period of enlightened positivism, one attributes to oneself these numinous experiences, and in so doing forgets one's own limitations and ignores the shadow side, then the chances of repeating the conflictual fate of a Friedrich Nietzsche in one's own particular way are considerable. How might we come to terms with these indelible experiences, so that they could be profitably integrated into human existence? The author denies that a generally valid answer can be given. She proceeds to guide the reader to an individual appraisal of this profound problem: she does so by highlighting important aspects in the psychological development of a man who was destroyed by his own search for his soul. Not only, therefore, does the author cast new light on the life of Friedrich Nietzsche as reflected in his works, but she also illuminates some of the problem areas of psychology that are of great concern to us all.

We are very pleased that this passionate and genuine contribution by Liliane Frey is now becoming available to English-language readers.

*Robert Hinshaw and Lela Fischli*

# PREFACE
## by Helmut Barz

In *On the Genealogy of Morals* (1887), Nietzsche wrote:

"Our educated people of today, our 'good people,' do not tell lies – that is true; but that is *not* to their credit! A real lie, a genuine, resolute, 'honest' lie (on whose value one should consult Plato) would be something far too severe and potent for them: it would demand of them what one *may* not demand of them, that they should open their eyes to themselves, that they should know how to distinguish 'true' and 'false' in themselves. All they are capable of is a *dishonest* lie; whoever today accounts himself a good man is utterly incapable of confronting any matter except with *dishonest mendaciousness* – a mendaciousness that is abysmal but innocent, true-hearted, blue-eyed and virtuous. These 'good men' – they are one and all moralized to the very depths and ruined and botched to all eternity as far as honesty is concerned: who among them could endure a single *truth* 'about man'? Or, put more palpably: who among them could stand a *true* biography?"

A hundred years later, an "educated person of today" has written a monograph of Nietzsche's work which, it seems to me, fully deserves to be called a "true biography" – not because it traces the dates and events of Nietzsche's life, but because it reconstructs his inner development.

xiii

Nietzsche is treated here neither with "true-hearted" nor "blue-eyed" nor "virtuous mendaciousness," but, as the careful reader will note, by an author who knows how to "distinguish 'true' and 'false' in [her]self" because she has "opened [her] eyes to (her)self."

Just as Nietzsche himself struggled with terrifying intensity to gain knowledge of himself, so his work is analyzed here in the pursuit of self-knowledge: neither objective learning nor subjective attachment and aversion are displayed in this book, which represents a search for "truth about man."

The tools employed in the course of this search consist predominantly of insights gained from depth psychology, those insights into the soul that Nietzsche had intuitively anticipated in such diverse and painful forms, but which were only fashioned into manageable implements after his death, during the development of the spirit *From Freud to Jung* (Liliane Frey's previous major work).

However, the apparatus of depth psychology has not, as often happens, become an end in itself by the insidious means of moulding the examined phenomena to close the circle and fit the initial theory. Quite the opposite is true: using the example of Nietzsche's life and fate C.G. Jung's psychology has once more demonstrated its validity, since it can help to "open [one's] eyes to [one]self" and give a clearer impression of "true biography," including one's own.

# FOREWORD

Whoever involves himself with Nietzsche finds himself both forced into a dialogue with this fervent spirit and compelled to take sides over his biting criticism of culture. Hardly any other thinker of the previous century has been the subject of so many contradictory assessments, with unconditional veneration standing alongside brusque rejection. Condemned by some as a precursor of National Socialism and praised by others as the creator of a new vision of life, Nietzsche's reputation is such that no one can remain indifferent to him. The clashing evaluations of his personality are evidence enough of the profundity of his world of ideas, which always went directly to the central human core. It was the extent to which the individual felt addressed by him that determined his (mis)understanding of Nietzsche, and it was mainly Nietzsche himself who was responsible for such a clash of interpretations. He wrenched men out of their comfortable self-satisfaction not only through the radically new direction of his thought, but also by virtue of the untimeliness of his concerns, whether they dealt with the demise of the Christian God, the 'will to power' or the inevitable nature of evil. These comments of mine are not intended to lessen the standing of Nietzsche. On the contrary, I am interested in shedding light on the exceptional greatness of this thinker who, haunted by prophetic misgivings, anticipated the nihilistic chaos of the future; who, profoundly moved by his conception of the 'great man,' regarded it his mission to perform a universal act of world-historical liberation that would ultimately prove his downfall.

Various phases may be determined in the reception of Nietzsche's ideas that correspond to the high demands set by his writings. After a period in which he was almost totally ignored, Nietzsche's tragic breakdown brought him into the public eye. It was amongst the youth of Germany in particular that a veritable storm of enthusiasm broke out. Constricted by the rigidity of the bourgeois moral code prevalent at the end of the 19th century, they saw Nietzsche as the man who would free them from the pressure of the family home and a traditional morality still influenced by the Victorian era. They were fascinated by the freedom of the individual and affirmation of life embodied by the 'overman' – though it must be added that they only seemed to grasp the deeper meaning of his work insofar as it coincided with the excesses of the movement they represented. We will only briefly mention the fact that similarly strong movements existed in France, Italy and Latin America, albeit in more moderate forms.

Although critical voices – among them Gerhart Hauptmann's – were raised in all quarters, the enthusiastic response to Nietzsche's writing lasted on into the 1930s. However, as his distressing fate grew more distant and forgotten with the passing of time, and with political events in Germany beginning to take a striking turn, the waves of excitement died down considerably.

Lou Salomé was the first to give an objective insight into Nietzsche's work and personality in *Friedrich Nietzsche in seinen Werken* [*Friedrich Nietzsche in his Works*] (1894), a study based on her real-life experience of the man. Significant exponents of the reader-response approach to Nietzsche's work were Heinrich Mann and, more importantly, his brother Thomas, who attempted to grasp the import of Nietzsche as a philosopher and cultural critic. For the latter, Nietzsche embodied a lifelong and highly valued spiritual phenomenon that was principally related to those of his early ideas influenced by Schopenhauer and Wagner. He became more moderate in his enthusiasm as a result of the atrocities perpetrated during the Hitler era and began to emphasize the dangers of interpreting Nietzsche too literally. In *Doctor Faustus,* he created an unforgettable monument to Nietzsche's "awe-inspiring fate."

Gottfried Benn, another admirer of Nietzsche's writings, wrote retrospectively of him: "In my time he was the earthquake that shook the epoch," the "greatest shock Germany had ever had." He was particularly concerned to prove that Nietzsche had nothing to do with the catastrophe of National Socialism, a defence that confronted many a charge levelled against Nietzsche after the Second World War.

In this respect, Ernst Bertram assumed a curious position. On the one hand, he praised the mystical ascension of Nietzsche's madness, which he compared to the crucifixion of Christ, while on the other, he made insinuations about the ambiguity of his philosophical views that made an issue of Nietzsche's reputation amongst the National Socialists. He thus establishes a link with notions of the dubious role Nietzsche was rumored to have played as a pioneer of this movement. Nietzsche's sister, Frau Elisabeth Förster-Nietzsche, also had a hand in suggesting such supposed connections. By means of clever deceptions, she clearly intended that her brother should emerge as one sympathetic to anti-semitism and the National Socialist cause in order to increase the prestige of her husband, himself an inveterate anti-semite. Among other things, the quite tendentious and arbitrary assembly of parts of his literary bequest and their publication in the one-volume *Will to Power* was an aspect of this intention, and produced an entirely distorted picture of Nietzsche. The various falsifications, suppressions and omissions made in the first editions of his works, and later uncovered by Schlechta and Podach, were similarly designed to serve this end. It was substitutions such as these that formed the basis of the so-called legend of Nietzsche pieced together by Bäumler, a writer and philosopher in the service of National Socialism.

In truth and deed, Nietzsche fought against both anti-semitism and German nationalism, not least as embodied by the whole Bismarckian era. He had already described nationalism as "the malady of the century" at the time of his professorship in Basle, and it was a thought as alien to him as racism. Yet it cannot be denied that Nietzsche's glorifications of power and strength easily lent themselves to certain misinterpretations of him as a harbinger of National Socialism. So much for the initial reception of Nietzsche's work in Germany, which tended to be a confusion of disparate interpretations derived from a lack of reliable information, a situation that was only remedied with the publication of Curt F. Janz's biography of Nietzsche some 80 years after his death.

Janz's three-volume work is extremely reliable and as such immeasurable valuable in filling a crucial gap in our knowledge of the life and work of Nietzsche. Equally helpful is the critical edition of his works brought out by Colli and Montinari, who follow a strictly chronological order in the publication of the literary bequest and thus facilitate an historical understanding of Nietzsche's gradual development and of the specific motivation behind the isolated and often disconnected aphorisms scattered throughout the works.

My own interest in Nietzsche, the human being, stretches back to my high school days. An early fascination on my part for Richard Wagner inevitably spilled over to the figure of his sometime friend Nietzsche. My thesis on Wilhelm Dilthey then brought me into contact with Nietzsche's philosophy of life. Some years later, I deepened my psychological understanding of him by attending a seminar, held for many years by C.G. Jung, on the work *Thus Spoke Zarathustra*. I shall never forget Jung's illuminating comments on Nietzsche's sufferings of the spirit, which he experienced both as a cruel hammer and a tortured anvil. When I was later occupied with the psychology of evil, Nietzsche's 'revaluation of values' once more proved invaluable. Last but not least, throughout those years I was also able to recognize that his aphorisms on self-deception and the untruthfulness of morality reflected my own pain when moral values were corrupted.

The more I became involved with Nietzsche's personality, the more intense my desire grew to understand – as far as one may understand a creative figure at all – the work and fate of this thinker who stands at a turning point in the history of western culture. My study on the gradual formation of his world of ideas limits itself to the presentation of a picture of Nietzsche based on my experiences in the field of psychology.

I remained uncertain for a long time whether to opt for a systematic or a chronological method of presentation. Being principally concerned with tracing the process of development and change undergone by Nietzsche, I decided on the latter. The division of my work into the periods before, during and after *Thus Spoke Zarathustra* is the result of the special position occupied by that work, which I regard as the most valuable document for a plotting of his inner development. Here we see spontaneous experience erupting forth directly from the unconscious and revealing an inner path of rare and inexhaustible richness to the student of psychology.

Before proceeding to this inner process and turning my attention to how Nietzsche's life is reflected in his works, I would like to supplement this with a look at Nietzsche's external development, at the Nietzsche who emerges from such biographical data as his profession, his friendships and his illness.

As a psychologist I have had to forgo an assessment of his historical and philosophical significance in order to get close to what finally turned out to be the unfathomable mystery of his influential power. I sought to close my study with a comprehensive critical appreciation in the form of an epilogue.

I would like to extend warmest thanks to my friend, Aniela Jaffé, for her invaluable encouragement throughout the course of my work. I am equally indebted to Dr.

Helmut Barz, President of the C.G. Jung Institute, for kindly revising my manuscript and for his many fruitful comments. I would like to thank the Psychological Club of Zürich, the Linda Fierz Foundation and the C.G. Jung Institute of Zürich for their financial support of the original German edition of this book, and the latter for renewed assistance with the present edition.

I am also grateful to Lela Fischli for her invaluable suggestions in working on the original manuscript, to Dr. Gary Massey for his faithful translation, index and general assistance with this English edition, and to Dr. Robert Hinshaw, the publisher, for his many contributions and unflagging support of this project from the very beginning.

Last but not least, I would like to express my deepest gratitude to my revered teacher, C.G. Jung, for opening my eyes to the hidden secrets of the soul.


Zürich, April 1988     *L.F.-R.*

> "You sought the heaviest burden
> and you found *yourself* –
> it is a burden you cannot throw off..."*

# INTRODUCTION

## 1. Personality

Friedrich Nietzsche represents a complex and contradictory figure who may be counted as one of the turn of the century's most controversial thinkers. After an initial period of almost total obscurity for a number of years, he was discovered at the beginning of the 20th century and since the Second World War has undergone something of a renaissance. Even today, no one seeking out his work remains unaffected by it. His writings exert a fascination that arrests and captivates.

What I am repeatedly impressed by in Nietzsche is the inexorability of his struggle with existence, a struggle conducted, despite early physical weaknesses and a confusing multiplicity of talents, with admirable heroism to the very point of his breakdown. Compelled from within to confront his *daimon* and find expression for his plight, he allowed his urgent inner need largely to take control of him.

Nietzsche's unswerving loyalty to his own experience of life and to himself is moving. Following his emotions

---

\* Friedrich Nietzsche, *Gesammelte Werke,* vol. VIII, p. 423, or Nietzsche, *Kritische Studienausgabe* by Colli-Montinari, vol. 6, p. 391.
  Henceforth 'Ges. W.' will refer to the Kröner octavo edition in 16 vols., and 'CM' to the critical edition by Colli-Montinari.

without prejudice, he only felt obliged to recognize what he had wrested from life. It is an attitude that does not shy away from anything novel or unfamiliar, that is able to cast doubt on previous judgments, and that can unflinchingly sacrifice cherished values. The liveliness of his thought process unavoidably draws the reader into his questioning and enables him to become involved with problems no serious-minded person of today can afford to neglect or set aside. What occupied Nietzsche was fundamental to the culture of his age, and included such questions as: Why is there so much untruthfulness? What is genuine culture? What are the real motives behind human actions? What is good, what is evil? And finally: Is there a divine power beyond man and the human ego – beyond tradition and morality?

What distinguished his questioning was it untimely character; indeed, in *Twilight of the Idols,* Nietzsche described himself as untimely. The more he matured, the closer he came to his true self, the more he set himself against the values of his times. With a fanatical devotion to truth that became increasingly obvious, he denounced both the untruthful and spurious attitude and writing of his day and the erroneousness of traditional idealistic and metaphysical constructions – in short all those intellectual illusions he felt called upon to challenge and do battle with over and over again.

Quite apart from his bold venture to overthrow moral values and establish something beyond good and evil, he stood out by virtue of the unusual rigor of his ethical strength. His consciousness of having a mission to fulfil, the conviction that he had an inner vocation to complete a great work, represented the immutable constant in his restless existence and helped him overcome the many adverse blows of fate suffered in the course of his life. In his art of self-overcoming, he attained the near unattainable; it enabled him to subordinate everything to the pursuit of the self and of God, which were always deemed the higher goals.

2

Nietzsche fascinates his reader not only through his many-sided and multi-layered questioning, but also through the unique charm of his language. He knew how to breathe life into the long ineffable in the most subtle of ways, an ability he owed to the direct contact he possessed with the inner depths of his own nature.

His open-mindedness found further expression in the extreme sensitivity of his perceptions, his seismographic awareness, so to speak, of the dark and obscure sides of the unconscious processes at work in him and others. We must therefore not be surprised that such an inwardly open and vibrant personality should have been subject to changes of mood that ranged from devoted adoration to hate-filled loathing, from states of depressions to suicidal urges. Again and again his sensitivity formed the battleground of the contrasting tendencies within himself, a struggle made manifest in the form of a painful conflict between a pronounced 'Yes' and an equally pronounced 'No.' His receptivity to the tensions of his epoch was also due to his intense sensitivity, enabling him to be dimly conscious of, and anticipate, future happenings that were already taking shape – a gift of the gods that turned out to be more of a burden! And because his intuitions were always interwoven with his personal sorrow at contemporary events, it was not rare for the path of his own suffering to accord with his presentiment of the future.

Irrespective of the tension of opposites inherent in his nature, a tension that always pressed him into taking up the very opinion he was calling into question, one may discern in his work a unifying thread. Nietzsche doggedly followed a path he regarded as fateful right from the early work *Fate and History,* through to *The Antichrist* and *Ecce homo.* In his very contradictions he remained, to the end, and despite becoming progressively more aggressive in tone, true to himself.

In view of the revolutionary content of his world of ideas Nietzsche was largely misunderstood and even ignored by his contemporaries and this was what caused him the most suffering; it was far more painful than the torture of his painful illness. Thanks to the unbending strength of his self-discipline, he managed to find in both his physical pain and the suffering caused by his increasing isolation from the world the inspiration for a deepening and intensification of his personality. It is therefore not surprising that the saying: "Profound suffering makes noble: it separates" should come from him.

It was, of course, inevitable that his growing alienation from friends and contemporaries would loosen his grip on external reality to a degree that rendered his writings increasingly subjective and strained, and the rift between life and work wider and wider. Although right up to his mental breakdown, his intellect lost virtually none of its clarity or acuteness, the hectic tone of his language and the pathos of his self-expression in later works – above all the tendency towards excessive self-glorification and near idolization – openly display the shadow of his mental illness.

## 2. Biographical Data and Friendships

Nietzsche was born on the 15th October, 1844, in the village of Röcken, near Lützen (Germany); he was the son of a rural Protestant clergyman.* It was noted as a particular omen that he shared his birthday with King Wilhelm IV of Prussia, and not only his family, but he himself would later judge this coincidence an indication of future greatness.

Nietzsche's father was a modest man with a quiet temperament who valued austerity and had a love of order. He had royalist sympathies and possessed as the intermittent tutor of princes an acute sense of the aristocratic. In keeping with his origins he represented the rationalistic wing of Protestantism. His early death, striking his delicate and dependent boy at the age of five, plainly constitutes the traumatic childhood experience that was to leave deep scars on

* I have largely relied on Curt Janz's excellent biography for the external data on Nietzsche's life.

Nietzsche's later development. The depressive character trait that was already his own may well have been intensified by this, his childhood trust in fate shaken. As he himself pointed out, it certainly denied him the direction to be offered by the strict guidance of a superior, and also the opportunity to come to an understanding of the male intellect. It was not just the fact of the premature death so much as its cause – his father died of cerebral softening – that was to disconcert Nietzsche and awaken fears in him that his own headaches and eye trouble from an early age were symptoms of the same cerebral disease. The loss of his father was exacerbated by the fact that he could find in his mother, Franziska Oehler, neither the spiritual counterbalance to, nor an understanding of, his intellectual development. She was, instead, of a rather cool disposition, and though she cared for her son, he clearly missed the instinctive warmth she lacked.

Another factor responsible for hindering Nietzsche's growth into manhood was the family's move upon the death of the father to Naumburg, a small town on the Saale staunchly loyal to the monarchy. Nietzsche grew up there amid a circle of relations that was exclusively female. This, on the one hand, strengthened the feminine side of his being – his impressionability, contemplativeness and need of love and adoration –; on the other, it caused him to repress in his unconscious the image of his father, which found no nourishment in such an overpoweringly feminine environment. Living on as the original symbol of the 'great man,' this image was ever poised for projection onto a suitable figure.

The existence of a family tradition in which Nietzsche was rooted further handicapped his development. That powerful tradition had been shaped by the spiritual heritage of a number of clerical personages, but Nietzsche opposed it with an equally strong conviction of his own inner vocation. The conflict between his sense of duty to the spirit of his forefathers and his own individual sense of destiny produced within Nietzsche's soul a psychical field of tension that would be the focal point of further and repeated conflicts, and of attempted resolutions.

Isolated on the one side from the after-effects of both the French Revolution of 1848 and its bourgeois German counterpart, which manifested itself in the form of fermenting social unrest, and on the other from the rapid progress of the Industrial Revolution, Nietzsche's upbringing took place in an atmosphere of Christian piety and rural tranquility. During those years, he was depicted as a pious, well-behaved child with impeccable manners. His experiences of the natural world – wandering around "yellow, tall cornfields," delighting in the "thickly leaved nut trees" and the colorful splendor of "yellowing autumn"[1] – left a deep and lasting impression on his being. Until he was about ten years old he enjoyed a feeling of security that he himself reported as suddenly disappearing without apparent reason, bringing the happiness of his childhood to an end. This loss left behind a yearning in his soul 'to drink his fill' and, in the last analysis, a feeling of loneliness. Early compositions already betray his involvement in the world of music, a world in which he could give vent to his feelings.

At the age of ten he attended the *Gymnasium* or grammar school in Naumburg, and at fourteen gained a free place at the nearby monastery school of Schulpforta, from where many a poet and philosopher had gone out into the world (Fichte, Hölderlin and Klopstock, to name but three). Here he came into contact with a spirit of Prussian conservatism that was nevertheless open to the influence of humanism. It was during these years that Nietzsche acquired the discipline and self-mastery that continued to be his distinguishing characteristics. He also stood out by his fanatical adherence to adopted principles, which cast light on later and equally fanatical attempts to break loose from the constraints of law, tradition and order. His unexpected de-

1 Mazzino Montinari, *Nietzsche lesen* [*Reading Nietzsche*], p. 31. Reference to: Ges. W. vol III/1, p. 36, aph. 49; CM vol. 2/II/1 p. 401, aph. 49.

scription of God as "the father of Evil"[2] as part of his questioning on the origin of evil when he was about twelve, arising like some sort of erratic block amid the untroubled serenity of those days, is a notable anticipation of later thoughts. For the first time, a feeling for the "darkness of existence" (Benedetti) had taken hold of his soul.

It is extraordinarily stimulating to follow the process of change in him from a sensitive, impressionable youth to an independent, individual personality who, once free of the burden of familial and religious obligations, would mature into one of the most significant cultural critics of his time.

Notwithstanding the strength of his spirit, his self-discipline and his not inconsiderable self-assertion, Nietzsche suffered at an early age from an inner anxiety that seems to be the result both of being intellectually over-burdened and of poor health. He was very susceptible to infectious disorders of the throat with fevers, rheumatic illnesses and bouts of headaches and sleeplessness, and his near-sightedness also proved a lasting handicap. It needed an heroic will to live to be able to unify his physical delicacy, the sensitivity and 'musicality' of his soul, with his passionate desire to attack and win, in order to form a more or less consistent whole. In a process lasting more than 24 years, Nietzsche struggled with these unusually harsh provisions of fate, which finally overcame the strength of his body and soul to resist and brought on his mental breakdown.

His inner wrestling is already evident in his autobiographical entries between the ages of 14 and 18,[3] which reveal Nietzsche's early critical mentality. Even then he was

2 CM vol. 11, p. 253 (bequest): "When I was twelve years old I devised an eccentric Trinity: namely God the Father, God the Son and God the devil. My conclusion was that God, reflecting on himself, created the second divine being: but that in order to reflect on himself he had to reflect on his opposite, had therefore to create it. – This is how I began to philosophize."

3 *Der Werdende Nietzsche* [*Nietzsche Becoming Himself*], vol. 1, only available in vol. 1 of the Kröner Musarion edition and in the Colli-Montinari critical edition, as well as in a work edited by Elisabeth Förster-Nietzsche.

questioning Christian standards of behavior: both the coercion of conscience and implicit faith of Christian ideals represented a thorn in his flesh.

At the early age of eighteen (1862), when he was still at Schulpforta, Nietzsche wrote a short work entitled *Fate and History*,[4] remarkable for the fearlessness of its thought. Influenced by the writings of Feuerbach and Darwin, it anticipated later findings. Not only does one recognize here his doubts about the spiritual authority of Christianity (the existence of God, immortality, the absolute nature of morality),[5] but also his compensatory esteem for the world and for the individual. His glorification of the 'great personality' who renews humanity by virtue of his strength of will is equally clear. Equally important are the beginnings of a relativization of good and evil and of the opposition of fate and free will – a thought that would return twenty years later in his affirmation of *amor fati* (love of fate).[6]

The sincerity of his religious feeling remained unaffected by his early reflections on the dark side of the divine and found expression in both his musical improvisations and in his poetry. At 20, on the occasion of his departure from Schulpforta, he wrote a hymn to 'The Unknown God,' whose religious intensity is reminiscent of the 'Magician's Song' in the fourth part of *Zarathustra*.[7]

Shortly afterwards he began to study at the University in Bonn (1864). Although he was registered in the theological

---

4 Cited by Curt Janz, *Nietzsche*, vol. 1, p. 98 ff.
5 *Ibid*, p. 99.
6 Ges. W., vol. V, p. 209, §276; CM, vol. 3/3, p. 521, §276.
7 The first verse reads:
> "Once more before I go on
> And direct my looks forward
> Do I lift up my lone hands
> To Thee, my refuge,
> Whose altars I have solemnly consecrated
> With devotion from the depths of my heart,
> That your voice may ever
> Call me back."
>
> *Der Werdende Nietzsche*, p. 239.

faculty, he did not restrict himself to a particular field of study but pursued his many and varied interests. Here he met the philology professor F.W. Ritschl, whom he then followed to Leipzig, finally deciding to study philology. His admiration for Ritschl, as well as his friendship with Erwin Rohde, played a large role in this period of his life.[8] His relationship with Rohde was kindled by a shared enthusiasm for Greek culture and lasted many years. After a fairly long period of separation, it cooled, largely because Rohde was inwardly no longer in a position to follow Nietzsche's train of thought. Jaspers' comments on the friendship between Nietzsche and Rohde are illuminating: "After both had found common ground in the 'exuberance of willing' and in the awareness of 'boundless possibilities,' they both went in opposite directions; Nietzsche remained young and created a bottomless faith in his mission, Rohde became old, bourgeois, static and unbelieving...".[9]

Nietzsche's relationships with his boyhood friends from his time at Pforta continued to be significant: with Carl von Gersdorff, for instance, who supported him financially over the years, and with Paul Deussen, who became an historian of religion.[10] Although the relationship with Deussen was initially the result of a pedagogic attitude in Nietzsche, it gradually developed into a much closer one in the final period of his life.

Fundamental to all these relationships formed at school and university was, in Nietzsche's estimation, the bond of shared intellectual interests and ideals as opposed to anything elementary or spontaneous. Even then, one could detect a tendency in him that stressed the self and the 'pathos

---

8 Erwin Rohde (1845-98), Prof. at Heidelberg after 1886. Author of *Psyche* (1890), see also p. 202.

9 Karl Jaspers, p. 62.

10 Paul Deussen (1845-1919), Professor in Kiel, devotee of Schopenhauerian philosophy, who made a name for himself principally through his works on Indian philosophy, particularly Vedanta. Unlike Nietzsche he stayed true to the Schopenhauerian doctrine of the denial of the Will as the highest goal all his life.

of distance': it is indicated, to give one example, in a comment taken from a letter to Deussen:

"In all seriousness, my friend, I must ask you to speak of me with greater respect when you talk about me."[11]

Despite the many relationships Nietzsche had established, the influence of the loss of his father on his spiritual development made itself painfully clear in these years. Always the strongest member of his circle of colleagues, Nietzsche himself missed the presence of a strong figure he could look up and submit to, as we learn from his diaries. In his bequest we read in retrospect that it was essential to his early path to wisdom to have "admired better, obeyed better and learned better than anyone."[12]

In this respect, his Leipzig years (1865-69) were decisive. Two extraordinarily significant events occurred in this period that would determine his life's direction: the reading of Schopenhauer's *World as Will and Idea* (1865) and the overwhelming meeting with Richard Wagner.

Schopenhauer, described later by Nietzsche as "his first and only teacher," became the embodiment of his heroic ideal.[13] He regarded both his moral commitment and his total engagement in the search for truth as exemplary – characteristics, he felt, which corresponded to the striving for truth in which he himself was gradually becoming involved. Without Schopenhauer's world of ideas he would hardly have put up with the rather dry study of philosophy. We will become more familiar with Nietzsche's attitude when we discuss his essay, *Schopenhauer as Educator*.[14]

His relationship with Wagner was completely different.[15] At the very first meeting, he was struck by the extraordinary greatness of this man and his demonic per-

---

11  Paul Deussen, *Erinnerungen an Nietzsche* [*Memories of Nietzsche*], p. 62. Such passages weaken the conception that Nietzsche's later overestimation of himself was caused by his progressive paralysis.
12  Ges. W. vol. XIII, p. 40; CM vol 11, p.159.
13  Arthur Schopenhauer (1788-1860).
14  See p. 32 ff.
15  Richard Wagner (1813-83).

sonality. For three years (1869-72), he fell under the spell of this personality, in which he recognized the quintessence of the German artist. He not only projected onto him the role of a guiding father figure, but also experienced, through the medium of his music, the fascination for the Dionysian that never left him even after his later renunciation of Wagner.[16] He still confessed in his last work, *Ecce homo,* that the days he spent in the Wagner home at Tribschen, near Luzern, belonged to the most striking and unforgettable impressions of his life.[17] His emotional response to Wagner's music derived equally from its exuberant, elementary power and from the receptivity to the musical world that was his from earliest childhood. The latter was so pronounced that for a long time he was unsure whether he should actually devote himself to music; but it was his passion for knowledge that finally won out.

In 1869 Nietzsche moved to Basle, where his teacher Ritschl, in recognition of his excellent achievement in this field, had recommended him for the vacant Chair of Philology. At barely twenty-five years of age, and before even obtaining a doctorate, Nietzsche took up the honorable post at the university. As Janz emphasizes, the motive for his acceptance had less to do with his enthusiasm for philology than with his desire to be closer to Wagner's abode – a grave error with regard to his further development!

From early 1869 until 1879 Nietzsche taught at the University of Basle, which reflected the conservative and petty bourgeois spirit of the town, and at the Philological Seminar (the *Paedagogium*). The initial enthusiasm with which he devoted himself to his studies of Greek literature and mythology was unexpectedly destroyed by the outbreak of the Franco-Prussian War. Shaken by his experiences of the war as a volunteer medic, and infected with dysentery and diphtheria, he returned to Basle. The pessimistic attitude of his soul that had already existed since the death of his father was strengthened, and led to his doubting the meaning of

16  See p. 37
17  Ges. W. vol. XV, p. 37.


11

human existence. The work, *The Birth of Tragedy,* which appeared in 1872, and its dark and untimely depiction of the heaven of the Greek gods, and of the figure of Dionysus, whom Nietzsche portrayed both as the bringer and destroyer of life, casts light on the tragedy of his spiritual background. As the critical reception of his work confirmed, he was an outsider – an impression also established by the *Untimely Meditations.* Fearlessly and publicly he exercised his criticism, not just of the educational aims of his age but also of the intellectualism and historicism that were predominant then.

The Basle years demonstrate his literary ambitions and his impatient search both for a style of his own and his philosophical mission. His occupation as a philologist did not satisfy him, he was discontented with the burden of his profession and the lack of free time, and he increasingly considered himself a philosopher. Schopenhauer was still the model for his creative activity, the great educator whose genius he glorified. Nevertheless, he was already complaining about his isolation, about the "loneliness of the last philosopher." Thus we read in his bequest: "My heart refuses to believe that love is dead, it cannot bear the horror of the loneliest loneliness and forces me to speak as if I were two persons."[18]

Seen from the outside, he was, however, by no means alone: his position as Professor opened doors for him to the most distinguished houses of the town. But the large circle of acquaintances did not change the fact that he was friendly with only a few people and that he was on only distant terms even with his professional colleagues. Thus, despite his esteem for Bachofen, to whose symbolic approach to mythology he was attracted, he was nevertheless unable to establish a deeper relationship with him.[19]

The Basle lecturer Jacob Burckhardt was one of his few

---

18  Ges. W. vol. X, p. 146,147; CM vol. 7, p. 459,460.
19  Johann Jakob Bachofen (1815-87).

friends[20] He was well disposed towards Nietzsche's inspired ideas, but without abandoning his reserve. In contrast, Nietzsche openly announced his deep admiration for this temperate, balanced scholar whose image as a great teacher left a lasting impression on him. Although contact was never broken, Burckhardt was alienated by the untimely thoughts of his younger colleague, which tended to lose themselves in vertiginous heights, and withdrew more and more, but never quite made his intentions clear. Although they shared a common love of Greek culture and the Italian Renaissance, it was primarily on Nietzsche's initiative alone that they remained in touch.

Two further friendships that would possess a similar importance in Nietzsche's life can also be traced back to the Basle period, although they varied considerably in nature: with Franz Overbeck, the historian of religion, and Peter Gast (rebaptized Heinrich Koeselitz by Nietzsche), the musician. Both stood unswervingly by him to the end of his life and represented a constant factor in an existence so turbulent within.

In Overbeck, Nietzsche's lifelong helper in the practical questions of life, he valued a superior sort of cleverness and reason, and a loyalty that displayed both reliability and constancy.[21] Overbeck's doubts about the Church's doctrine of revelation were also of value to him, especially the open confession of his own secularity. Although it gave rise to fierce criticism, it represented for Nietzsche himself a welcome link with his own intuitions. Jaspers' words characterizing this relationship are appropriate: "The depth of *this* loyalty, and not the depth of a destiny that fulfilled itself in friendship, was what united both."[22]

Nietzsche's friendship with Koeselitz (Peter Gast)

20 Jacob Burckhardt (1818-97), Professor of Cultural History at Basle. See also p. 232 for his views on war.
21 Franz Overbeck (1837-1905), Professor for the Exegesis of the New Testament and the History of the Church at Basle.
22 Karl Jaspers: *Nietzsche*, p. 83.

followed a very different pattern[23]: on the one hand, he expected from it the satisfaction of his unquenchable yearning for discipleship, and on the other, he projected onto him the image of a creative musical spirit strong enough to eventually overcome Richard Wagner's music drama and to bring about a new form of music. In neither case were his hopes fulfilled, as Koeselitz did not have the stature to live up to them. Nevertheless, he did manage to aid the creative efforts of his ailing friend by copying out his manuscripts and advising him on corrections. It would be an exaggeration to say that Nietzsche's work would have been impossible without him, but he certainly brought a degree of security into his life.

The meeting with Paul Rée, with whom Nietzsche stayed on friendly terms for seven years, also occurred during the Basle period.[24] The discussions he held with this subtle, intelligent and, above all, philosophically-schooled doctor, who had already emerged as the author of the *Origin of the Moral Senses,* primarily covered the fields of psychology and morality. They had an extremely stimulating effect on Nietzsche, in whom the moral crisis that would throw him back on himself was already beginning to take form: they strengthened his own tendencies to break loose from bourgeois rules.[25] Parts of the work he wrote in this new spirit, *Human All-Too-Human,* go back to this time.[26]

The period in Basle was also significant insofar as Nietzsche then began to cultivate friendships with women. Despite his passionate nature, *his physical dependency on*

23  Heinrich Koeselitz (1854-1918), an unsuccessful composer, in whom Nietzsche had great hopes. Nietzsche's aphorism may well have been referring to him: "One repays a teacher badly if one always remains nothing but a pupil." Ges. W. vol. VI, p. 114; CM vol. 4, p. 101.

24  Paul Rée (1849-1901) was a doctor and writer. The work cited above came out in 1895, and, in the same year, the *Psychological Observations* appeared, whilst his work on *Philosophy* was published posthumously (1903). See Curt Janz, vol. 1, p. 640 ff.

25  See p. 40.

26  See p. 38.

*female help* cast a shadow on these relationships. Not only did his dependency on mother and sister, the result of his physiological weakness, impair his emotional development; it was also the standard of their spirituality, characterized by a traditional piety, that constricted him. The lack of a father-image was no less of a barrier blocking the way to a healthy emotional life.[27] Neither the strict upbringing at Schulpforta nor the freer atmosphere of university had been suitable for providing him with an adequate picture of the female sex.

Nietzsche's experience with women began, apart from unimportant student crushes, with an extremely embarrassing situation in a Cologne brothel, where he was unlucky enough to contract a syphilitic infection.[28] Nevertheless, it seems that he was not unimpressed by the colorful goings-on around him for, in his 'Zarathustra period,' he still made wistful mention of the "flimsy little fan-flutter and tinsel-skirts" of the prostitutes.[29]

The meeting with Wagner's partner Cosima left an initial and indelible impression. He had got to know her shortly after moving to Basle during his visits to Tribschen (1869-72). She embodied less an earthly woman than an unattainable goddess.

It was only in Basle that he gained the inner freedom necessary for establishing relationships with women, where his success in public brought with it an active but superficial social life. Of some note was his friendship with Marie Baumgartner in Lörrach, a woman who "loyally took care of him"; she had great sympathy for his existential difficulties, also completing translations of his works into French.[30] His relationship with Malvida von Meysenburg was closer; her fascination for Wagner first brought the two

27 See p. 5f.
28 Curt Janz, *Nietzsche*, vol. 1, p. 138.
29 See p. 161 on the 'Song of the Wilderness,' and Ges. W. vol. VI, p. 448; CM vol. 4, p. 384.
30 Marie Baumgartner (1831-97), née Koechlin, a well-read intellectual from Lörrach.

together, but later became a bone of contention between them.[31] As a sensitive writer famous for her *Memoirs of an Idealist* and a warm-hearted mother-like friend, she was in a position to lend Nietzsche support in various periods of change and detachment in his life. This friendship lasted until 1888, ending abruptly after the publication of the polemical work *The Case of Wagner*.

The moral crisis already indicated worsened appreciably. It would be one-sided merely to explain it in terms of illness and professional dissatisfaction. What preoccupied Nietzsche more was the extremely questionable attitude towards established morality he had by now adopted, and the awareness of his own inner destiny.[32] His mental anguish gradually became more and more intolerable and induced him to give up his Professorship in Basle in 1879, at the age of thirty-five. I will return to this subject when discussing his activity as a writer: an activity that had already seen the publication of several works *(The Birth of Tragedy, Untimely Meditations* and *Human All-Too-Human).*

From this time onwards, Nietzsche's life consisted of a restless wandering from place to place between – to name only the major stations – the Engadine, the Riviera and Turin. Where he lived was largely determined by choice of a suitable climate and altitude for his health, partly the result of his illness. Of these, Sils-Maria, the place where he had his vision of the 'eternal recurrence,' was his favorite. It is painful to follow Nietzsche on his travels, undertaken in conditions of utmost poverty. He survived as best he could in unheated rooms as a lodger in cheap hotels, barely able to manage on his modest pension and with occasional financial help.

In these early years of freedom regained, he first encountered Lou von Salomé, a woman who would lead him to both the towering heights and the blackest depths of ex-

31 Malvida von Meysenburg (1816-1903). The memoirs cited above appeared in 1876. Further references on p. 36.
32 See p. 36.

istence.[33] From the very first meeting, arranged by Frau von Meysenburg, he was overwhelmed by the unusually intellectual charisma of this woman in whom astuteness, courage and girlishness all came together as one. In her he thought he saw his future assistant and lifelong companion, a woman capable of understanding and fostering his ideas. Nietzsche's flashing enthusiasm was soon dampened when Lou showed herself unwilling to accompany his thoughts and not at all interested in being converted. His passionate inclinations towards her were not reciprocated. Despite having some things in common she possessed neither the emotional maturity nor the inner warmth to satisfy his expectations, and particularly his ethical demands, as Nietzsche would all too soon be forced to recognize. The 'cat in her' that could only take and never give was repellent. Kurt Janz's description of the incompatibility of the relations between Nietzsche and Lou is striking. In his opinion they diverged too greatly for any inner closeness to have been possible between them, in spite of certain traits they shared, such as the early loss of a father, an anti-nationalistic view of Europe, an anti-idealistic conception of the world, and, not least, the sacrifice of a Christian view of God. Lou laughed at Nietzsche's mystical fantasies and had no feeling for the mystic experience on Montesacro, which contained for Nietzsche the significance of a "mystery of love."[34] She understood just as little about Nietzsche's attitude to music. She responded to the great vision of the 'eternal recurrence' with mocking laughter.[35]

Their friendship was clouded from the start by the concurrent relationship she had with his friend Paul Rée, which he kept from Nietzsche. In complete ignorance, Nietzsche confided to Rée his love for Lou; it was a situation doomed to failure, due to the double role of friend and rival that Rée was playing, but not admitting to.

33 Lou von Salomé (1861-1937). In 1886 she married Charles Andreas, a philologist and professor.
34 Curt Janz: *Nietzsche,* vol. 2, p. 164.
35 *Ibid.*

Through the intervention of Nietzsche's sister Elisabeth, who was not prepared to play second fiddle to another woman in Nietzsche's life, the situation was considerably worsened. Nietzsche was exposed through her to the whole inferno of a woman whose love is scorned and self-esteem offended.

Nietzsche himself, however, was made most embarrassingly aware of his own reactions of hatred and revenge, which manifested themselves in fierce emotional outbreaks such as that seen in the chapter 'The Adder's Bite,' in *Zarathustra*. That love and hatred should be mutually dependent, and that his love should have been so demanding, would occupy him for a long time to come. After a short time this extraordinarily intense friendship suddenly broke down when the situation had been rendered intolerable by intrigues and defamation.

In the bequest covering those days (summer and autumn, 1882) some moving remarks about Nietzsche's relationship with Lou are to be found:

> "For *men, love* is something completely different than for women. For most of them love is clearly a type of *possessive greed*; for the rest of the men, love is the worship of a suffering and veiled deity."[36]

Or:

> "What does he know of love who must not despise what he loves?"[37]

Or:

> "What shook me was not that you lied to me, but that I no longer believed you."[38]

36  CM vol. 10, p. 37.
37  CM vol. 10, p. 57.
38  CM vol. 10, p. 95.

Or:

*"To hurt the man we love* is truly devilish. . . ."[39]

A further aphorism dating from this time illuminates his suffering:

"My love is so fastidious, it is frightening! I cannot love without believing that the one I love is destined to do something immortal. And guesses what what I believe – what I demand."[40]

Nietzsche seems to have emerged a more mature man from this painful experience of love. His aphorism on love as the worship of a suffering and veiled deity betrays a surprisingly new spirit. One cannot help feeling that as a consequence of having to retrieve what he had projected upon Lou he had become conscious of the reality of his soul – the *anima*. Belonging to this period is the impressive aphorism:

"A labyrinthine person never seeks the truth but always his Ariadne alone – in spite of what he may also tell us,"[41]

in which "labyrinthine" in all probability means 'hopelessly entangled' and "Ariadne" a 'Dionysian abyss of the soul.'

Roughly two years after the separation from Lou, Nietzsche set his hopes on another equally-matched person to accompany him on his path. He thought he had found this person in Baron Heinrich von Stein, a young philosophy lecturer at the University of Berlin, of whom much was expected.[42] After an extremely fruitful three-day meeting at Sils, Nietzsche wrote the following, rather curious words

39  CM vol. 10, p. 28.
40  CM vol. 10, p. 88.
41  CM vol. 10, p. 125. See my remarks on the *anima*, p. 118 f.
42  Heinrich von Stein (1857-1887).

to his friend Overbeck: "At last someone else who is mine and respects me instinctively."[43] Not only do they reveal the demanding and egoistical character of Nietzsche's relationships, they also show to what degree he felt deprived of friends. His poem, 'From High Mountains,' which he sent to Sils in memory of von Stein, testifies to this: "Looking all day and night, for friends I wait: For new friends! Come! It's time! It's late!"[44] Stein's premature death at the age of thirty was a bitter blow.

Amongst the many visitors he received in the following years, three figures would attain a special significance: Helen Zimmern, who translated his works into English, Resa von Schirnhofer,[45] who recorded her memories of Nietzsche in *On Nietzsche the Man,* and Dr. Meta von Salis-Marschlin,[46] with whom he had a great deal in common. She became a valued companion with whom he discussed much in his final years, a friend who stood by him.

As late as 1888, Nietzsche was holding stimulating conversations with the theologian Julius Kaftan,[47] who stayed in Sils for all of three weeks and accompanied him daily on his walks. From the memoirs and impressions Kaftan left to posterity it can be seen that, in spite of the approaching catastrophe, he received an undoubtedly positive impression of Nietzsche's behavior as regards his mental alertness. On the basis of his conversation he was also convinced that the worsening of his illness shortly afterwards had a religious cause. As a true theologian he recognized the core of Nietzsche's mental stress as the loss of God. He

43 Letter of Sept. 1888, to Franz Overbeck.
44 'From High Mountains.' Aftersong to *Beyond Good and Evil.*
45 Resa von Schirnhofer (1855-1948), an Austrian. Awarded a doctorate in Zürich in 1889. *Vom Menschen Nietzsche [On Nietzsche the Man]*, 1968.
46 Meta von Salis (1855-1929). The first woman from Graubünden to obtain a doctorate (philosophy). *Philosoph und Edelmensch,* 1897.
47 Julius Kaftan was called to the University of Basle in 1873, where he had already met Nietzsche, and ten years later was appointed to Berlin University.

thus based his suffering on the fact "that he was never able to forget Christianity and ignore it. He destroyed it over and over. But what must be destroyed again and again proves to the destroyer its indestructible vitality. The tragic end to his existence, his insanity, might well be explained by this ... That he was godless, without God, that he had lost God, that is the tragic destiny of his life...."[48] Though Kaftan was right to draw attention to the religious background of Nietzsche's conflicts, he is too concerned with tracing them back to a betrayal of traditional Christianity. At the end of my study I shall examine the religious problem more closely. Kaftan singled out from his conversations the simple politeness of his nature as well as his streak of ethical greatness – both characteristics that contrasted so much the aggressive tone of his works and their hostility towards morality.[49] Kaftan's impressions were shared by many friends who visited Nietzsche in his final year.

A few months after the meeting with Kaftan in Sils, Nietzsche had a mental breakdown in Turin, followed by eleven years of total derangement.[50]

## 3. Illness

I would not like to end my introduction before first casting light on the etiology of Nietzsche's illness. Although little precise information exists either on the prehistory of his disease or on the way it developed, the medical diagnosis at the time of the breakdown in December, 1888, still seems to have been beyond dispute: P.J. Moebius was the first to refer to a progressive paralysis resulting from a syphilitic infection, presumably contracted

48 'Aus der Werkstatt des Uebermenschen,' *Deutsche Rundschau* 31, (1905).
49 See Curt Janz, *Nietzsche*, vol. 2, p. 621.
50 See p. 265f.

between 1864 and 1865.[51] Whilst there was a general consensus of opinion on this point, the same cannot be said with regard to the timing of the secondary and tertiary stages of the illness. Psychiatric views also vary on the possible connection between the disease and the regular attacks of the migraine he suffered since childhood, his gradual loss of sight and frequent bouts of vomiting. The question of whether symptoms of paralysis existed before the breakdown remained similarly unanswered.

On the other hand, it seems highly likely that certain psychic changes had repeatedly led to transformations in Nietzsche's behavior and condition. It was principally Karl Jaspers who drew attention to such mental and spiritual factors, differing greatly from Moebius' intention of working out a faultless medical history stretching from the very first physical signs of the illness to its fatal end. Jaspers thus stressed the factor of repeated "shifts in the overall condition of his mental and physical existence," such as those occurring at the time when Nietzsche relinquished his professorship, when the *Gay Science* originated and during his great vision of the 'eternal recurrence.'[52] According to him, it was characteristic of such shifts that they were accompanied by a new self-awareness, by an increased intensity of feeling and inner openness, but that, at the same time, they were also related to unexpected fits of depression and a blackening of mood.[53] As far as

51  See Lange-Eichbaum's pathological study.
52  Karl Jaspers, *Nietzsche*, p. 93.
53  Thus we read in Jaspers: "Nietzsche visualizes the ineffable with marvelous vividness in the image: 'I am standing still, I am suddenly tired. In front it seems to go downhill, quick as a flash, into some sort of abyss – I don't like to look. The mountains tower up behind me. Trembling, I reach out for a hold. What! Has all around me become stone and precipice? Here are some bushes – they are breaking apart in my hand ... I shudder and close my eyes. – Where am I? I am looking into the purple night, it attracts me to it and greets me – and how do I feel? What has happened to make my voice suddenly fail, and you feel as if you were buried under the weight of drunken and opaque emotions?' " Ges. W. vol. XII, p. 223; CM vol. 9, p. 612.

Jaspers is concerned, such phenomena point to the existence of an as yet unknown 'biological factor' affecting Nietzsche's entire constitution. Arguments in favor of this appear to him to lie both in Nietzsche's paroxysmal states and in sudden and contradictory moods that would switch from fervent enthusiasm to a strange form of absent-mindedness.

Indeed, the inflated view of himself which Nietzsche displayed in his last works, a view that was frighteningly divorced from reality and betrayed clear signs of an incipient split personality, seems to indicate the presence of such a factor.

Jasper's remarks are rendered doubly illuminating by his assumption that a biological constituent should in no way be interpreted as devaluating intellectual creativity. On the contrary, for he saw in the existence of this biological influence the cause of Nietzsche's enormous intellectual inspiration in the last decade of his life. He did not doubt that, in contrast to all materialistic interpretations, "the value of an inner creation" should be "seen and judged solely by what the intellect has produced."[54]

I would like to concur with the judgment of this experienced psychiatrist and attempt to understand Nietzsche's world of ideas on its own terms. Illness does not seem to me a valid objection to an unprejudiced evaluation of his work, and it certainly does not invalidate his greatness. Although in time the syphilis did obscure his sense of reality, intensify his visionary side and affect his speed of working, it did not necessarily impair the genius of his intellect. Quite the opposite: his illness turned out to be the very "fish-hook of knowledge."[55] Nietzsche himself regarded his suffering as the very thing that provoked his depth of insight. He wrote that illness had led him to reflect on reason.[56] I find the view of Udo Rukser worth noting, which states that the urge caused by the illness to explore

54 Karl Jaspers, *Nietzsche*, p. 101.
55 Ges. W. vol. II, Preface (4); CM vol. 2, Preface (4).
56 Ges. W. vol. XV, p. 31; CM vol. 6, p. 282.

the secret of the soul drove Nietzsche to confront the incomprehensible and ineffable aspects of the numinous and finally broke him. His 'personal consciousness' was not able to withstand domination by the greater impersonal reality of the soul, whose dangers he was only dimly aware of.[57]

In all probability a meaningful link does exist between Nietzsche's inexorable will to know and his illness – a connection, however, that we must accept as lying beyond the dimension of causality.

57  Udo Rukser, *Nietzsche in der Hispania*, p. 121.

# NIETZSCHE'S WORK

## A. The Period Before Zarathustra

### *I. The Birth of Tragedy out of the Spirit of Music (1872)*

Nietzsche's first lengthy publication, *The Birth of Tragedy out of the Spirit of Music,* originated in Basle in 1871. It represents an immortal monument to both the music of Wagner and the spirit of Schopenhauer. But anyone expecting an objective, historical study of the origins of Greek tragedy will be disappointed. The work has more the character of a personal document and a declaration of belief in the 'greatness' of Richard Wagner. Nietzsche was essentially interested in justifying and even glorifying Wagner's music drama or more precisely, in showing that his artistic program was not a modern discovery but a *creative revival of Greek art.*

Under the influence of Schopenhauer's pessimism, he was also concerned with demystifying the prevalent conception of a serene Olympian Heaven of the gods and unveiling the cause of the tragic darkness that existed within Greek culture. Insofar as the Greeks were constantly dogged by the terrors of life and the might of the Titans, survival for them became a matter of opposing these things with the illusionary world of appearance. In the two figures of Apollo and Dionysus, Nietzsche sought to capture this opposition of light and darkness, the one representing all moderation and balance, the other intoxication and ecstasy. Even at this time, one may recognize the secret attraction

25

exerted upon him by Dionysus, the embodiment of the affirmation as well as the annihilation of life.

In the divine figures of Apollo and Dionysus he also brought together two forms of artistic outlook: Whilst Apollonian art was derived from the "beautiful illusion of the world of dreams" and was inculcated with the conscious striving for moderation, proportion and beauty, Dionysian art was rooted in the depths of life, "in primal being," and embraced both life and death. Both artistic drives, whose opposing tendencies of the inebriation and transfiguration of the soul manifested the deep rift in mankind, had, Nietzsche believed, been mystically synthesized principally in Aeschylean, but also in Attic tragedy. This synthesis presented, so to speak, a "higher possibility of existence in which the art of Apollonian appearance was unified with that of Dionysian 'truth' in tragic art."[1]

Inasmuch as such a mystical renewal was the deepest concern of the Attic tragedy, it also become Nietzsche's own *model* for his *mythic interpretation of "tragic art."*

What, however, were the artistic methods that would prove adequate to produce such a synthesis of 'Apollo and Dionysus'? In accordance with the emotional impression made on him at that time by Wagner's art, Nietzsche fell back on the latter's creation of music drama, whose major feature was the union of myth and music. Nietzsche discovered an analogy to this in the way Attic tragedy combined mythic narrative, on the one hand, and an ecstatic state of intoxication on the other. He attributed a high degree of significance to both artistic forms: without myth and its symbolic illustration of the depth of being, it would have been more difficult to understand the action, whilst without the Dionysian revelation contained within the music, it would have been impossible to captivate the individual and afford him a metaphysical experience of the eternal.[2] The direct experience in tragedy of the unity of both artistic forms acted like a cure for man's "eternal wound of exis-

1 Ges. W. vol. IX, p. 91; CM vol. 1, p. 571.
2 Ges. W. vol. I, p. 117; CM vol. 1, p. 108.

tence,"[3] and was the equivalent of a "metaphysical comfort."[4] Nietzsche found the key to the understanding of this action in the teachings of the Greek mysteries,[5] which answered both the question of the fundamental evil suffered by mankind and of the possibility of redemption. Just as the suffering of Dionysus-Zagreus could be traced back to his dismemberment, so all of mankind's suffering rested on the fact of "individuation,"[6] the loss of original oneness. And just as the rebirth of Dionysus was an omen for the Epopt of guaranteed redemption, so man in his pain could also hope for salvation; that is, for the spell of individuation to be broken and for the simultaneous experience of a new path leading to "the mothers of being" and the "innermost heart of things."[7]

In formal terms, this miracle came to pass through the symbolic and mythic revelation, by means of Apollonian form, of primal being hidden within the Dionysian and manifest in the chorus. As a consequence of the intermingling of chorus and work, of music and myth, *primal oneness was restored in symbolic form,*[8] in other words the mystery of "fusion with primal being"[9] became a reality actually experienced in the tragedy. The emphasis Nietzsche placed on the existence of a mythic symbolism in art appears to me to be highly significant. Art seemed to him characteristically to express itself in the creation of images,[10] and as such was virtually predestined to convey an "understanding of the world in symbols."[11]

For the spectator, the redeeming effect of tragedy lay in looking at the mysterious course of events taking place; in short, it lay in the *aesthetic contemplation.* This corre-

3 Ges. W. vol. I, p. 125; CM vol. 1, p. 125.
4 Ges. W. vol. I, p. 123; CM vol. 1, p. 114.
5 Ges. W. vol. I, p. 74; CM vol. 1, p. 73.
6 Ges. W. vol. I, p. 73f; CM vol. 1, p. 72.
7 Ges. W. vol. I, p. 110; CM vol. 1, p. 103.
8 Ges. W. vol. I, p. 74; CM vol. 1, p. 73.
9 Ges. W. vol. I, p. 62; CM vol. 1, p. 62.
10 Ges. W. vol. IX, p. 86; CM vol. 1, p. 564.
11 Ges. W. vol. I, p. 74; CM vol. 1, p. 73.

sponded to Nietzsche's consistently aesthetic approach to things, which consciously ignored, as Jung correctly observed, the religious and moral meaning of the symbol of redemption.[12] Apart from clarifying Attic tragedy, Nietzsche saw it as the principal aim of his work to advance the breakthrough of the music drama in Germany and thus to open up new cultural possibilities for German opera in general. He discovered in the synthesis of music and myth, of music and dramatic action, indicated in Aeschylean tragedy, the meaningfulness of a model for opera *per se.* He expected of opera nothing less than the renewal of German art, an expectation that proved no more than a utopian fantasy.

Despite the youthfully fantastical and unrealizable nature of Nietzsche's picture of the future, he nevertheless continued to yearn subliminally for the means to reveal the mythic basis of being hidden within the Dionysian. Although it appeared as if this vision had been submerged when he was experimenting with freethinking, it was later resurrected by the appearance of the mythical Zarathustra and the myth of the 'eternal recurrence.' By then, however, it had become part of worldly outlook as opposed to a metaphysical one.

According to Nietzsche, the tragic conception of the world, and with it Attic tragedy, were both destroyed by Socratic teaching, which proclaimed the significance of knowledge and understanding. With Socrates came the rise of *morality,* the doctrine of virtue and the conviction that "virtue is equivalent to knowledge." For the first time in history, the life instinct was confronted by reason. Regardless of his inclination towards myth and art, Nietzsche had to acknowledge with a certain admiration that Socrates had helped the "archetype of the theoretical genius" to win the day. Indeed, he did more: as a "mystagogue of sci-

---

12 C.G. Jung: *Die psychologischen Typen,* Ges.W. vol. VI, p. 149. Standard English translation: C.G. Jung, *The Psychological Types,* in *Collected Works* (henceforth referred to as 'C.W.'), vol. 6, p. 140. See Translator's Note.

ence,"[13] introducing his contemporaries to the "mysteries of science" and knowledge of life's depths, he represented a "turning point and vortex" in world history. Thanks to his instinct for science he understood both how to live and how to die, emptying the poisoned cup without fear of death.[14] But at the same time his doctrine of "knowledge as a universal medicine" produced the painful result of having annihilated the mystical contemplation of the world. Nevertheless, the Socratic avowal of the "fathomability of nature" would never completely let go of Nietzsche, and his *oscillating between logos and myth* can be traced right through to his final works.

As Nietzsche retrospectively stressed in the foreword added in 1886 to the *Birth of Tragedy*, the polemic he had written at this time against the absolute claims of science was aimed not only at Socratic teaching but also at the rise of science in general. It was in this work that science first appeared to him as something questionable and problematical, lending his criticism a romantic and irrational flavor.[15] In this foreword he also mentioned that not only had he directed himself against Socrates but was being equally critical, even at this early stage, of Christianity's overemphasis upon moral values and simultaneous denial of the instincts and of life.

Nietzsche's initial work suffered as much from a lack of objectivity as from the unclarity and mysticism of its presentation. It is not unlikely that the emotional shock he

13 Ges. W. vol. I, p. 170; CM vol. 1, p. 154.
14 Ges. W. vol. I, p. 106; CM vol. 1, p. 99.
15 Ges. W. vol. I, p. 3; CM vol. 1, p. 13. After the appearance of the *Birth*, the spirit of romanticism and irrationalism did indeed receive a strong impetus. On this subject we read in Jung: "Since the 'Birth of Tragedy' (1872), the dark, earthy feminine side, with its mantic and orgiastic characteristics, has possessed the imagination of philosophers and poets. Irrationality gradually came to be regarded as the ideal; this is found, for example, all through the research of Alfred Schuler (1923) into the mystery of religions, and particularly in the writings of Klages (1872-1956), who expounded the philosophy of irrationalism...." C.G. Jung: Ges. W. vol. X, p. 205 (C.W. vol. 10, p. 181).

received in 1861 at the hands of a performance of *Tristan* at Pforta had left imprinted on his soul the nearly inexpressible archetype of mystic oneness.

The *Birth of Tragedy* was to become the target of fierce criticism. It was primarily the mythic, intuitive approach this work embodied that met with strong resistance, for it correspondingly neglected the philological and historical points of view. Curt Janz mentions the subjectively colored and at times immoderate criticism of Nietzsche's colleague at Basle, Wilamowitz-Moellendorf; and also the equally critical, but much more controlled discussion of the work by Nietzsche's former teacher Ritschl. Both critics objected to the unscientific nature of this aesthetic consideration of the subject.[16]

## II. Untimely Meditations (I-IV)

In the years that followed, Nietzsche's mind was preoccupied with essentially art-historical interests. His thoughts continued to revolve around the advancement and renewal of German art and culture. He was worried by growing indications of cultural decline: religion had become nothing but show, art was surrendering its creative energy, the machine robbing man of his humanity, and the spirit of the herd and mediocrity spreading everywhere.

The four *Untimely Meditations,* in which Schopenhauer is revealed as Nietzsche's most impressive model, provide a living impression of Nietzsche's *cultural and philosophical ambitions.* [17] In these writings, Nietzsche appeared as the 'untimely' critic exposing the cultural deficiencies of his age – the decline of educational institutions and their preoccupation with the sciences, as well as the excessive cultivation of intellectualism and historicism. The thorn in the side

16 Curt Janz, *Nietzsche*, vol. 1, pp. 463-477.
17 The *Untimely Meditations* contain four essays: *David Strauss, the Confessor and the Writer; On the Uses and Disadvantages of History for Life; Schopenhauer as Educator;* and *Richard Wagner in Bayreuth.*

that the spuriousness of contemporary ideals represented was by no means the least of his concerns, either. In *Ecce homo* Nietzsche wrote of the first of the *Untimely Meditations,* aiming at the theologian David Strauss and calling *David Strauss, the Confessor and the Writer* (1873), in the following way:

> "The *first* attack (1873) was directed against German 'culture,' on which I looked down even then with contempt. Without meaning, without substance, without aim: mere 'public opinion' ...."[18]

Nietzsche saw in Strauss, who enjoyed considerable acclaim in theological circles, the exponent of a type widely present throughout the German Empire, and to whom he applied the expression "cultural philistine." Above all, his criticism sought out the intellectual world of his contemporaries, although it was also directed against their insubstantial and barbarous language and its overuse. The positive reception of this work amongst his contemporaries gave Nietzsche the strength to start work on his second *Untimely Meditation* just six months later.

In this second *Untimely Meditation,* Nietzsche emerges principally as a philosopher of culture. It bore the title, *On the Uses and Disadvantages of History for Life* (1874). Here he is battling with the "poisonousness of the pursuit of science," that is, with a torpid intellectualism and an overstressed "historical sense," both of which paralyze the life instinct. Wherever intellect and knowledge were held in too high esteem, symptoms of a spurious and overinflated culture showed themselves. But it was also excess, an "excessive regard for history," that impaired spontaneity in the living and clearly indicated signs of decline, i.e., signs of the "malady of history."[19] The highly commended pur-

18 Ges. W. vol. XV, p. 68; CM vol. 6, p. 316. Nietzsche knew Strauss primarily through his two books on the *Life of Jesus* and *Ancient and Modern Faith.*
19 Ges. W. vol. I, p. 378; CM vol. 1, p. 329.

suit of objectivity in thought and of an attitude free from personal interest was recognized by Nietzsche as an illusion: he considered the opposite notion of the historian lovingly immersing himself in empirical data to be far more essential to a fair assessment of the past. In the same way that all living things "needed an atmosphere, a mysterious circle of vapor," historical writing had to have the "veiling cloud." As Nietzsche stressed, history had to stand "in the service of life" and the living if it wished to create any sort of culture. It belongs to the greater of his merits that he should have been one of the first to point out the *discrepancy between knowledge and culture,* between *history and life.*

In his opinion, genuine culture was based on the "unity of life, thought and willing." The nobility of the spirit was founded on this unity. Neither the intellectual constructions of the world process, nor those concerning the ultimate goal of human history expounded, for instance, in Eduard von Hartmann's *Philosophy of the Unconscious* and Friedrich Hegel's historical philosophy, brought us any further. The honor of creating "a sort of bridge across the wild torrent of becoming" was, Nietzsche proceeded, bestowed upon the individual and not upon theories.

> "No, the *goal of humanity* cannot lie in its end but only in its *highest exemplars.*" [20]

Even then, when Nietzsche was about thirty, the "procreation of genius" seemed to him to be the highest aim,[21] an attitude that betrayed Schopenhauer's praise of genius and foreshadowed his own concept of the overman.

In the third *Untimely Meditation* (1874), which bears the title *Schopenhauer as Educator,* we possess a moving testament to Nietzsche's admiration and love for Schopenhauer, whom he described as his "teacher and taskmaster." In it his pain felt at the early loss of his paternal guide and

20 Ges. W. vol. I, p. 364; CM vol. 1, p. 317.
21 Ges. W. vol. I, p. 411; CM vol. 1, p. 358.

32

his search for a "great spirit" to whom he could devote himself finds particularly strong expression. In pursuance of his self-confession Nietzsche had invested this work with his own "innermost history, his *becoming*."[22] It therefore describes less of what Schopenhauer was than of what he himself was.[23] This is shown, for example, in the way he portrays Schopenhauer's suffering, his "despair of the truth,"[24] or in how he stresses his isolation and "ethical obduracy." Apart from this, Schopenhauer represented for him genuine human greatness and a unique personality expressing itself in the courage "to be free and entirely himself"[25] and "to bring to light all that is false in things"[26]; to be nothing but "a servant of the truth." With reference to Schopenhauer he tried to perceive the meaning of culture in the cult of genius – in the "production of true human beings."[27] The goal he had in mind was to educate the individual to become the "great man" whose strength derived from the creation of a "free manliness of character."[28] As far as he was concerned, this had nothing to do with furthering the sort of scholarship that was unfortunately taught in the higher institutions of learning in Germany. On the contrary, his aim was to reflect on life and thereby cultivate wisdom and inwardness. In culture, everything depended on the individual. It was, therefore, a valid means of receiving the "consecration of culture" "to set one's heart on a great man" (which was, incidentally, Nietzsche's own position at the time). Culture was for him:

22  Ges. W. vol. XV p. 72; CM vol. 6, p. 320.
23  He writes in *Ecce homo,* vol. XV, p. 72, and CM vol. 6, p. 320: "What I am today – at a height where I speak no longer with words but with lightning bolts – ah, how remote from this I still was at that time! – But I beheld the land – I did not deceive myself for a moment about the way, the sea, the danger – and success ... Here every word is experienced, is deep, is *inward* ...."
24  Ges. W. vol. I, p. 408; CM vol. 1, p. 411.
25  Ges. W. vol. I, p. 416; CM vol. 1, p. 362.
26  Ges. W. vol. I, p. 431; CM vol. 1, p. 375.
27  Ges. W. vol. I, p. 445; CM vol. 1, p. 387.
28  Ges. W. vol. I, p. 474; CM vol. 1, p. 411.

"the child of each individual's self-knowledge and dissatisfaction with himself."[29]

The advancement of culture always remained of the utmost importance to Nietzsche, even if the content of what he understood by this term varied considerably over the years. In place of the stress on traditional values came a growing sense of the power and strength of the individual. Even then he was similarly displaying open disapproval of the cultural aspirations of Christianity, regarding them as hypocritical and mendacious.

Irrespective of his objections to contemporary culture, he unswervingly looked upon the greatness of Schopenhauer's view of the whole as founded upon the fact that:

"greatness lies in having set up a picture of life as a whole, in order to interpret it as a whole. . . ."[30]

He was similarly fascinated by Schopenhauer's belief in a purely spiritual world that was, in contrast to the world of appearance, without illusion and without lies. Inspired by him, Nietzsche was the first to affirm the metaphysical position of a 'spirit in itself,' which promised the possibility that 'pure' knowing may exist free of subjective embellishment. Nietzsche was also impressed by the heroic character of Schopenhauer's outlook, which not only denied the will of life and worldly happiness but also included the "smothering of the individual will."

Although Nietzsche was already beginning to detach himself from the metaphysical notion of a 'spirit in itself' – of a true world – in his next longer work, the Schopenhauerian picture of man, based as it was on truthfulness and self-discipline, remained enduringly meaningful. It is of no small significance that Nietzsche's later conception of the 'will to power' may well have represented an unconscious concession to Schopenhauerian metaphysics, though

29 Ges. W. vol. I, p. 443; CM vol. 1, p. 385.
30 Ges. W. vol. I, p. 409; CM vol. 1, p. 356.

34

he adopted neither the life-denying aspect of Schopenhauer's work (the self-denial of the will in favor of an ascetic attitude), nor his morality of pity.

The fourth *Untimely Meditation, Richard Wagner in Bayreuth* (1876), was intended to be a work thanking Wagner but it already displayed a secret resistance to him. With it, an important chapter in Nietzsche's life drew to a close. It was the end of a period still by and large sustained by a faith in the genuineness and truth of the ideals of his age. What then followed, as if severed by a caesura, was a complete transformation of the positive evaluation of culture that had comprised his view of the world up to this point.

Whereas until now, having turned thirty-two in 1876, he had followed the example of great figures[31] and respected human beings and life, a gradual *detachment from hitherto existing ties of sentiment and emotional evaluations* set in. It was, so to speak, a farewell to the past, a "desecratory reaching and glancing backward, to where it (the soul) had until then worshipped and loved."[32]

It was to become a basic feature of his life that he should repeatedly break away from those he loved and admired, especially from figures onto whom he had projected the image and spirit of his father. This was matched only by his early tendency towards mastering himself. During his adolescence, he had already attempted to tear himself away from his Christian beliefs. It seems that his readiness to self-sacrifice was, even in his youth, an offering he had to make to his inner voice, his inner *daimon*.

A free spirit began to stir in Nietzsche, a 'spirit of criticism,' independent within and untied by bourgeois concepts of morality. Nietzsche needed to escape the con-

---

31  A view he later amended in *Ecce homo* by stating that he had already distanced himself from these models by this time.

32  Ges. W. vol. II, Preface, p. 7; CM vol. 2/I, Preface, p. 16. Since several writings are collected in each volume of the Colli-Montinari edition, the second [Roman] numeral (e.g., 2/I) will refer to the appropriate section within the volume.

stricting, artificial ideals of the decorous inhabitants of Basle, whose small-town atmosphere was desperately intent upon upholding Christian values and continuing to live off its humanistic past. Although freethinking did not mean freedom from moral responsibility, it still pointed in a direction away from narrow-minded bourgeois rules and behavior, a direction consistent with the individual's ability to determine things for himself. In this period of feeling his own way, Nietzsche became acquainted with Malvida Meysenburg, a highly talented writer and adherent of Wagner. It was her main concern to underpin young Nietzsche's faith in his own destiny and to give him the courage to confess it.[33] This also involved lending him understanding support in his battle against the absolute claims of Christian ideals. Marie Baumgartner was another friend whose maternal qualities aided and sustained him in his doubts with sympathy and interest. In a letter to her of 1877, we read:

> "I know, I feel that there is a higher destiny for me than that declared in my so estimable position at Basle; I am also something more than a philologist, even though I can use philology as well for my higher task. 'I thirst for myself' – this has really been the constant theme of my last ten years."[34]

It is noticeable that Nietzsche makes an increased number of references to his growing certainty of being subject to a "higher destiny." Thus he wrote in the foreword to *Human All-Too-Human* (1878):

> "Our destiny commands us, even when we don't know what it is; it is the future which gives the rule to our present ... like an unsuspected pregnancy." [35]

33 Curt Janz, vol. I, p. 687.
34 Letter to Marie Baumgartner of 30.VIII, 1877. See also p. 16ff.
35 Ges. W. vol. II, p. 12; CM vol. 2/I, p. 21.

An aphorism from this time shows that he did not find it easy to abandon his ideals and fall back on himself. In it he describes the expression "time of darkness" as an image for all thinkers for whom "the sun of the future of mankind has temporarily disappeared."[36] All of this indicates an acute crisis. What had happened?

His letters reveal that the labor pains of his new attitude were accompanied by a considerable worsening of his health: he suffered incessantly from headaches, stomach pains and from bouts of vomiting and fainting. His eye trouble even got so bad that he could only read or write for a quarter of an hour at a time. All of these symptoms displayed an extreme weakening of his nerves, a factor presumably connected with the rejection of his application for a philosophical professorship at Basle, as well as with the frosty silence that followed the publication of the *Birth of Tragedy*. Furthermore, it is likely that the cause of his crisis lay in the growing conflict he felt between profession and vocation, which ultimately drove him away from the academic corner of Basle in 1879. The immediate reason, however, was probably supplied by his disillusionment with Richard Wagner, in whom the pathetic and theatrical sides, manifest in the monumentality of his recently constructed *Festspielhaus* in Bayreuth, in short the 'Germanness,' had gained the upper hand and forced Nietzsche to withdraw. Fascination can so easily turn into its opposite, and the degree to which Nietzsche had been moved by Wagner was now matched by the seriousness of his break with him and of the criticism he poured upon him. Both expressed one and the same commitment, only in differing circumstances. Despite further, often vehement, attacks, Nietzsche's encounter with Wagner remained his most deeply-felt human experience. In his own way, he even appears to have stayed loyal to his former idol, as a com-

36 Ges. W. vol. III/2, p. 300, § 191; CM vol. 2/II, p. 638, § 191.

ment made in 1885 shows.[37] Yet in the end it was the sacrifice of this friendship that would enable him to achieve the 'birth of Dionysus' within his own soul.

Nietzsche's severance from the figures that constituted his ideals was paralleled by a change in his attitude to music. To develop the clarity of his thought, he first had to rid himself of the danger of being overwhelmed by the world of music, and particularly that of Wagner. Karl Jaspers' observation seems to me to shed light on this: "What Nietzsche philosophizes on has been wrested from the musical sphere, and has then been used to conquer it."[38] Likewise, it may be said that the psychological insights gained in Nietzsche's later years, though they came less from his musical inspiration, were nevertheless wrested from the direct and creative sources of experience. Just as previously music and knowledge had been the same, so now it was the turn of experience and creativity. Life and work were increasingly becoming one.


## III. Human All-Too-Human

The first evidence of his radical change in attitude was provided by the work *Human All-Too-Human, a Book for Free Spirits* (1878). The book reveals him taking his leave of accepted values, ideals and beliefs, and betrays a spirit who had liberated his self from personal models and was once more in possession of his own being.[39] This spiritual liberation culminated in him ruthlessly breaking free from

37 "I have loved and adored Wagner more than anyone else, and if he had not finally ... sadly had to make common cause with 'spirits' of highly dubious quality as far as I was concerned, with his adherents, the Wagnerians, I would have had no reason to bid him farewell while he was still alive: him, the deepest, boldest and most misunderstood of all the figures that are difficult to understand today, to have met him has advanced my knowledge more than any other encounter." CM vol. 12, p. 80.
38 Karl Jaspers, *Nietzsche*, p. 37.
39 Ges. W. vol. XV, p. 74; CM vol. 6, p. 322.

38

the views on Wagner and Schopenhauer that had hitherto been a constant factor in his life.

This work contained a sceptical and critical attitude to culture that was very difficult from the tone of his earlier writings. It was the expression of his tormenting struggle with 'self-overcoming,'[40] and referred not only to the testing of himself, but also to the sacrifice of romantic and dearly-held convictions. At the same time, this criticism represented a freer acceptance of *ratio,* reason and science. It was one of his principle aims to clarify his relationship with Schopenhauerian metaphysics. He was forced to acknowledge that the latter's assumption that pure knowledge existed 'in itself,' and was directed towards a 'true world,' was unjustified. His own experience made clear to him the fact that the human being was basically dependent on *instinctual needs,* which ran completely contrary to the hypothesis of a 'truth in itself' and upset any claims of objectivity for truth and knowledge. In view of the presence of the errors and deceptions that such instinctual drives cause, a subjective truth, i.e., the subjectification of convictions and values, is the inevitable result. If man wished his knowledge to remain relatively free, then this could only be attained, Nietzsche realized, by means of a fundamental reassessment of the existence and nature of traditional values and ideals. It was thus that Nietzsche, under the influence of his freethinking period, came to see the necessity of thoroughly *becoming conscious of human drives and motivations.* What was needed, above all, was to replace metaphysical and rational questioning, discredited through the impossibility of making objective statements, with *questioning of a psychological sort:*

---

40 His preface to *Human All-Too-Human* begins with the following words: "One should only speak when one cannot be silent; and then only speak about the things one has *overcome,* – all the rest is just empty chatter ... My writings only speak of my overcoming: 'I' am in them, with everything that was once inimical to my *ego ipsissimum.*" Ges. W. vol. III/1, Preface, p. 3; CM vol. 2/II, p. 369.

"Whoever attacks his age can only attack *himself:*
What can he possibly see if not himself?..."[41]

His inner need to investigate his own motivations, and
partly also the influence of his intensive discussions of
psychological themes with his friend, Paul Rée,[42] turned
him rather hesitantly in the direction of the "art of the psychological dissection"[43] of human behavior. With his support, Nietzsche detached himself from the metaphysical
models to whom Schopenhauer had guided him and subjected himself to the "rigorousness of science" and "its
crisp air," i.e., to the dispassionate and sober world of the
intellect. Both Dionysian intoxication, which had fired him
during the *Birth of Tragedy* period, and the compulsive
adoration of genius of his 'untimely' days now gave way to
cool Socratic judgment. He even went so far as to dedicate
the first edition of his new book *(Human All-Too-Human)*
to the memory of Voltaire – something he would later drop,
however. Under the spell of Socratic intellectualism,[44] he
devoted himself to a rigorous criticism of the dominant
drives. The spirit that manifested itself was a tribute to the
strictest of intellectual discipline and put an abrupt end to
the cult of genius and all idealism.

His achievement rested on the ruthless self-torment of
exposing the errors and self-deceptions that crept into day-
to-day conceptions of a moral and ideal sort. As C.G. Jung
rightly emphasized, he discovered that ideals were "figurative expressions for secretive motives." Using his intuition,
Nietzsche found the courage to minutely examine his own

41  CM vol. 8, p. 500.
42  See p. 14. Their friendship was broken up by the circumstances
surrounding Nietzsche's separation from Lou Salomé.
43  Ges. W. vol. II, p. 57; CM vol. 2/I, p. 57, § 35.
44  Ges. W. vol. III/2, p. 248; CM vol. 2/II/2, p. 591, § 86. "If all goes
well, the time will come when we will prefer picking up Socrates'
memorabilia to the Bible for moral improvement, and when Montaigne
and Horace will be used as the forerunners and guides to an
understanding of the simplest and most unforgettable of the mediator-
sages, Socrates."

motivations and seek out many a 'hiding-place' in which ideals had made themselves at home. What he was able to portray in this respect are masterpieces of psychological analysis and reveal an extraordinary grasp of the processes of the mind. Nietzsche had found out that he was a psychologist at heart. His newly gained freedom was also expressed by the aphoristic style he used, which, apart from being forced on him by his eye trouble, corresponded to his true nature.

The words contained in the retrospective Preface of 1886 to this book were characteristic of his new attitude:

> "Cannot all values be overturned? And is Good perhaps Evil? And God only an invention of the devil?"[45]

For the first time, we can read that the world is neither good nor evil and that, instead of resting on general principles, moral values only have meaning with regard to the individual.[46] This represents a complete reversal of the concept of ethics put forward in the *Untimely Meditations*. Such a precipitous reversal in Nietzsche's thinking betokened not only his basic disposition towards antithetical thinking which repeatedly led him to tear away at cherished convictions and confront every 'Yes' with a 'No';, but also his remarkable openness to all things new.

Yet, the inner change he underwent in coming to a critical view of human ideals cost him great pain. For it included having to sacrifice the hardened ideal, schooled in him by Schopenhauer, of a transformation of human society through sublimation of instinctual drives[47] and through the combating of the 'brutalization of the instincts.' What he had expected was the advancement of the cultural values of selflessness and pity. Nietzsche turned further and fur-

45  Ges. W. vol. II, 1886 Preface; CM vol. 2/I, Preface, p. 17, § 3.
46  Ges. W. vol. II, p. 46; CM vol. 2/I, p. 49, § 28.
47  Ges. W. vol. II, p. 110; CM vol. 2/I, p. 104, § 107. "Good actions are sublimated evil actions; evil actions are good actions become coarse and stupid."

ther away from such didactic ideals, his present state of rigorous intellectual self-analysis helping him to see in them the tyrannical suppression of instinctual needs. He was already giving advanced notice of his 'revaluation of values.'[48] It seemed to be growing more and more necessary for him to dig down into the depths of his own being and light the way into his own true 'source of experience.' Clear-headed perception became more important to him than the ideal of selflessness. He attributed immeasurable significance to the need:

> "to see the bottom in the dark well of your being and knowing. . . . Toward the light – your last movement; a joyful shout of knowledge – your last sound."[49]

The psychologist within him had triumphed. Nietzsche had cleared the path before him and could now expose the true motivations behind ideals, developing a *method for unmasking the truth* that was all his own.

We can read what lay behind his inward gaze in a sharply critical aphorism taken from *Ecce homo:*

> "One error after another is cooly placed on ice; the ideal is not refuted – it *freezes to death*. Here, for example, the genius freezes to death. . . . the saint ... the hero: in the end 'faith ... pity also cools down considerably, and almost everywhere 'the thing in itself' freezes to death."[50]

Thus "the saint" disguises not only "voluptuousness," but also traits of "cruelty."[51] Pity for instance, is, upon closer observation, nothing but a "hypochondriac illness" or a tendency towards "egotistic pleasure," while Nietzsche wrote of curiosity and hypocrisy in the following way:

48  See p. 122f.
49  Ges. W. vol. II, p. 267; CM vol. 2/I, p. 237, § 292.
50  Ges. W. vol. XV, p. 74; CM vol. 6, p. 323.
51  Ges. W. vol. II, p. 150f.; CM vol. 2/I, p. 138, § 142.

"....curiosity sneaks into the house of the unfortunate and needy"[52]

"To speak about oneself not at all is a very refined form of hypocrisy."[53]

In contrast to the *Untimely Meditations,* he now regarded the "cult of genius" and glorification of human genius essentially in terms of gushing vanity and self-love.[54] Indeed, vanity represented for him one of the basic motivations in human nature. Yet, whereas he now saw vanity as "the skin of the soul,"[55] revealing all the characteristics and advantages it was presumed to contain, he would later equate it with the power-drive. "Vanity," for example, resided in the following aphorism:

"One is twice as happy to dive after a man who has fallen into the water if people are present who do not dare to."[56]

The motive for acting here is not a love of mankind, but a repressed tendency towards self-admiration. The following comment also testifies to his psychological perceptiveness:

"Mothers are easily jealous of their sons' friends if they are exceptionally successful. Usually a mother loves herself in her son more than she loves the son himself."[57]

The projection onto the child of ambitions the parent has not been able to realize her or himself is all too familiar to

52 Ges. W. vol. II, p. 288; CM vol. 2/I, p. 255, § 363.
53 Ges. W. vol. II, p. 367; CM vol. 2/I, p. 321, § 504.
54 Ges. W. vol. II, p. 169; CM vol. 2/I, p. 151, § 162.
55 Ges. W. vol. II, p. 90; CM vol. 2/I, p. 86, § 82.
56 Ges. W. vol. II, p. 277; CM vol. 2/I, p. 245, § 323.
57 Ges. W. vol. II, p. 302; CM vol. 2/I, p. 266, § 385.

psychology! Another aphorism pointing to "the skin of the soul" reads:

> "There are women, who have no inner life wherever one looks for it, being nothing but masks. That man is to be pitied who lets himself in with such ghostly, necessarily unsatisfying creatures, but just these women are able to stimulate man's desire most intensely: he searches for their souls – and searches on and on."[58]

Nietzsche's statement contains the remarkable assertion that there is nothing like the soullessness and emptiness of a beautiful woman to encourage projections.

The following aphorism is also of psychological interest, since it refers to the mother as the archetype of femininity:

> "Everyone carries within him an image of woman that he gets from his mother; that determines whether he will honor women in general, or despise them, or be generally indifferent to them."[59]

In view of the fact that, in the moral sphere, everything is in a "variable and unsteady" state of flux, there can be no continued distinction between good and bad actions, between 'good and evil' as such. The observation that follows already anticipates the thoughts of *Beyond Good and Evil:*

> "Good actions are sublimated evil actions; evil actions are good actions become coarse and stupid."[60]

I will return to Nietzsche's understanding of sublimation later...[61]

58 Ges. W. vol. II, p. 306; CM vol. 2/I, p. 270, § 405.
59 Ges. W. vol. II, p. 301; CM vol. 2/I, p. 266, § 380.
60 Ges. W. vol. II, p. 110; CM vol. 2/I, p. 104, § 107.
61 See p. 125

Seen from a psychological viewpoint, one cannot praise too highly Nietzsche's role in properly evaluating the rational consciousness, and so in bringing to light the fact that unconscious motivations traverse conscious ideals. Conscious beliefs were less important to him than basic, instinctual impulses. He recognized that such convictions were steered by secret and largely hidden forces. Whenever the individual focused on ideal concepts, he merely saw a facade that obscured more than it betrayed. Only later would Nietzsche be able to formulate the notion that decisive value lay not in conscious intention, but in the opposite and unconscious tendencies that, to a large extent, forsook human personality. In psychological terms, this caused the individual to do, and make come true, just what he did not actually want. In accordance with this fact, Nietzsche wrote in *Beyond Good and Evil:*

> "that the decisive value of an action lies precisely in what is unintentional in it, while everything about it that is intentional, everything about it that can be seen, known, 'conscious,' still belongs to its surface and skin – which, like every skin, betrays something but *conceals* even more."[62]

His expositions on self-deception set in motion a process that led to Breuer's and Freud's studies on the relationship between the conscious and unconscious mind in the 1890's. It is astonishing that he not only used the word 'repression,' which was to become central to Freud's psychology, but also ascertained the inclination repressed emotions had at times to prematurely force their way into consciousness. This could lead to the reverse of conscious intention and cause unconsciously and without the individual wishing it, a negative effect upon him. This insight drew attention both to man's dark side and also to the dynamism that existed between his 'conscious' and

62 Ges. W. vol. VII, p. 53; CM vol. 5, p. 51, § 32. See also L. Frey-Rohn: *Das Böse [Evil]*, p. 166.

45

'unconscious' mind. Nietzsche's investigations were, as Klages acknowledged, no less important to the study of character. In his opinion, the study of character and graphology were unthinkable without Nietzsche's discovery about self-deception.[63]

## III. Human All-Too-Human, 3: The Wanderer and his Shadow

In the work that followed – *The Wanderer and his Shadow;* (1879) – which Nietzsche included as the third part of *Human All-Too-Human* (the second being the *Mixed Opinions and Maxims*), he continued his examination of the dark side of man, referring to it for the first time as the *shadow.* He confessed that this was a phase in which he had withdrawn from mankind and the world, and so lacked any deeper sort of contact with figures onto whom the shadow was projected . He therefore had no alternative but to elect himself the subject of his discussion and give free rein to his desire to speak out, an attitude Nietzsche himself referred to as 'vanity.' His essential aim was to find out *who he himself was.*

In the course of his search, the first thing he discovered was that the 'dark side,' the ever-present but rarely noticed unconscious tendency within him, that is to say, 'man's shadow,' was "just as necessary as the light."[64] Only the shadow improved one's character and gave beauty and expressive power to one's face. But although Nietzsche's accomplishments were remarkable, they appear to have been products of the head rather than of the heart. As an avowed

---

63 Ludwig Klages, *Die psychologische Errungenschaft Friedrich Nietzsches,* p. 46.
64 Ges. W. vol. III/2, p. 188; CM vol. 2/II, 2, , p. 538,. This aphorism from the bequest is interesting: "Truth, like the sun, should not be too bright: else people will flee to the night and make it dark." CM vol. 8, p. 513.

"disciple of the light" it was extremely difficult for him to accept that there was an inferior side to man, one that was "banal, trivial and ugly."

For the present, the way his freethinking had unmasked ideals and established value-systems still had hold of him. He underlined the importance of the normally despised "little, insignificant truths," which he regarded as indispensable. He was thus the first to stress the value of bodily functions such as eating, dwelling and dressing, an early indication of the appreciation of the body present in *Zarathustra*. The value of man and his needs was gradually making headway. In his literary bequest he exclaims impressively:

> "Let us become *what we have yet to: good neighbors to the things closest to us*."[65]

In the *Wanderer and his Shadow* he writes of those smallest of things:

> "... not knowing about *the smallest and most everyday things* and not having a sharp eye – this is what makes the earth a 'meadow of calamity' for so many ... one should consider that *nearly all bodily and mental ills* of the individual result from this shortcoming...."[66]

– an extraordinary realization for those times!

Despite his intuitions, he continued to put the main accent on knowledge and the intellect clarifying which of the small things man could use and benefit from. At this stage, however, there was no question of his grappling with the shadow, let alone of including the dark side within his portrayal of man as a whole. It is, therefore, not surprising that, at the end of the work, the relationship between wanderer and shadow should break down again, since the

65  CM vol. 8, p. 588.
66  Ges. W. vol. III/2, p. 192f.; CM vol. 2/II, p. 542f., § 6.

shadow personality finds the intellectual too icy for itself. The conversation ends thus:

> "The wanderer: And could I not quickly do you some kindness? Don't you have a wish?
> The shadow: None, apart from the wish, perhaps, that the philosophical 'dog' had before Alexander the Great: You're blocking my sun, I'm getting too cold.
> The wanderer: What should I do?
> The shadow: Step under the pines and look around for the mountains; the sun is sinking.
> The wanderer: – Where are you, where are you?"[67]

Through the exposure of unconscious ideal images in *Human All-Too-Human,* Nietzsche embarked on a voyage of self-examination and knowledge that would characterize him as a "lonely wanderer."[68] The way led not only to a reconsideration of the rigid principles of the psychology of the conscious mind, but, at the same time, to the 'irrational' emerging as compensation for the scientific spirit of contemporary research. That, in time, he would also turn out to be the first cultural critic of his century was of no lesser importance.

It is understandable that *Human All-Too-Human* should have caused so much displeasure amongst contemporaries, given not just Nietzsche's sarcastic and critical unmasking of cherished values, but also the obvious break with his own previous admiration for Schopenhauer's ethics and Wagner's cultural program. Though he was suffering a growing spiritual isolation and an increasing lack of appreciation on the part of his fellows, Nietzsche never wavered as he pursued the pathway of inner destiny that led away

67 Ges. W. vol. III/2, p. 374f.; CM vol. 2/II, p. 704, § 350.
68 Ges. W. vol. II/1, p. 413; CM vol. 2/I, p. 362, § 638.
    "He who has come only in part to a freedom of reason cannot feel on earth otherwise than as a wanderer — though not as a traveller towards a final goal, for this does not exist."

from the rationalistic spirit and down towards the core of his inmost soul.

## IV. The Dawn

In his next work, *The Dawn* (1881), the withdrawn and lonely wanderer took upon himself the demanding task of looking into the fundamentals of morality. As he mentioned retrospectively in *Ecce homo,* it signified a "veritable campaign against morality"[69] and its prejudices. The attempt he now made at uncovering moral prejudice served a similar end to his unmasking of ideals: the undermining of confidence in morality. The later Preface of 1886 referred to *The Dawn* in this way:

> "... in this book faith in morality is withdrawn – but why? *Out of morality.*"[70]

His critical attack on the unassailable "fortresses of moral security" and the steadfast belief in the 'eternal principles' of morality paved the way for the 'revaluation of values' already hinted at in the title, *The Dawn.*

What did Nietzsche understand by traditional bourgeois morality? In broad terms it represented for him the embodiment of ethical obligations that had more to do with the age-old "sanctity and indisputability" of morals than with what our ancestors had deemed useful or damaging.[71] He regarded the vital factor of morality as its constant demand for absolute obedience to authority, whether in the form of

69 Ges. W. vol. XV, p. 81; CM vol. 6, p. 329. In the preface to *The Dawn,* we can read: "In this book you will discover a 'subterranean man' at work, who tunnels and mines and undermines. You will see him – presupposing you have eyes capable of seeing this work in the depths – going forward slowly, cautiously, gently inexorable, without betraying very much of the distress which any protracted deprivation of light an air must entail."

70 Ges. W. vol. IV, Preface p. 8; CM vol. 3/I, Preface p. 16.

71 Ges. W. vol. IV, p. 28; CM vol. 3/I, p. 32, § 19.

custom, bourgeois principles or political prescriptions. It was this that provoked Nietzsche's most bitter criticism. Morality required nothing less than the sacrifice of one's personal freedom of choice, it paralyzed the will and halted all thought; in short, it dragged the individual down to the level of a slave.

Nietzsche was principally fascinated by the unconscious motivations that encouraged the individual to behave ethically, and, sparing none, he exposed the in large part disguised motives behind the individual's moral actions; motives like fear, giving way to protective measures, the desire for distinction[72] or power, and finally, even cruelty. Fear caused the individual to subject himself to the judgments of others, and out of fear he "glorified security as the highest divinity"; while it was fear of the incursion and deception of others that lay behind dissemblance and hypocrisy.[73] This barbed comment has often been quoted:

> "The lie is, if not the mother, then the nurse of goodness."[74]

If Nietzsche had already exposed *vanity as a hidden motivation* in *Human All-Too-Human,* then, in *The Dawn,* he characterized it as a desire for recognition, *esteem and power.* This instinct, in collective terms, may well have only started out as fear and impotence, but Nietzsche saw it as one of the strongest impulses we could ever have. He did not hesitate to draw parallels between the development of the power-drive and the drive of cultural history in general. It was not only the force that drove politics forward, but one that motivated every individual and every event. Nietzsche even went so far as to postulate the power-drive

72  Ges. W. vol. IV, p. 110; CM vol. 3/I, p. 102, § 113.
73  Similarly, in *The Dawn,* we find: "Whenever a person reveals something one can ask: what is it supposed to conceal? From what is it supposed to divert the eyes? What prejudice is it supposed to arouse?"
Ges. W. vol. IV, p. 338; CM vol. 3/I, p. 301, § 523.
74  Ges. W. vol. IV, p. 230; CM vol. 3/I, p. 204, § 248.

as the root of cruelty,[75] the desire to hurt others. "For to practise cruelty is to enjoy the highest gratification of the feeling of power,"[76] in the same way that "cruelty" belongs to "the oldest festive joys."[77] He even believed he saw lust for power in the ascetic's "self-torment." Finally, he thought he recognized in the love of power nothing other than the demon of man itself.

> "Not necessity, not desire – no, the love of power is the demon of men. Let them have everything – health, food, a place to live, entertainment – they are and remain unhappy and low-spirited: for the demon waits and waits and will not be satisfied."[78]

Small wonder that Nietzsche's subversive ideas invited the indignation of his contemporaries. It was a dangerous thing to draw back the veil that covered up the reality behind moral motivations, given the lasting power held by the phantom of ecclesiastical Christianity and its doctrines of goodness, justice, pity and truth.

Another target of Nietzsche's anger was therefore the hypocrisy on which Christian moralism was based, an hypocrisy that held tightly onto values that were rapidly disappearing. His quarrel was with the so-called spirituality of Christianity, which sought to suppress the "values of life" and the human instincts "blindly and one-sidedly," and which even "decried Eros" (meaning sexual impulses). For the first time, he chanced a direct assault upon Christian values, questioning whether the Christian God was not, in fact, cruel for not interfering in the pathetic suffering He could see in mankind. He even dared call faith in such a God a cowardly act; indeed, he regarded the very principles of morality as founded on the individual's cowardice, laziness and dishonesty. For this reason, it was only logical

75 Ges. W. vol. IV, p. 36; CM vol. 3/I, p. 40, § 30.
76 Ges. W. vol. IV, p. 26; CM vol. 3/I, p. 30, § 18.
77 Ges. W. vol. IV, p. 25; CM vol. 3/I, p. 30, § 18.
78 Ges. W. vol. IV, p. 235; CM vol. 3/I, p. 209, § 262.

that the greatest problem the future would pose would, in his eyes, be that of *abolishing traditional moral concepts* and freeing morality from conventional prejudice. The absolute nature of this undertaking made it an extremely dangerous one, in that it left the unprotected individual at the mercy of the powers of good and evil. For the moral code only proved psychologically destructive when the individual took its commandments and prohibitions to be absolute ends in themselves. The doctrine of morality itself should not be held responsible for any negative effects, only the moral attitude of the human being.[79] Nevertheless, Nietzsche did stress the *rational* and *metaphysical premises of the Christian view of the world* in his questioning.

That is why he disputed the absolute validity of truth, goodness, justice and brotherly love, and particularly, the concept of a moral goal man should strive for. It was consistent that he should also criticize Kant's philosophy, which was itself based on Christian ideas; it was the premise of a 'categorical imperative' valid for all human beings and the assumption of a 'thing in itself' that Nietzsche singled out for special attack. Even Schopenhauer's hypotheses of the 'true world' and the ethic of pity became an increasing source of irritation for Nietzsche. He contradicted both philosophers by emphasizing that to presuppose a 'morality in itself' ignored the individual for the sake of the unworldly and unreal, and so was inimical to life. "All absolutes belong to pathology," he expounded later in *Beyond Good and Evil*.[80] It was a viewpoint that culminated in the notion that "*there is no absolute morality*,"[81] and that *all morality was relative to the individual*. Every moral statement and every sort of human action was basically subjective and founded on instinctual impulses common to the whole of humanity. All of his discoveries proved to him that neither moral commonplaces nor universal values had an objective existence. Such hypotheses served both to re-

79  L. Frey-Rohn, *Das Böse*, p. 168.
80  Ges. W. vol. VII/1, p. 107; CM vol. 5/I, p. 100.
81  Ges. W. vol. IV, p. 143; CM vol. 3/I, p. 131, § 139.

pudiate the individual and his right to live and to undermine our valuation of life and instinct.

This was Nietzsche's first decisive formulation of the idea that it was not just ideals, but also the moral motivations of the individual that rested principally on instinctual drives.

"There is nothing 'moral in itself': these are opinions *produced by the instincts, which in turn influence these same instincts again.*" [82]

Even when the purpose and cause of moral judgments and motives are well-known, the latter were the result of unconscious instinctual drives that the intellect saw as absolute. In each case it was a question of a "*battle of instincts* taking place within the mind,"[83] with victory going to the stronger. In representing the view that morality was subject to the physiological functions,[84] Nietzsche finally broke free from Western metaphysics. What started out in *Human All-Too-Human* as thoughts on unconscious impulses had now become, in meaning, if not in the words themselves, the notion that the instinctual unconscious lay behind all our motivations and value judgments.

It was something totally new to have discovered the *irrational basis* of the human understanding of the world, and it would have a lasting influence on psychological research. For the time being, Nietzsche experienced certain difficulties with his discovery. The fact that all conscious motivations were acted out against a backcloth of unconscious drives made them hard to pin down. Nothing was certain anymore, now that the human being had found himself grossly deceived about the world. What was really happening belonged largely to the unconscious and the unknown. It makes a great impact when Nietzsche states that

82  CM vol. 9, p. 363.
83  Ges. W. vol. XI, p. 201, § 113; CM vol. 9, p. 229.
84  CM vol. 9, p. 42.

one "is more likely to be done to than know what one is doing."

"However far a man can go in self-knowledge, nothing may be more incomplete than his image of the totality of drives which constitute his being."[85]

Though these comments may appear naive by today's standards, they nevertheless represented, in his day, a sensitive *blow to the ethical rationalism of his age*.

Nietzsche went on to develop the idea that man could only comprehend the tiniest part of what constituted his actions.

"Moral actions are, in reality, 'something other than that' .... all actions are essentially unknown."[86]

The things we believed we knew were just images, dreams and fantasies caught up with the instincts that had found their way into the conscious mind and been interpreted by the intellect. For anyone who, like Nietzsche, thirsted for the truth, this could only represent a highly problematic situation! Did this not make objective moral judgments precarious? Did blind anarchy prevail? Was not every interpretation subject to constant reassessment and merely the result of a basically vague and unknown process? He seemed to have at first regarded the individual as incarcerated within his own cage of instinctive drives and devoid of the opportunity to get at the reality and truth of his experience. It was an opinion he was compelled to moderate in the course of *The Dawn*. Everything depended on how the instinctive core might be more clearly defined. If the instincts, as he supposed, lacked direction and intellectual substance, then the following statement had a right to be made:

85 Ges. W. vol. IV, p. 120; CM vol. 3/I, p. 111, § 119.
86 Ges. W. vol. IV, p. 118; CM vol. 3/I, p. 109, § 116.

"The habits of our senses have woven us into lies and deception of sensation: these again are the basis of all our judgments and 'knowledge' – there is absolutely no escape, no backway or bypath into the *real world* : we sit within our net, we spiders, and catch nothing at all except that which allows itself to be caught in precisely *our* net."[87]

To deny so totally an objective knowledge of truth was impossible for Nietzsche in the long run. His inexorable desire for truth, therefore, drove him to look for ways to endow the instincts with a certain sublimity that went beyond lies and deceptions. It was not beyond the realms of possibility that the instincts were not without some meaning, even if one did have to disclaim their rational value and admit that as "interpretations of mere nervous stimuli," they were free, unrestrained and obeyed only "the motions of the blood and intestines."[88] It is characteristic of the genius of Nietzsche's perception that he should uncover such meaning in *the instincts' own self-awareness*. The quotation below illustrates how he envisaged an attribute that, though it could never be known, could still be felt:

"... that our moral judgments and evaluations too are only images and fantasies based on a physiological process unknown to us ... that all our so-called consciousness is a more or less fantastic commentary on an unknown, perhaps unknowable, but felt text ..."[89]

The assertion that the instincts contain a proportion of meaning is important in shedding light on the neglected values of knowing how we feel and experience things. Yet at the same time it makes clear the enormous significance Nietzsche gave to feeling in his own life. Despite the meticulousness of his conceptual thinking, Nietzsche's

87 Ges. W. vol. IV, p. 119; CM vol. 3/I, p. 110, § 117.
88 Ges. W. vol. IV, p. 122; CM vol. 3/I, p. 113, § 119.
89 *Idem.*

search for truth was primarily determined by feelings and emotions, and not just by thought.[90]

The detection of meaning inherent in instinctive life gives Nietzsche the honor of having discovered that knowledge of the unconscious was possible. It was this *growing awareness of the unconscious* that would become very important for the later discipline of depth psychology.[91]

Nietzsche was thus in the position of having referred to certain psychological processes that, to a degree, accepted that the truth could be stated. What he was thinking of was the experience of dreams, whose content appeared to point back to an absence of nourishment on the previous day. His psychological genius led him to deduce from this that *the unconscious acted to compensate* for the foregoing absence.[92] Although he did not postulate a connection as such between the meaning of dreams and an "unknowable but felt text," it still seemed probable to him that feelings contained the deeper meaning of one's physiological being, one's instinct and one's inclinations. It was this that lent specific color, tone and shading to everything that happened in the unconscious, and constituted its very essence. *Zarathustra* illustrates this clearly when Nietzsche describes the body as the bearer of "higher reason," of meaning and even the self.[93] In *Beyond Good and Evil* he also mentions the fact of an unchanging perception of the self, a feeling that "this is I,"[94] capable of stabilizing the physiological processes. These references may be only incidental, but they nevertheless seem to be highly important, inasmuch as they express a solid core of feeling residing within his own

90 In the course of this book, we shall see that Nietzsche finally had to abandon this insight after his painful experience of the ultimate "truth abolishing itself." See p. 219.

91 However, we must not overlook the fact that when Nietzsche stresses the meaning of instinct, the meaning of unconscious drives, he is already betraying signs of what would later become the abolition of absolute truth.

92 Ges. W. vol. IV, p. 121; CM vol. 3/I, p. 112, § 119.

93 See p. 96.

94 See p. 180.

56

personality. The concepts of 'overcoming' and 'becoming oneself' ("become what you are") later confirm this fact.

In *Human All-Too-Human*, Nietzsche writes of the hallucinatory aspect of dreaming as constituting the memory of what man had once been in primordial times. Thus the dream itself acquired sense and meaning:

> "Thus, in our sleep and dreams, we go through the work of earlier mankind once more."[95]

The following sentence puts it even more clearly:

> "This old aspect of humanity lives on in us in our dreams, for it is the basis upon which higher reason developed ... the dream restores us to distant states of human culture and gives us a means by which to understand them better."[96]

Another aphorism, discussing the reshaping of the world through the ideas and imagination of the individual, extracts a certain value and meaning from dreaming and poetry, and even seems to do the same with delusion:

> "World of phantoms in which we live! Inverted, upside-down, empty world, yet dreamed of as *full* and *upright*."[97]

Experiences such as these, which attribute meaningfulness to dreaming and the imagination, hint that it may be

95 Ges. W. vol. II, p. 27; CM vol. 2/I, p. 32, § 12.
96 Ges. W. vol. II, p. 28; CM vol. 2/I, p. 33, § 13. Though Nietzsche was correct to describe "thought in dreams as a philogenetically older type of thinking," he went much too far when he interpreted the content as nothing more than the archaic remains of an older type of mankind. For, as C.G. Jung emphasized, they are "not only relics or vestiges of earlier modes of functioning; they are the ever-present and biologically necessary regulators of the instinctual sphere...." C.G. Jung, Ges. W., VIII, p. 231 (C.W., vol. 8, p. 201).
97 Ges. W. vol. IV, p. 120; CM vol. 3/I, p. 111, § 118.

possible to gain knowledge of unconscious happenings. But Nietzsche had considerable doubts about how much could be established on the basis of such "pictures and sorceries," doubts that were reinforced by a fear, bordering on despair, that nothing could be known for sure. Yet he was still driven by the need to seek the truth and was able to wrest something positive from his despair in the form of a restrengthened desire to overcome the self.

How Nietzsche was finally able to bridge his ambivalent attitude towards the possibility of knowing the life of the unconscious makes fascinating reading. His doubts were dispelled with the help of an overwhelming experience, which gave him access to a wholly new dimension of knowledge. In the middle of his reverie about the beauty of the sea, he was struck by its 'eloquent' muteness and silence. This awareness of how powerful and expressive silence could be was, for Nietzsche, tantamount to discovering a profound truth. During his mute contemplation, he realized that the acts of merely *seeing* and *feeling* had a significance more valuable than speech, and possibly more useful than thought itself.

> "I begin to hate speech, to hate even thinking: for do I not hear behind every word the laughter of error, of imagination, of the spirit of delusion?"[98]

His mind's eye conjured up the Greeks, who, unlike his "color-blind" contemporaries, could appreciate the beauty of the world. This inspired his growing awareness that, far from being the rational and purely conceptual process he had always held it to be, the very *act of knowing itself* probably contained the same *emotive* element that characterized the instincts. This wholly new insight was rendered more intense by Zarathustra's own experiences and completely reversed Nietzsche's previously critical attitude towards feelings. Nietzsche's own later work was pioneered

98 Ges. W. vol. IV, p. 292; CM vol. 3/I, p. 260, § 423.

by his discovery that there was also an *irrational, emotional dimension* to knowledge, a dimension not unakin to passion and which is commonly described in terms of the 'spirit.'[99]

Until now, he had been working from the premise that instinct and intellect were two separate things; but, from this point on, he was prepared to acknowledge that such a contrastive approach was unnecessary. Indeed, he believed that these opposites could be reconciled and overcome by unifying word and feeling, word and seeing. Although he understood that it "obscured the pure vision of the intellect" to assume knowledge was based on instinct and emotion, he nevertheless saw one great advantage to counteract any loss: conceptual supremacy of the mind. Consciousness was pushed aside so that the human personality could participate undisturbed in life as a whole. It was the first time in the study of philosophy that instinctual and intuitive knowledge was regarded as containing the truth. What Nietzsche had already looked on as the unity of culture in the *Untimely Meditations,* the unity of thought, willing and life, now received more substantial treatment. It was used to oppose the prejudice of modern science that considered the thought process to be exclusively intellectual and free of all emotion and any values.[100]

After the radical flirtation with positivism that brought him under the sway of Rée, Nietzsche returned to his own path. This time, the task he set himself was of an altogether more comprehensive sort, now including the irrational and seeking to harmonize life and thought. His nature compelled him to try to understand problems not just through 'pure' thinking but also by means of experience and suffering. *His experience and his work represented a unified whole,* and it was this discovery that was of fundamental significance both to himself and to the later development of

99 Ges. W. vol. IV, p. 296f; CM vol. 3/I, p. 264, § 429.
100 See the philosophy of Max Weber, Prof. of National Economy at Heidelberg.

philosophy and science in general.[101] As a result of his suffering Nietzsche began to realize that a "thinker who thinks against the grain," i.e., against his own most personal experience, will become ill, whilst fruits that "grow in one's own soil" are the most nourishing. It became increasingly clear to him that the world of experience and "the passion for knowledge" formed what was the core of his own search for the truth:

> "Just as the Italians appropriate music by absorbing it into their passion ... so I read thinkers and repeat their melody; I know that behind all the cold words a longing soul is in motion, I hear it singing, because my own soul sings when it is moved."[102]

Yet his path was not without danger. It could have been that, in lifting its emotional barriers, the human personality would be overpowered by passions, a risk Nietzsche himself occasionally ran. Despite being conscious of how bottomless the passions could be, often irredeemably so, he could still write in *The Dawn* :

> "Knowledge has in us been transformed into a passion which shrinks at no sacrifice and at bottom fears nothing but its own extinction ..."[103]

In accordance with his ecstatic nature, it was more meaningful to him to be consumed by the passion for knowledge than forego all contact with the source of life. With fiery enthusiasm, he continued:

> "We would all prefer the destruction of mankind to a regression of knowledge. And finally, if mankind

---

101 I am thinking not only of the philosophers Dilthey and Bergson, but also of psychoanalysis, founded by Freud and developed further by C.G. Jung and A. Adler. See p. 64f.
102 CM vol. 9, p. 320.
103 Ges. W. vol. IV, p. 296f.; CM vol. 3/I, p. 264, § 429.

does not perish from a *passion*, it will perish from a *weakness:* which is preferable? This is the main question. Do we desire for mankind an end in fire and light or one in the sand?"[104]

Yet, as Montinari stresses, the desire for passion was held in check by an equally strong inclination towards a strict and upright honesty. Both were necessary to him: the passion for knowledge and for probity.

It is interesting to trace Nietzsche's path to himself in the aftermath of this realization, a path that led into the "desert of loneliness," where he hoped to drink "water from the well of the self." In the meantime, he wrote:

"I am not quick-moving; I have to wait for myself – it is always late before the water comes to light out of ' the well of my self, and I often have to endure thirst for longer than I have patience. That is why I go to solitude – so as not to drink out of everybody's cistern."[105]

The way was now clear for him to be true to himself, to his feelings and conscience. In *Human All-Too-Human,* Nietzsche had already intuitively anticipated the fact that such a relationship to the self required total submission to the processes of the unconscious; and, writing about the creative achievement of self-discovery, he stated:

"Everyone has his good day, when he finds his higher self ... [many] fear their higher self because, when it speaks, it speaks demandingly."[106]

104 *Idem.*
105 Ges. W. vol. IV, p. 325; CM vol. 3/I, p. 290, § 491.
106 Ges. W. vol. II, p. 400; CM vol. 2/I, p. 351, § 624. Nietzsche never defined the expression 'self': he hated all intellectual definitions. He spoke of the self as the "path to me," to himself, and also as the indefinite feeling for what we are deep down. See p. 96.

An aphorism from the *Mixed Opinions and Maxims* conveys the same spirit:

"... *will* a self and you will *become* a self ..."[107]

Nevertheless, it was a big step to achieve this aim by way of risking one's whole existence. Loyalty to oneself demanded, in addition, loyalty to the ideas secretly nurtured, particularly to the idea that the highest authority in life no longer existed; in other words, that "God is dead."[108] Similarly, such loyalty also required the constant searching of one's conscience, followed by the strain of total obedience to it.

> *"What does your conscience say?* – You should become who you are."[109]

An observation in the literary bequest made at this time bears witness to the far-sightedness of his mind:

> "They will call you the destroyers of morality, but you are nothing but the discoverers of yourselves."[110]

The "discovery of the self" was important to Nietzsche all his life, even when he was lapsing into mental illness and beginning to learn how dangerous loyalty to the self and the search for truth could, in fact, be. The poem, 'Amid Birds of Prey,'[111] published in the *Dionysus Dithyrambs,* illustrates the point, when Zarathustra-Nietzsche is described as a *"self-knower"* and *"self-hangman."* The final aphorism of *The Dawn* sounds just as pessimistic with regard to the vast and infinite passion of the spirit:

107 Ges. W. vol. III/1, p. 173; CM vol. 2/II/1, p. 524, § 366.
108 See p. 70.
109 Ges. W. vol. V, p. 205; CM vol. 3/3, p. 519, § 270.
110 Ges. W. vol. XII, p. 266; CM vol. 10, p. 212.
111 Ges. W. vol. VIII, p. 421; CM vol. 6, p. 389f. See p. 168f.

"And whither then would we go? Would we *cross* the sea? Whither does this mighty longing draw us, this longing that is worth more to us than any pleasure? Why just in this direction, thither where all the suns of humanity have hitherto *gone down* ? Will it perhaps be said of us one day that we, too, *steering westward, hoped to reach an India* – but that it was our fate to be wrecked against infinity? Or, my brothers? Or?"[112]

Did Nietzsche already sense his decline? Retrospectively, it may be stated that Nietzsche's exposure of moral prejudice *(The Dawn),* like his unmasking of human motives and ideals, broke new ground in contemporary philosophy and psychology. With his concepts, he once and for all broke the mould of the traditional philosophical view of the world expounded since Descartes. At a time when there was still a strong belief in the accuracy of scientific knowledge, Nietzsche's ideas virtually revolutionized our fundamental understanding of reality. In the period that followed, he anticipated important discoveries in psychology, depth psychology most of all, as all as in the natural sciences. His insights into the manifold sources of self-deception and moral prejudice provide, even by today's standards, a wealth of psychological information of particular use to the interpretation of dreams and the psychoanalysis of neuroses. In recognizing the unconscious as the irrational foundation of conscious processes, Nietzsche also struck a decisive blow to the positivism of the late 19th century.

Nietzsche was probing the irrational sphere of the mind at a time when Freud, then aged twenty-nine, was still a medical student in Bruecke's laboratory. More or less contemporary with this were Charcot's famous investigations

112  Ges. W. vol. IV, p. 371; CM vol. 3/I, p. 331, § 575.

of *idées fixes,*[113] and a decade later came Pierre Janet's demonstration of the existence of *idées subconscientes.*[114] Nietzsche managed to uncover the significance of *unconscious phenomena as the basis of the intellect and primary source of the vital and instinctual processes.* It was unprecedented in the contemporary psychology of the unconscious for him to have discovered the *irrevocable* connection of all *thought and knowledge* with *affective states* of instinct and emotion. No less revolutionary was his view that all intellectual activity was conditioned by life itself.

Of equal importance was Nietzsche's realization that dreams and the imagination fulfilled a compensatory role: this, too, was to prove deeply enlightening to posterity. Later developments in psychology were also anticipated by his unflinching demand for *loyalty to oneself.*[115] Nietzsche, then, may rightly be seen as one of the most significant psychologists of the second half of the 19th century.

Freud rarely mentioned Nietzsche's work, and then only hesitantly and in his later years, references appearing chiefly in his writings on the dream,[116] in *The Psychopathology of Everyday Life,*[117] and in the work, *Some Character-Types met with in Psycho-Analytic Work.*[118] The following observation on Nietzsche, made in Freud's *Selbstdarstellung* [*An Autobiographical Study*], should be of interest:

---

113 Jean-Martin Charcot (1825-93) worked at the Salpêtrière in Paris, where he was the first to do scientific research into hypnotism, and where he also made a name for himself with his investigation of hysterical states.
114 Pierre Janet (1859-1948), a pupil and colleague of Charcot, became famous through his research into psychic automatism.
115 See C.G. Jung's *Analytical Psychology.*
116 Sigmund Freud, Ges. W. vol. II/III, p. 554 (S.E. vol. 4/5).
117 Freud, Ges. W. vol. IV, p. 162 (S.E. vol. 6). Reference to Nietzsche: Ges. W. vol. VII, On the Memory.
118 Freud, Ges. W. vol. X, p. 391 (S.E. vol. 14, p. 332). Reference to 'Criminals from a Sense of Guilt.'

"Nietzsche, another philosopher whose guesses and intuitions often agree in the most astonishing way with the laborious findings of psycho-analysis, was for a long time avoided by me on that very count; I was less concerned with the question of priority than with keeping my mind unembarrassed."[119]

C.G. Jung, on the other hand, was interested in making it known that he had begun his career in psychology "well-prepared by Nietzsche," this being a reference to his psychology of the shadow. Nietzsche also concerned him later on, which, alongside the repeated references to him in his works, is revealed by the seminar (unpublished) he held from 1933 until 1939 on *Thus Spoke Zarathustra*. Jung referred to many aspects of Nietzsche's work but was particularly absorbed by his views on the dream, on art and the Dionysian, on power and evil, and finally on Zarathustra and the death of God. Unfortunately, I am not allowed to quote from this seminar, since it has not been released for publication.

## V. The Gay Science

*The Dawn* preceded *The Gay Science* (1882), another product of the freethinking period, but with its own lighter and fresher touch. Written after a mental and physical

---

119 Freud, Ges. W. vol. XIV, p. 86 (S.E. vol. 20, p. 60).Although by his own testimony, Freud is supposed to have read only half a page of Nietzsche, he was rather well- informed about his opinions: as early as the now famous Wednesday Meetings in Vienna, two evenings (1908/09) had been reserved for a discussion of 'The Nietzsche Phenomenon,' at which Freud was also present. In addition, Freud discussed Nietzsche with Lou von Salomé, Thomas Mann, Arnold Zweig and O. Gross. There can be no doubt that he valued Nietzsche for his forward-looking and intuitive flashes of genius, and he did not hesitate to describe him as a harbinger of psychoanalysis. See also Paul-Laurent Assoun, *Freud et Nietzsche,* p. 60.

breakdown[120] that brought Nietzsche close to death, it exudes the hope of renewed health and enjoyment in life. It was a work sustained by Nietzsche's exuberant gratitude for having overcome death despite his feeling that, at 35, he would go the same way as his father. The *affirmation of life* was still the tenor of this book, but it took on a new form, matured by illness, and communicating the knowledge that pain can be a purifying and ennobling factor. According to the 1886 Preface, life appeared to Nietzsche "as a process of continuous change" in which "constantly our thoughts are born out of our pain"[121]:

> "Life – that means for us constantly transforming all that we are into light and flame – also everything that wounds us; we simply cannot do otherwise."[122]

Nietzsche's new, restrengthened belief in himself and his task are beautifully expressed in the motto to the 4th book of the *Gay Science:*

> "With a flaming spear you crushed
> All its ice until my soul
> Roaring toward the ocean rushed
> Of its highest hope and goal,
> Ever healthier it swells,
> Lovingly compelled but free:
> Thus it lauds your miracles,
> fairest month of January."[123]

---

120 Eye disorders, headaches, bouts of fainting and vomiting.
121 "We are not thinking frogs, nor objectifying and registering mechanisms with their innards removed: constantly, we have to give birth to our thoughts out of our pain, and like mothers, endow them with all we have of blood, heart, fire, pleasure, passion, agony, conscience, fate and catastrophe." Ges. W. vol. V, p. 8; CM vol. 3/3, Preface, p. 349.
122 *Idem.*
123 Ges. W. vol. V, p. 207; CM vol. 3/3, p. 591, motto.

His apotheosis of destiny springs from the same feeling of renewed vigor:

"I want to learn more and more to see as beautiful what is necessary in things ... *Amor fati:* let that be my love henceforth! ... Looking away shall be my only negation. And all in all and on the whole: some day I wish to be only a Yes-sayer."[124]

A different tone of inner freedom is struck here, which goes beyond mere humor, approaching ridicule and malevolence. In the work as a whole, Nietzsche gives himself room to balance opposites and so avoid any sort of fanaticism. The serene and the tragic, evil and good, knowledge and life are reconciled. At the very start of the work, Nietzsche champions the *unreasonable in history,* which he deems as important as reason, duty and morality in preserving the human species. Thus, he wrote:

"Not only laughter and gay wisdom but the tragic, too, with all its sublime unreason, belongs among the means and necessities of the preservation of the species."[125]

In his view, part of the principle of "unreasonableness" was the realization that it was generally the strongest and most evil spirits that brought mankind forward, "just as what is new is always evil." It was the so-called evil spirits who always rekindled passions that were going to sleep and roused them to contradiction.[126] Nietzsche was already

---

124  Ges. W. vol. V, p. 210; CM vol. 3/3, p. 521, § 276. Was Nietzsche aware at this stage of how far he was going with his affirmation? Saying 'Yes' to existence was tantamount to accepting the dark side of his being as well; to wanting to say 'Yes' as much as to say 'No' to the monstrous dynamism that was lurking in the background. See also: C.G. Jung, Ges. W. vol. 7, p. 33 (C.W., vol. 7, p. 29f.).

125  Ges. W. vol. V, p. 37; CM vol. 3/3, p. 372, § 1.

126  Ges. W. vol. V, p. 41; CM vol. 3/3, p. 376, § 4.

revealing the revolutionary spirit that would radically question prevailing morality.

Whoever wishes to pursue the irrational gives himself a considerable task, and Nietzsche was no exception. Such an undertaking meant that all manifestations of instinct, passion and superstition would have to be investigated and considered, including everything "that had until now given color to existence," like greed, envy and even cruelty – in short, everything that contradicted the 'moral' spirit. By illuminating human passions, Nietzsche believed, a new *instinctive morality* derived directly from all the drives, the passions, the good and the evil of living experience would enrich and enlarge our knowledge to a far greater extent than was possible under a conventional moral code based on conscious values. Contemporary science-oriented morality failed in this respect because it sought to prove either the goodness and wisdom of God, or the usefulness or uselessness of knowledge. In either case, it was always careful to omit the "evil impulses in man,"[127] which Nietzsche regarded as essential. He wanted to cultivate the passions instead of suppressing them, allowing the art and imagination for which they are responsible to live. All these aspects of life were part of a living whole that encompassed the consciousness, the light of being as well as its shadows, the world of darkness and appearance.

In *The Dawn,* Nietzsche had emphasized that knowing was related to instinct. Now he did not hesitate to go further and see in *life* in general the decisive *condition of knowledge*. For the sake of knowledge, life should be loved and fostered,[128] irrespective of the fact that our image of what it represents has inevitably been faulty in the past. It was the first time Nietzsche dared to ignore established scientific method and trust himself to an experimental approach to life. That these experiments also contained much uncertainty, chance and irrationality was further cause for him to celebrate life. Thus, he wrote:

127 Ges. W. vol. V, p. 75; CM vol. 3/3, p. 406, § 37.
128 CM vol. 9, p. 504.

"Life as a means of knowledge – with this principle in one's heart one can live not only boldly but even gaily, and laugh gaily too."[129]

Besides assuming life to be superior to knowledge, he called into question the claim that judgments could represent truth. Since all knowledge is relative to the experience of the individual, it could lay no possible claim to an objective authority. Nietzsche unequivocally expressed his scepticism about truth in the aphorism:

"What are man's truths ultimately? Merely his irrefutable errors."[130]

Every statement has a different meaning, according to the personal interpretation of the individual and his instinctive sensitivity. In notes taken around this time, we find Nietzsche's first indication that knowledge could never be anything but an *importation of meaning* by the individual: "The more eyes the individual regards the world with, the more complete the picture becomes" that he builds up for himself; i.e., it grows to correspond to the meaning of his own experience.

"Task: to *see* things *as they are!* Means: to be able to look at them through a hundred eyes, through *a lot of persons*."[131]

I will concentrate on this important perspectivistic subject of knowledge in the section on *Beyond Good and Evil,* and therefore will not proceed any further with it at this point.[132]

Nietzsche found it difficult to renounce the total objectivity of truth and knowledge, but it was easier for him to

129  Ges. W. vol. V, p. 245; CM vol. 3/3, p. 553, § 324.
130  Ges. W. vol. V, p. 204; CM vol. 3/3, p. 518, § 265.
131  Ges. W. vol. XII, p. 13.
132  See p. 176.

cope with the errors of science, since art provided him with a more than adequate compensation. As an aesthetic phenomenon, standing for the playful side of existence, art guaranteed a 'freedom above things' that was an agreeable complement to the deceptions of knowledge. Indeed, art even possessed a "cult of the untrue"[133] and of the lie, and it was of particular significance to him that, within the cult, the beauty, dance and rapture of life should have been preserved.

Nietzsche's affirmation of life and renunciation of objective knowledge was to have wide-ranging consequences. It was inevitable that the *relativization of values* would bring with it the collapse of faith in the absolute truth of Christian valuations. A certain collective fatigue within mankind was unmistakable with regard to the belief in important Christian symbols.[134] With this change in attitude came a broadening of man's intellectual receptivity to thoughts that had long kept him busy, but now had sufficient evidence to be made public. For the first time, he found the courage to declare something that had occupied him for a long time, namely that "God is dead."

> "God is dead; but given the way of men, there may still be caves for thousands of years in which the shadow will be shown. And we – we still have to vanquish his shadow, too."[135]

Although this idea corresponded more or less openly to the mood of the age since the French Revolution and had been put almost beyond all doubt by the hints of Hegel and the unequivocal statements of Strauss and Feuerbach, Nietzsche had been very reluctant to admit it outright, as it

---

133  Ges. W. vol. V, p. 142; CM vol. 3/3, p. 464, § 107. In *The Birth of Tragedy,* Nietzsche had paid tribute to art for symbolically reconciling Dionysian and Apollonian attitudes; now art represented a counterbalance to the deception of the intellect. See p. 27.

134  Ges. W. vol. X, p. 289; CM vol. 7, p. 711.

135  Ges. W. vol. V, p. 147; CM vol. 3/3, p. 467f., § 108.

meant acknowledging what had always been left obscure and undefined. That was the invalidity of faith not only in the concept of "the saintly and powerful," in the highest value the world had ever known, but also in the concept of God creating everything for the sake of man's salvation. This reluctance was also responsible for him placing the idea of the death of God in the mouth of a madman.

The text reads as follows:

> "Have you not heard of that madman who lit a lantern in the bright morning hours, ran to the market place and cried incessantly: 'I seek God, I seek God!' – As many of those who did not believe in God were standing around just then, so he provoked much laughter ... The madman jumped into their midst and pierced them with his eyes. 'Whither is god?' he cried; 'I will tell you. We have killed him – you and I. All of us are his murderers.... What was holiest and mightiest of all that the world has yet owned has bled to death under our knives: who will wipe his blood off us? What water is there for us to clean ourselves?... Is not the greatness of this deed too great for us? Must we ourselves not become gods simply to appear worthy of it? There has never been a greater deed; and whoever is born after us, – for the sake of this deed he will belong to a higher history than all history hitherto.' Here the madman fell silent and looked again at his listeners; and they, too, were silent and stared at him in astonishment. At last he threw his lantern on the ground, and it broke into pieces and went out. 'I have come too early, ' he said then; my time is not yet. This tremendous event is still on its way, still wandering; it has not yet reached the ears of men."[136]

The madman's unexpected silence is indicative of Nietzsche's half-conscious, half-unconscious awareness of the

136  Ges. W. vol. V, p. 163; CM vol. 3/3, p. 480f., § 125.

71

enormity of his words. Was it the terrible thought that the murder of God would finally lead to self-adoration and "identification with the gods"?[137]

Nietzsche concludes by adding that the madman forced his way into various churches and began to sing his *Requiem aeternam Deo*. Asked why by those present, he repeatedly answered:

> "What, after all, are these churches now, if they are not the tombs and sepulchres of God?"[138]

Nietzsche was only too aware that the thought that God was dead challenged what had hitherto been man's center of gravity, burning all the safe bridges behind him and placing him in the clutches of the 'eternal void.' Nietzsche allowed his madman to articulate the following fears:

> "What were we doing when we unchained the earth from its sun? Whither are we moving? Away from all suns? Are we not plunging continually? Backward, sideward, forward, in all directions? Is there still any up or down? Are we not straying as through an infinite nothing?"[139]

This feeling of anguish points to a bond with the Christian God hidden deep within the soul, a bond that made him shy away from a full awareness of his heresy. The 'murder' of God signified nothing less than the *rejection of Christian metaphysics* and of faith in *the absolute, the unconditional and the perfect,* as represented in Christian doctrine. Nietzsche himself stressed that to be conscious of

137 Nietzsche's notes make a clear reference to the consequences of the murder of God: "We wake up as murderers! How does someone like that console himself? How does he cleanse himself? Doesn't he have to become the most omnipotent and holy poet himself?" CM vol. 9, p. 590.
138 Ges. W. vol. V, p. 164; CM vol. 3/3, p. 481, § 125.
139 Ges. W. vol. V, p. 163; CM vol. 3/3, p. 481, § 125.

the loss of God would result in disillusionment with a now bankrupt tradition of reason, and the crisis of having sacrificed the idea of an all-embracing, divine love and all hope of eternal rest after death.[140] Yet, the illness from which he had recently recovered roused his defences for combatting the bottomless nihilism and despair at the void of his soul (the invalidity of values), enabling him to reassert his inner destiny. In overcoming his fear of 'God's shadow,' he rediscovered the inner freedom to look himself in the eye. The sentences that follow attempt to formulate that destiny:

> "*In what do you believe?* – In this, that the weights of all things must be determined anew.'
> 'What does your consciousness say? You shall become the person you are.'
> '*Where are your greatest dangers?* – In pity.
> *What do you love in others?* – My hopes.
> *What is the seal of liberation?* – No longer being ashamed in front of oneself.' "[141]

A stronger belief in himself was accompanied by a reconsideration of what belonged to greatness. We read:

> "*What belongs to greatness?* – Who will attain anything great if he does not find in himself the strength and the will to inflict great suffering. Being able to suffer is the least thing: ... But not to perish of internal distress and uncertainty when one inflicts great

140 Ges. W. vol. V, p. 126; CM vol. 3/3, p. 527, § 285.
"You will never pray again, never adore again, never again rest in endless trust; ... you have no perpetual guardian or friend for your seven solitudes ... there is no longer any reason in what happens, no love in what will happen to you ... you resist any ultimate peace; you will the eternal recurrence of war and peace: man of renunciation, all this you wish to renounce? Who will give you the strength for that? Nobody yet has had this strength."
Georg Lukàcs' *The Destruction of Reason* (1955) is interesting in this context.
141 Ges. W. vol. V, p. 205; CM vol. 3/3, p. 519, § 269-275.

suffering and hears the cry of this suffering – that is great, that belongs to greatness."[142]

It was, indeed, very hard for the sensitive Nietzsche to inflict pain on, and bear the suffering of, others out of loyalty to his convictions. Such behavior demanded greatness. It was less a problem for him to develop the capacity of 'the great' for consciously realizing their significance to the future of mankind, in spite of the danger of delusion.

> *"The most dangerous point of view.* – What I do or do not do now is as important for everything that is yet to come as is the greatest event of the past ..."[143]

In this respect his heroes, Napoleon and Shakespeare, were exemplary – the former, because he had had the courage to stand by himself,[144] and the latter, for the ability to create free spirits. Confronted by such figures, Nietzsche became more and more convinced that neither he nor mankind could afford to give in to nihilism without a fight. The age demanded that we overcome it. It was necessary to risk scaling heights of one's own, though it exacted the sacrifice of desiring to do so above all considerations of pity for the suffering of oneself and others. The affirmation of life and strength, the wish for greatness and a decided aversion to unworldly concepts, these things formed the foundation of Nietzsche's overwhelming vision of the 'eternal recurrence,' the most moving event of his lifetime.
It was first mentioned thus:

> *"The greatest weight.* – What if some day or night a demon were to steal after you into your loneliness and say to you: 'This life as you now live it and have lived it, you will have to live once more and innumerable times more; but every pain and every joy and every

142  Ges. W. vol. V, p. 245; CM vol. 3/3, p. 553, § 325.
143  Ges. W. vol. V, p. 197; CM vol. 3/3, p. 512, § 233.
144  Ges. W. vol. V, p. 66; CM vol. 3/3, p. 397, § 23.

thought and sigh and everything unutterably small or great in your life will have to return to you, all in the same succession and sequence – even this spider and this moonlight between the trees, and even this moment and I myself. The eternal hourglass of existence is turned upside down again and again, and you with it, speck of dust!' "[145]

We shall see that neither the idea of physical reincarnation nor the notion of the transmigration of the soul bound Nietzsche to the concept of recurrence. What inspired him was the idea of an *eternally incomplete cycle,* in which the same phenomenon recurred an infinite number of times without any sort of change. Though this concept had impressed him earlier, whilst studying Greek philosophy, it was only now that it took up a central position in the structure of his thought. Unlike the teachings of the pre-Socratics which had inspired him at that time, his own theoretical formulations seemed somewhat flat. Whereas, in Heraclitus, the idea of the cycle was supported by the metaphysical notion of the world fire,[146] in Nietzsche it assumed the form of a fantastical vision that was very difficult to reconstruct. Its contradictoriness, as well as its abstruseness, aroused resistance. On the one hand, Nietzsche founds his argument on a cosmophysical hypothesis of the world,[147] which I deem untenable; on the other, he cites the revelatory character of this idea. As he often admitted, the moment in which he had his vision can be equated with a profound experience of the *immortality and eternity of life,* an impression whose strength can leave no doubt as to its validity. Although the evidence he felt was in

145 Ges. W. vol. V, p. 265; CM vol. 3/3, p. 570, § 341.
146 *Die Vorsokratiker [The Pre-Socratics]*, ed. W. Capella, Fragment 52, p. 140: "Every event occurs in the form of contrast, and all thinkgs are caught in a constant flux ... and the world is periodically bron from, and returned to, the fire, in an eternal process of continuous change. But this will only take place after the catastrophe (that will befall the home-armies)."
147 Ges. W. vol. XII, p. 62 and 51; CM vol. 9, p. 498 and 523.

no way objective proof, the event that occurred within him was of an extraordinarily high order. Even when wrestling with nihilism in his later years, the religious experience of these days helped to strengthen him in his conviction that fear and danger could only be overcome by the idea of the 'eternal recurrence.' He, therefore, directed the following appeal at mankind:

"Let us print the likeness of eternity on *our* life!"[148]

As far as Nietzsche was concerned, the subjective significance of the concept bore no relation to its objective value. It was highly likely that the concept was sustained by a wish for eternity and eternal life, and so we read:

"My doctrine is: live so that you must *wish* to live again ... *eternity* is what counts!"[149]

In another passage, there is a similar mood:

"You feel that you must take your *leave,* perhaps soon ... Heed this testimony: it means that you love life and yourself, and that you love life as you have known it and it has shaped you – and that you *aspire to its eternization. Non alia sed haec vita sempiterna.*"[150]

It is clear that, for Nietzsche himself, the vision of the 'eternal recurrence' was related to the mystery of numinosity. The very moment this vision took place – the midday hour when the sun is highest in the sky and casts no shadows – retained for him a numinous character all his life. What fascinated him most was the paradoxical sounding *mystery of earthly immortality*. It was a paradox inasmuch as, on the one hand, he felt he was subject to the inevitability of fate, while, on the other, he did not wish to renounce

148  Ges. W. vol. XII, p. 66; CM vol. 9, p. 503.
149  Ges. W. vol. XII, p. 64; CM vol. 9, p. 505.
150  Ges. W. vol. XII, p. 66; CM vol. 9, p. 652.

the claim to being an earthly lord. Worldly life and eternity, will and fate were seen as one, in a drastic attempt to reconcile opposites on the ultimate basis of the irrationality of existence.

Nietzsche's early work on *Fate and History*[151] had already stressed the earthly aspect and depicted man at the center of the world. Likewise, that work had also expressed Nietzsche's secret resistance to Christianity. It is, therefore, no surprise that sixteen years later, he should have developed as his most important thoughts the death of God, the 'eternal recurrence' and the overman, all struggling, in turn, with the Christian notions of God's omnipotence and other-worldliness. The best counterargument to the Christian view of God was undoubtedly the eternal cycle of events, since the necessity of its process was irreconcilable with the idea of an omnipotent God intervening in what occurred on earth whenever it suited Him.

"He who does not believe in the *cyclical process of the universe must* believe in an *arbitrary* God."[152]

We must not overlook the fact that, despite his satisfaction at God's dethronement, Nietzsche regarded the thought of an unbroken chain of eternal repetition without possible progress as a crippling one. The question was whether man was at all capable of bearing the prospect of such a hopeless future, one devoid of initiative and in which the weak must perish. Nietzsche met this objection by showing that the fateful necessity of the recurrence itself could inspire the strong and powerful to master the difficulties of life, such impulses coming, for example, from hope that an overman will appear. In his opinion, such an assumption called for an extraordinary ability to overcome the self. Could Nietzsche have been mistaken? Is anything 'new' possible when things are supposed to repeat themselves in an eternal cycle?

151 See p. 8.
152 Ges. W. vol. XII, p. 57; CM vol.9, p. 561.

Whatever the answers, Nietzsche's expectation was founded on his hope for a godlike man to lead the world to a new future.[153] His foresight was the product of a Dionysian, almost presumptuous awareness that it was he who should save the world from destruction. The figure of Zarathustra was to be a projection of Nietzsche's redemption for mankind.

The 'death of God,' i.e., Nietzsche's nihilistic experience, the anticipation of the overman and the notion of the 'eternal recurrence,' are all interwoven, forming a unified whole that determined Nietzsche's image of the world to the very end of his life.

---

153 Conscious of the difficulty of this idea, he wrote: *"At the prospect of the overman,* the doctrine of the *recurrence:* now horribly *tolerable."* Ges. W. vol. XIV, p. 265.

# B. The Zarathustra Period

*Thus Spoke Zarathustra*

Nietzsche called *Thus Spoke Zarathustra* the "highest and most profound book" he had written, and "an inexhaustible well from which everyone could draw." The importance he attached to this work and its profundity justify a close examination of it, particularly with regard to its psychological significance in relation to the rest of Nietzsche's output.[1]

Like the vision of the 'eternal recurrence,' the *Zarathustra* experience can be traced back to the inspiration he received some months later in Rapallo, when the Zarathustra *numen* took hold of him. He retold the shattering effect this realization had on him:

> "... If one has the slightest residue of superstition left in one's system, one could hardly reject altogether the idea that one is merely incarnation, merely mouthpiece, merely a medium of overpowering forces. The concept of revelation – in the sense that suddenly, with indescribable certainty and subtlety, something becomes visible, audible, something that shakes one to the last depths and throws one down – that merely describes the facts. One hears, one does not seek; one accepts, one does not ask who gives; like lightning, a thought flashes up, with necessity, without hesitation regarding its form – I never had any choice."[2]

What happened to him in psychological terms could be described as an *encounter with the image of the autono-*

1  The individual parts of *Zarathustra* were each written in ten days.
2  Ges. W. vol. XV, p. 90; CM vol. 6, p. 339.

*mous numen of the 'wise old man,'*[3] an archetype existing within man's unconscious since time immemorial in the individual form of a redeemer 'beyond good and evil.' Nietzsche was simply overwhelmed: his experience of the coming of the redeemer was tantamount to meeting an inner companion, which inspired him to conduct a dialogue with himself. "One became two, and friend Zarathustra passed me by!" The intensity of this relationship was seen when he designated Zarathustra his "son." The dialogue with his own soul, already conducted in *The Wanderer and his Shadow,* was continued as a reconsideration of the pressing moral problems of his age. His short, passionate, but painful encounter with Lou Salomé, which occurred at *Zarathustra's* inception, left its mark on the forcefulness of the diction. The variable perspective of the book, focusing, in turn, on the contrasting aspects within it, is also reminiscent of the emotional conflict within his own soul: "What does he know of love, who must not despise what he loves."[4]

It is hardly surprising that he chose the name 'Zarathustra,' a direct allusion to Zarathushtra (called Zoroaster by the Greeks), the founder of the Persian faith. In doing so, he was carrying forward the old Persian legend of the 1,000-year reincarnation of their redeemer. Nietzsche thought that the moment had come to concentrate on the approaching task of the revaluation of values. He viewed the time as having arrived not least because the century he was living in had invalidated Christian answers to good and evil. The relationship between the spiritual and the material worlds needed to be redefined, to which the 'Zarathustra' figure was admirably suited for, having introduced in his own day (600 B.C.) a new moral attitude to the world. After adapting the ancient Aryan concept of a light, 'well-intentioned' world to one pregnant with the dualism of the ruling powers of light struggling with those of darkness, his name became associated with the moral conflict of the

3   See footnote 6 p. 81.
4   CM. See p. 18.

world. As an extension of his confrontation of good and evil, Zarathustra would now free the world from the oppressive tension between light and darkness; in Nietzsche's opinion, a task that could only be fulfilled beyond good and evil.

The 'Zarathustra' figure became the mouthpiece of thoughts Nietzsche had long held within his unconscious, but had as yet been cautious about articulating. The creation of *Zarathustra* was a tremendous confession of the soul arising from the unconscious. Totally unlike Nietzsche's earlier, more reflective and intellectual works, this one possessed the character of a *revelation* from *within*. In a series of spontaneous, unconscious images and visions, a *new conception of the world* gradually unfolded within him to compensate for the Christian spirit of the age in which Nietzsche found himself.[5] The symbols and metaphors used were mainly linked to archetypal experiences of the spirit (C.G. Jung's archetypes[6]) and remained in an unconscious, and therefore archaic, form. The book is bewitchingly direct, and its language reminds us of the pathos of Holy Scripture. Its ideas concern the pressing problems of the 19th century as they emerge from various reflections on culture, religion, science and art.[7]

From the outside, Zarathustra is a godlike figure, bearing for mankind a new gospel of the overman's descent and promising the 'eternal recurrence.' From the inside,

5 As C.G. Jung recognized, it was part of the uniqueness of the "unconscious spirit of the age to compensate for the attitude of the consciousness and anticipate future changes." See C.G. Jung: Ges.W. vol. 10, p. 334 (C.W. vol 10, p. 303).

6 By archetype, C.G. Jung understands a basic form of human conception that can be equally traced in dreams, fairy tales, imagination and, more generally, in the documents of the history of mankind. The archetype is a representation of typical modes of experience and reaction, and the numinous effects they produce.

7 The philosophical expression of these basic conceptions is largely found in *Beyond Good and Evil,* but also partly in the *Genealogy of Morals.* The latter, like *Zarathustra,* is closely related to notes in the literary bequest (1882-84).

Zarathustra stands for the spiritual experience of an archetype that has arisen from the unconscious and inspired modern forms of age-old religious images. From a subjective point of view, Zarathustra's statements represent the sustained reflection of an *inner process of transformation,* reaching deep into the collective unconscious – the embodiment of the general experience of humanity – and preparing for Nietzsche's self-realization. Such religious processes of the soul tend to occur when prevailing collective concepts of religion lose their effectiveness and symbolic value.[8] As a result, images driving at a *new image of God* suddenly and spontaneously rise up from the unconscious.

Whenever an archetypal event takes place, there is some danger that the human ego will be overcome by the numinosity of the image and experience an inflation. It is as if the content of the symbol were too powerful to be fully assimilated by the ego. The ego is then absorbed by the unconscious, losing its objectivity. Nietzsche himself indicated how immediate a danger Zarathustra's descent presented when he predicted the beginning of a tragedy *(incipit tragoedia)* in the *Gay Science.*

Every time the individual is confronted with the image of God, he suffers a battle between life and death. It is moving to see how the problems mentioned in this work ultimately led to Nietzsche's breakdown. He was incapable of standing up to the extraordinary spiritual demands brought on by Zarathustra's vision.[9] The work portrays an exciting conflict between man and the image of God, between *man and archetype,*[10] in the course of which an overpowered inner Nietzsche was finally defeated.

8  When a symbol is dead, Jung sees it as having only historical importance, Ges.W. vol. VI, p. 516 (C.W. vol. 6, p. 474f).

9  It was a similar story with Hölderlin, van Gogh, Robert Mayer and others.

10  *Zarathustra* may be regarded as a gigantic attempt to create this archetype of the spirit in the image of the overman, resulting in Nietzsche's identification with that image and, in turn, his suffering at being overpowered by it.

This work is indispensable to an understanding of Nietzsche's personality and his destiny, combining as one his painful resistance to fate and its inevitability. As Thomas Mann wrote, his "destiny was his genius. But this genius goes by another name, and that is sickness ... ."[11] We may expand on this and contend that his genius was nothing other than madness.[12]

## Part One

At the very start of the work, Nietzsche announces his momentous struggle with traditional Christianity by proclaiming the now fully conscious notion of the 'death of God.'[13] In effect, when 'God dies – the central numen of an era – then His leadership must undeniably be replaced by another authority. Nietzsche realized a new image of God in the figure of Zarathustra, who casts off his previous existence in the world of light to provide man with a new awareness of good and evil. The latter is initially limited to *heralding the overman,*[14] a supra-personal being who will reveal new meaning for the earth. At the same time, this event calls for a great sacrifice, the downfall of conventional man, who has been rooted in a collective morality. The tragedy Nietzsche foresaw has thus declared itself. Zarathustra states laconically:

11  Thomas Mann: *Nietzsche,* p. 237.
12  I had the rare privilege of participating in C.G. Jung's seminar on *Zarathustra.* It lasted from 1935-39. The unpublished copy of the report on the seminar consists of 10 volumes in four parts, which, sadly, only go as far as the middle of the third part of *Zarathustra.* I am grateful to this seminar, rich in psychological and mythological insights, for many stimuli to my own thoughts.
13  With the death of God, Nietzsche wished to draw attention to the general fact that belief in the traditional God had already lost its conviction.
14  Later, the idea of the 'eternal recurrence' of mankind, already experienced as a vision, would be heralded.

"God is dead ... I teach you the overman. Man is something that shall be overcome.... The overman is the meaning of the earth.... Behold, I teach you the overman: he is the lightning, he is the frenzy."[15]

In setting himself this new aim, Zarathustra-Nietzsche diverges greatly from the traditional view of God. The *worldly realm* of corporeal reality has now usurped God's unworldly one, with earthly values replacing the absolute ideals of their impotent, afterworldly equivalents. Man entered the empty space left behind by the "old God" and prepared a new spirit of creativity. By announcing the "new tablets" of the "overman" the focus was shifted to a new type of man who would decide the fate of common humanity:

"What is great in man is that he is a bridge and not an end: what can be loved in man is that he [is] an *overture* and a *going under*."[16]

The earthbound destiny of man functioned as a bridge reaching across to the overman.

Zarathustra's proclamation fulfils the role of a revolutionary vision of the future rotating around the death of God, the overman and the downfall of existing man. Each of these concepts represents a shaking of the hitherto valid conception of the world. The nearly 2,000 year old conception of a suprapersonal God of light, truth and perfection is relentlessly called into question. With it, the idea of a kindly Father in control of man and His world collapses. Man is thrown back onto himself and deprived of protection and security in his life. Who or what can guarantee his

---

15 Ges. W. vol. VI, p. 12-15; CM vol. 4, p. 14-16. A certain problem in *Zarathustra* is the overlapping of 'Zarathustra' and 'Nietzsche.' According to the respective meaning conveyed at various points in the text, I will stress either one or the other figure, or both together as 'Zarathustra-Nietzsche.'

16 Ges. W. vol. VI, p. 16; CM vol. 4, p. 16f.

surviving this disastrous situation?

What Nietzsche had in mind was making mankind aware of an idea that was already latent within the unconscious. Although it had not yet been clearly stated, people had been touching on this repressed complex of ideas about God since the French Revolution. Along with theology – represented by David Strauss and Auguste Comte – science and philosophy had made progress towards ridding the world of God. We need only mention the works of Voltaire, Diderot, Hegel and Fichte. In a late work, Nietzsche put it this way:

> "Why atheism today? – 'The father' in God has been thoroughly refuted; likewise: 'the judge,' 'the rewarder.' Also his 'free will': He does not hear – and if he heard, he still would not know how to help."[17]

Experience teaches us that the individual's attitude towards the concept of God is highly important. From a psychological viewpoint, the existence of the suprapersonal, archetypal factor can be neither denied nor invalidated without endangering the soul. The psychological health of the human being depends to a great degree on acknowledging this, both externally and internally. If he denies its existence on the outside, the question arises as to whether he has accepted it on the inside. If he then also denies such a reality within, he will either fall prey to deflation and despair, or attribute the divine to his own ego (inflation). Whenever he identifies himself with this, he overestimates his own personality[18] to a dangerous extent, losing his detachment from things human and claiming for himself the power that belongs to God alone. Let us look at how C.G. Jung follows up the effects of such behavior:

> "Nietzsche was no atheist, but his God was dead. The result of this demise was a split in himself, and he felt

17 Ges. W. vol. VII, p. 77; CM vol. 5, p. 72, § 53.
18 C.G. Jung: Ges.W. vol XI, p. 344 (C.W. vol. 11, p. 315).

compelled to call the other self 'Zarathustra,' or at times, 'Dionysus.' ... The tragedy of *Zarathustra* is that, because his God died, Nietzsche himself became a god; and this happened because he was no atheist.... It seems dangerous for such a man to assert that 'God is dead': he instantly becomes a victim of inflation ... inflation and man's hubris ... elected the ego, in all its ridiculous paltriness, to become the lord of the universe.... The individual ego is much too small, its brain is much too feeble, to incorporate all the projections withdrawn from the world. Ego and brain burst asunder in the effort ... ."[19/20]

It is easy to trace how the *tendency to overestimate himself,* that had lain dormant in Nietzsche from the start – as a child he felt he was destined for something special – increased in strength as he grew older, this feeling. The early death of his father hindered the fortification of his character and, instead of being able to project inner images onto his father and thus develop a fully formed manliness, the archetype of the great man awakened in his unconscious. True to his dependent nature, Nietzsche became fascinated by those who bore the projection of 'higher men' and 'great educators' – I remind the reader of Schopenhauer and Wagner; but his overly high expectations were repeatedly disappointed.[21] With no one to turn to but himself, the idea of the overman[22] crystallized within him, and rather than establish an inner relationship to its overpowering content, he began to identify himself with it. The inclination to overestimate himself, which in *Zarathustra* had already reached a questionable level, steadily grew into the near self-deification of *Ecce homo.* The excessive pathos it held

19 *Ibid.* p. 93.
20 *Ibid.* p. 96.
21 "How I have looked for the man higher than I who can truly look over me! I did not find him. I should not compare myself to W[agner] – but I belong to a higher rank, irrespective of his 'power'." CM vol. 9, p.577.
22 The idea of the overman was already mooted by Herder and Goethe.

prefigures his insanity. The more vehemently he expressed himself, the more likely it was that he was in the throes of a repressed conflict between the identification of ego and God on the one hand, and inner doubt about his 'divine mission' on the other. Although he 'knew' from an early stage about the danger of killing God, which would replace security with isolation and slide him into the 'eternal void,' he was pulled along by an inner process and incapable of avoiding the catastrophe. At that time, he also wrote:

> "If we do not make a great *renunciation* and a lasting *victory over ourselves* out of the *death of God,* then we must *bear the loss.*"[23]

What Nietzsche meant was the creation of a greater being to supercede and excel Christian man. When he was still under the sway of the Schopenhauerian spirit, he had already tried to capture this notion of a godlike man in the concept of *genius.*[24] Even then, he had described this type of man as belonging to the "highest exemplars of humanity." This concept became less convincing with Nietzsche's exposure of ideals, and was replaced by that of the 'hero.' From then on, potency and strength characterized the "great man of the future" with Nietzsche increasingly affording him the attributes of the man of power, and thereby obviously compensating for his own physical weakness! In the end, it was the idea of the overman that won out, exhibiting a 'new will' capable of creating "meaning for the world" and originating "beyond good and evil."[25] He apportioned him the task of shaping the world anew and legislating over humanity. With this idea of a world-creator, the *image of archetypal man* had formed within him, probably an unconscious image lodged in man's psyche since the mists of prehistory. The archetype attempts to establish the unity of the world as its creator and the bringer of light. The loss of

23  Ges. W. vol. XII, p. 167; CM vol. 9 , p. 577.
24  Ges. W. vol. I, p. 446; CM vol. 1, p. 387.
25  Ges. W. vol. XVI, p. 384; CM vol. 13, p. 493.

the concept of God and the resultant transference of psychic energy to the unconscious made recourse to this most ancient of genotypes possible. Seen in terms of the dynamics of the psyche, no energy is, in fact, lost: the power-flow released by the concept of God activates latent archetypes of the world-redeemer that had been dormant in the unconscious. The form of the new symbol varies according to the religious expectations associated with it. In Nietzsche's day, this hope was projected onto the *déesse raison* – reason, – which had been elevated to its throne by the French Revolution. Nevertheless, the issue still arose as to who or what might now exorcise the threats emerging in this age of materialism and capitalism, i.e., onto which figures these powers may be transferred and projected.

Did Nietzsche's overman measure up to this expectation? The weakness in his vision clearly lay in his projecting the function of the redeemer onto the outside and into the future. It was thus removed from human control and transported into a mythical time span.

From a psychological point of view, it would have been much more fruitful to have *withdrawn the projection to the inside,* whence it came. As a symbol of the self or of a suprapersonal spiritual power, it would have had the advantage of allowing the individual a conscious relationship with the image or concept of God. Nietzsche had no feeling for such a possibility; his age was not yet prepared for a psychology of the unconscious that Freud was to initiate and Jung would carry forward.

As it was, Nietzsche's personal ego was sucked into the powerful maelstrom contained by his projection, with the result that he identified himself with the autonomous complex of a godlike being – the overman – and so cut himself off from the vital, regulating powers it also possessed.

Despite repressing the dangers posed to himself by the death of God, Nietzsche understood all too well the consequences of mankind divorcing itself from an unworldly concept of God. Thanks to the prophetic gift that led him to surmise the hidden connections behind the surface events of his age, he was able to predict the threat to the world caused by wars, the rise to power of tyrants and, equally important, the creation of huge power blocs. With the over-cultivation of the intellect, he expected a corresponding development in technology (airship travel), a vision that came all too true in the 20th century, with its explosion of technical inventions (space travel, electronics, atomic fission).[26] It would be a misreading of the facts to attribute to Nietzsche's prophecies on the growth of power-politics a direct causal effect on the political future, even though his remarks were frequently misunderstood, particularly with regard to National Socialism. On this subject, I would like to quote Mazzino Montinari, one of the two editors of the critical edition of Nietzsche's works. He writes:

"It is impossible to talk of a real National Socialist assimilation of Nietzsche's thought. Recent research has shown Nietzsche to have been virtually unknown to the founders of National Socialism. Alfred Rosenberg, who vindicated him with the 20th century myth that he stood as an antecedent of the 'movement,' puts Nietzsche in the dubious company of Paul de Lagarde (whom Nietzsche despised) and Houston Chamberlain (who, for his part, rejected Nietzsche from a racial and Wagnerian standpoint). Hitler himself had no connection with Nietzsche; it is doubtful that he even read him. It would be tantamount to carrying the 'owls to Athens' to quote the countless passages in which Nietzsche speaks out *against* the racial theories of the genuine forerunners of National Socialism in general and anti-Semitism in particular. He even had the occasion of corresponding with a future National Socialist deputy: his two letters to this man truly mock

26 In Jung's *Psychological Types,* p. 203f, we read: "Nietzsche's Zarathustra, in particular, brings to light the contents of the collective unconscious of our time, and in him we find the same distinguishing features: iconoclastic revolt against the conventional moral atmosphere, and acceptance of the 'ugliest man'...." C.W. vol. 6, p. 191.

the confused racial ideology of the 1880's with their –
as Nietzsche put it – dubious concepts of 'Aryanism'
and 'Germanism.' Shortly after this correspondence
with Nietzsche, Theodor Fritsch reviewed *Beyond
Good and Evil* (1887) and (rightly) found it a 'glorification of the Jewish people' and a 'curt rejection of
anti-Semitism.' Nietzsche was dismissed by him as a
'fisherman in philosophical shallows' on whom all
and any understanding of national existence is lost
and who grows philosophical 'cabbage like an old
woman.' According to Fritsch, Nietzsche's statements in *Beyond Good and Evil* concerning the Jews
were 'the intellectual fondlings and shallow chit-chat
of a Jewicised parlour-room academic'; 'luckily,' he
wrote, 'Nietzsche's books will be read by hardly
more than two dozen people.' These were Nietzsche's
concrete connections with anti-Semitism and Germanism during his lifetime. And yet, even today,
Nietzsche is regarded by the general public as the intellectual pioneer of National Socialism." Cf. R.F.
Krummel, *Nietzsche und der deutsche Geist* [Nietz-
sche and the German Spirit], Berlin, 1974.[27]

That such an image of Nietzsche could have lasted Montinari attributes to the work of Adolf Bäumler, one of the
editors of Nietzsche's work who, as we have seen in the
Foreword, propagated the view that Nietzsche's ideology
conformed to that of National Socialism.[28] The effect of
C.G. Emge's funeral speech at Frau Förster–Nietzsche's
burial tended in the same direction, with Nietzsche being
praised as a "pioneer of the future." Adolf Hitler's courtesy
visit to her Weimar home on her 90th birthday was also received as proof of the way Nietzsche's ideas were related to
those of National Socialism.

27 Montinari: *Nietzsche lesen*, p. 169f, ch. on Nietzsche between Alfred
   Bäumler and George Lukàcs.
28 Alfred Bäumler: *Nietzsche, der Philosoph und Politiker* [*Nietzsche,
   Philosopher and Politician*], Reclam, Leipzig 1931.

However, it cannot be overlooked that Nietzsche's glorification of power and his similar fascination for evil often deceived later rulers into thinking that Nietzsche's work actually confirmed Hitler's ideology – a temptation only possible if Nietzsche's ideas were taken in isolation from his overall work, and his basic aims and conceptions ignored.

As if to demonstrate how dangerous Zarathustra's proclamation of the death of God could be, at the very beginning of the work something terrible happens: a tightrope walker about to show off his talents is 'jumped over' by a buffoon who pops up behind him and is killed. This is a symbolic rendition of the sacrifice of man, the presumptuous scaler of intellectual heights and pretender to the overman. The buffoon appears as the sacrificer, Zarathustra's demonic opponent. Just as all *archetypes* show *sides* of both *light and shadow,* so Zarathustra also possesses a destructive, devilish side, to which attention is drawn at the very start of the tragedy. Insofar as the buffoon "is the greater personality who bursts the shell, and this shell is sometimes – the brain,"[29] his behavior is particularly important. The following prophecy of Zarathustra is also a gloomy one:

"Your soul will be dead even before your body: fear nothing further."[30]

The prophetic aspect of this comment is alarming: whom will the buffoon undo? The side of Nietzsche obsessed by the intellect, or the intellectual extravagance of mankind in general? It is a fact that in the ensuing century, countless people fell victim to a dark fate. It is, therefore, possible that Nietzsche's prophecies might also refer to centuries beyond his own.

In Zarathustra's next speeches, the *new spirit* of this work is conveyed. Symbols have already indicated this

29  C.G. Jung, Ges.W. vol. XV, p. 157 (C.W. vol. 15, p. 141).
30  Ges. W. vol. VI, p. 23; CM vol. 4, p. 22.

spirit as a union of pride and wisdom – the symbols of Zarathustra's two animals, the 'eagle' and the 'serpent.'[31] As the sun stood at its midday point, Zarathustra gazed "into the air, questioningly, for overhead he heard the sharp call of a bird. And behold! An eagle soared through the sky in wide circles, and on him there hung a serpent, not like prey, but like a friend: for she kept herself wound around his neck."

Though the two animals represent opposites in reality and, like heaven and earth, mind and body, are seemingly irreconcilable, here they are unified, the principle of light appearing to have overcome that of darkness. To what extent does this anticipate the future?

The chapter on the 'Three Metamorphoses of the Spirit' reveals how Nietzsche understood this new spirit. The metamorphoses corresponded to the three stages of his mission:

> "Of three metamorphoses of the spirit I tell you: how the spirit becomes a camel; and the camel, a lion; and the lion, finally, a child."[32]

The first thing to do was to transform into a spirit able to endure much and, like the camel, bear the demands of the desert – an attitude that accepts the obligations of life, patiently tolerating the loneliness of knowledge and suffering the hunger of the soul for the sake of truth. The second step, the transformation of the spirit into the lion, the embodiment of the concept 'I want,' is characterized by a striving for freedom and self-assertion. The spirit must now become liberated from the pressure of values that have existed for 1,000 years and aspire to new ones. This aim is achieved by the will of the ego – the will to create and revalue – battling with the dragon of 'thou shalt,' the keeper of traditional Old Testament morality. The final

31 Ges. W. vol. VI, p. 29f; CM vol. 4, p. 27f.
32 Ges. W. vol. VI, p. 33; CM vol. 4, p. 29.

stage is the metamorphosis of the lion into the child, into creative innocence. In the creativity of the child, the symbol of the divine power to transform, and in the "sacred Yes" lay the possibility of completing the great work with the ease of a self-turning wheel – that work being the creation of the overman and the heralding of the 'eternal recurrence.'

Such suggestions of the transformational process of the spirit are already hinting at an attack on the metaphysical premises of Christianity, indicated by Nietzsche's constant recasting of Christian symbols. Indeed, *Zarathustra* as a whole shows Nietzsche painfully separating himself from the Protestantism handed down to him by his forefathers.

In a bitter protest against the transcendental beliefs of Christianity and their devaluation of the world, Nietzsche repeatedly looked to his faith in the physical and the earthly, in man and his body. It was the individual's duty to have the strength to go his own way and assume responsibility for his own destiny. As already indicated in the *Gay Science,* he was secretly nurturing the idea of the 'eternal recurrence' of the worldly to counter any danger of hitherto transcendental values collapsing totally. The recurrence was the secret motor driving his efforts in *Zarathustra* to establish a new meaning for human existence and throw down the gauntlet for the natural world.

That is why Zarathustra-Nietzsche also urged the individual to affirm the body, the "belly of being,"[33] in the chapter on the 'Despisers of the Body':

> "But the awakened and knowing say: body am I entirely, and nothing else; and soul is only a word for something about the body."[34]

This is the first time we come across the expression 'body,' used by Nietzsche in a more specific sense than the

33 Ges. W. vol. VI, p. 42; CM vol. 4, p. 36.
34 Ges. W. vol. VI, p. 46; CM vol. 4, p. 39.

word 'life' to signify the *instinct of inwardness* in man. The body became the polar opposite of everything that was otherworldly in the individual. It embraced the functions of life in their totality – not just the physiological processes, but also feelings, valuations and even the self – and was thus an extremely important term, reinforcing the commitment to life already apparent in the *Untimely Meditations*. Nietzsche had a central notion in mind when referring to the 'body,' using it to counteract the prevailing over-valuation of the spirit in the philosophical and Christian world-view. When he put the body on a par with the concept of 'great reason,' he did not mean the 'spirit,' which he equated with abstract thought or little reason, but rather *instinctive wisdom,* the all-embracing sense of the instinctual world. He was careful to segregate 'great reason' and 'little reason,' the latter possessing only a subordinate significance as a function of the mind and an "instrument and toy of the body."

> "An instrument of your body is also your little reason, my brother, which you call 'spirit,' a little instrument and toy of your great reason."[35]

In *The Dawn* Nietzsche made the conscious functions dependent on the more extensive instinctual sphere of the unconscious. Likewise in *Zarathustra* he viewed the body as the more expansive background to life, reducing the 'ego' and its concepts to "leading strings." It was an idea not far from that of the 'collective unconscious' as the sum total of our ancestors' experience.

> "The body is a great reason, a plurality with one sense, a war and a peace, a herd and a shepherd ..."[36]

35 *Ibid.*
36 *Ibid.*

94

"There is more reason in your body than in your best wisdom ..."[37]

"What the sense feels, what the spirit knows, never has its end in itself. But sense and spirit would persuade you that they are the end of all things: that is how vain they are."[38]

It was only in the second part of *Zarathustra* that the 'spirit' came to be understood as a spontaneous and creative impulse in man. This turnaround was made possible with Nietzsche's own Dionysian experience of the super-personal dynamism of the spirit, no longer something abstract, but now the source, the "most blessed rejoicing," as well as the deepest pain.

Neither did Nietzsche think of the concept of the soul when speaking of the body. The 'soul' was, for him, an unscientific expression for an imagined subject within man, and also occasionally for something that deserted the body.

Thus we read:

"Belief in the body is more fundamental than belief in the soul: the latter arose from unscientific reflection on the agonies of the body (something that leaves it; belief in the truth of dreams)."[39]

This is not to say that Nietzsche did not employ the word 'soul,' which was indeed used frequently, principally to denote emotions and sentiments,[40] such as yearning, loving

37 Ges. W. vol. VI, p. 47; CM vol. 4, p. 40.
38 Ges. W. vol. VI, p. 46f; CM vol. 4, p. 39.
39 Ges. W. vol. XVI, p. 17.
40 Here I would like to mention the wonderful passage on his love of the soul: "O my soul, now I have given you all, and even the last I had, and I have emptied all my hands to you: That I bade you sing, behold, that was the last I had. That I bade you sing – speak now, speak: which of us has to be thankful now? Better yet, however: sing to me, sing, O my soul! And let me be thankful." Ges. W. vol.VI, p. 327; CM vol. 4, p. 280.

and dreaming.

By contrast, the concept of the self was enormously important to an understanding of the body. Previously, he had applied this term in association with 'self-determination' and 'self-becoming,' but in *Zarathustra,* he outlined it in another way:

> "Behind your thoughts and feelings, my brother, there stands a mighty ruler, an unknown sage – whose name is self. In your body he dwells: he is your body."[41]

As the unconscious 'master' and the creative impulse within, the self represented the cause, not only of desire and pain, but of "worth and will,"[42] too. However, Nietzsche does not go into greater detail. When he referred to the individual becoming himself, i.e., "what he is,"[43] alluding to the self as a feeling guiding from within,[44] he might have gone further and declared the self as a greater impersonal center, as a regulative personality within the human being. But he did not take this step, remaining satisfied to merely underline the necessity of regarding the self as part of any action, as is seen by the aphorism below:

> "O my friends, that your self be in your deed as the mother is in her child – let that be your word concerning virtue."[45]

It was especially important for Nietzsche to acknowledge *the body as the basis of the will and creativity.* This

---

41 Ges. W. vol. VI, p. 47; CM vol. 4, p. 40.
42 *Ibid.*
43 See p. 62.
44 See p. 180.
45 Ges. W. vol. VI, p. 139; CM vol. 4, p. 123. Jung once made the interesting remark that he originally came upon the concept of the self when reading *Zarathustra* for the first time at the age of 17. He adopted it and went on to pursue the concept in Hindu writings.

assumption betrays the influence of Schopenhauer,[46] who gave the Will precedence over knowledge. Willing and creating come increasingly to the fore in *Zarathustra*, particularly in relation to the creation of the overman.

In view of the extraordinary significance of the body to the whole personality, Nietzsche could not help but examine his own constitution and physiological disposition, aspects so intimately woven into the fabric of his work. He repeatedly emphasized his extreme impressionability as well as his unique way of starting out from "things experienced," never just from "mental processes."

> "I have always written my works with my whole body and life: I do not know what 'purely intellectual' problems are."[47]

His own intense excitability and sensibility already pointed him in this direction. On the one hand, his extremely sensitive nervous system caused him to be pathologically dependent on diet, climate, altitude and noise, whilst on the other, it was thanks to this that he was able to determine physiologically "the inmost parts, the entrails" of every soul.[48] It was this perceptive ability that also gave him access, psychologically speaking, to the archetypal background of his age.

It was fundamental to Nietzsche to 'interrogate' and heed instinctive and bodily impulses.

> "Listen rather, my brothers, to the voice of the healthy body: that is a more honest and purer voice."[49]

However remarkable this statement might have sounded,

---

46 Schopenhauer wrote in similar terms: "... the whole body is nothing other than the objectified Will, i.e., the Will become Idea..." *The World as Will and Idea,* Book 2, § 18.
47 CM vol. 9, p. 170.
48 Ges. W. vol. XV, p. 22; CM vol. 6, p. 275.
49 Ges. W. vol. VI, p. 45; CM vol. 4, p. 38.

it also had its dubious side: by harking the bodily impulses, the individual exposes himself all too easily to the chaotic multiplicity of his instincts and the 'Yes' and 'No' of his various instinctual drives. Such a danger was particularly apparent when, as in the case of Nietzsche, consciousness could no longer fulfil a regulative function. In such a case, the individual is left totally to his "passions and instinctive impulses," and the body is elevated to the position of being a basic source of knowledge and truth. This attitude throws light on Nietzsche's highly criticized 'contradictoriness.' By heeding the body, he not only experienced new things to the full, but also suffered the torture of being torn apart by conflicting drives. For him, *antithesis was a part of life.*

*The Wanderer and his Shadow* made it clear to him that the opposition of light and dark impulses also belonged to the conflict of instincts. At that time, he had already contrasted the "soul of light" with the "soul of shadow."[50]

> "Immediately adjacent to wholly nocturnal man there is ... a soul of light, as if tied on. It is the negative shadow, so to speak, cast by the former."[51]

The lasting confrontation of 'Yes' and 'No,' light and shadow, made dialogue with the self very wearisome and painful, at once a curse and a blessing for Nietzsche. He wanted a 'bloody' exchange involving and ensnaring the whole man.

We get an impressive picture of this conflict in the ensuing passages, in which the passionate emotion of darkness rapidly alternates with equally strong intellectual excitement. In accordance with his contradictory nature, Zarathustra-Nietzsche both rose to intellectual heights and sank into unlit depths of the instinctual drives. Though the conflicting demands of his instincts caused him suffering, they were necessary to provide the living substance of his thoughts and insights.

50 See p. 46f.
51 Ges. W. vol. III/2, p. 329f; CM vol. 2/II, 2, p. 664, § 258.

Such situations were responsible for the redemptive image of the tree in the section on the 'Tree on the Mountainside,' an ancient symbol that, whilst rooted in the earth, stretched up to the heavens and so represented the high tension of his soul. The image of the tree captured not only the dangerous and frosty isolation of the heights of the intellect, but also possession by baser desires. The aphorism below reveals profound psychological perceptiveness:

"But it is with man, as it is with the tree. The more he aspires to the height and light, the more strongly do his roots strive earthward, downward, into the dark, the deep – into evil."[52]

Nietzsche's account of the confrontation in himself, between a passion for intellectual clarity – projected onto the "youth in himself" – and the painful imprisonment of physical desires, is moving. The question was: would Nietzsche keep to the lonely path of his hero, or would his downfall be sealed by the clash of light and shadow?

Initially, it was tolerating the banal and everyday impulses of *'collective mankind'* that Nietzsche found difficult. Whenever he came into contact with other people, he was overcome by distaste at the "rabble" and the "small of spirit" who were slaves to conventional virtues and suppressed the "wild dogs in the cellar." It was the "flies of the market"[53] that disgusted him most for flattering the great whilst hating their greatness, which they attacked with their poisonous bites. The inferior, weak spirit that stood at the service of cheap virtues was an insult to the lifelong nobility of his own outlook. The intensity of his negative projections was such that one cannot avoid asking if Nietzsche had ever consciously realized the degree to which he fought the mistrust, jealousy and evil in his own heart.

The object of his contempt was the individual's subservience to the state, for he regarded the *new idol of the*

52 Ges. W. vol. VI, p. 59; CM vol. 4, p. 51.
53 Ges. W. vol. VI, p. 73f; CM vol. 4, p. 65f.

*'state'* as the greatest obstacle to the development of man. As the "ordering finger of God,"[54] it embodied no less than the slow suicide of all concerned.[55] Nietzsche did not hesitate to describe the state as the "coldest of all cold monsters" and a lie "in all the tongues of good and evil."[56]

All these people caught up in the collective spirit were, in Nietzsche's view, nothing but "preachers of death" attempting to escape life by mutilating themselves or by simply fleeing into eternal existence. Nietzsche's appeal to seek out the enemy within ourselves, to do battle with it and become fittingly brave and bold warriors, is noteworthy in psychological terms. It was in this context that Nietzsche wrote the famous words: "... it is the good war that hallows any cause."[57]

Setting aside the criticism of those inferior parts of the personality oriented towards collective values (expressly personal in nature, according to Jungian psychology[58]), Nietzsche was preoccupied with the archetypal shadow that represented a 'possibility of evil' hidden deep in the unconscious. He saw this as predominantly rooted in the figure of the 'ugliest man,' the murderer of God. But he was also fascinated by the pale criminal, that paradoxical, archetypal figure whose instincts were distinguished by both a latent, unconscious blood-lust and an impulse to control it.

In the *'pale criminal,'* Nietzsche tried to display the conflict between the murder instinct shared by all humans and man's inability to bear the thought of murder, let alone the deed itself. His subtle feeling for man's secret underworld – the "neurotically immoral" (C.G. Jung) – managed to

54  Ges. W. vol. VI, p. 70; CM vol. 4, p. 62.
55  Ges. W. vol. VI, p. 71; CM vol. 4, p. 62.
56  Ges. W. vol. VI, p. 70; CM vol. 4, p. 61. In contrast to this, his early writings had seen the state as the necessary guardian of culture.
57  Ges. W. vol. VI, p. 67; CM vol. 4, p. 59.
58  The expressions 'personal' and 'archetypal shadow' are derived from the psychology of C.G. Jung. By the 'personal shadow' is meant an unconscious personality, whilst the 'archetypal shadow' embodies a general potential for evil.

100

track down that gruesome, secret dichotomy between a tortuous thirst for blood, the "bliss of the knife,"[59] and the anticipation of guilt (often dreamt of or imagined) that held it in check. Nietzsche believed that the inner tension of unconscious opposites could become so strong as to approach *insanity*.[60] One wonders whether Nietzsche anticipated his own fate here and felt in himself the inclination towards criminality, as indeed the many references to this shadow figure suggest. The autobiographical significance of this archetypal complex can be seen in the statement below, made by the figure described as the "shadow" in Book 4:

> "With you I broke whatever my heart revered; I overthrew all boundary stones and images: I pursued the most dangerous wishes: verily, over every crime I have passed once."[61]

Elsewhere, he writes on the criminal:

> "The criminal type is the type of the strong human being under unfavorable circumstances: a strong human being made sick."[62]

Nietzsche was treading the dangerous ground of the unconscious with this aphorism on the 'pale criminal,' and could only expose its dark and abysmal nature with the utmost caution. There is wisdom in the ancient words: *Quieta non movere.*

Nietzsche's conflicting instinctual and intellectual tendencies made him long again and again for peace and soli-

59  Ges. W. vol. VI, p. 53; CM vol. 4, p. 46. C.G. Jung, Ges. W. vol.VIII, p. 28.
60  The following well-known aphorism makes the point: "But thought is one thing, the deed is another, and the image of the deed still another: the wheel of causality does not roll between them."
Ges. W. vol. VI, p. 53; CM vol. 4, p. 45f.
61  Ges. W. vol. VI, p. 397f; CM vol. 4, p. 340.
62  Ges. W. vol. VIII, p. 157; CM vol. 6, p. 146. See p. 272.

tude. He hoped to escape the inner tumult and find quietude for his soul far from the "flies of the market" and the "spirit of the herd," a wish that was not to be fulfilled. For, on the contrary, it was most probably his isolation 6,000 feet above sea level that increased the dissociation between his ego and the world.

As the dramatic plot of *Zarathustra* unfolded, it was obvious that Nietzsche felt increasingly torn between the demands of the instincts and the spirit. This reached its climax in the highly problematical 'Ass Festival,' demonstrating Zarathustra-Nietzsche's dilemma of *spurning and worshipping the concept of God.*

To begin with, Zarathustra-Nietzsche, as he wrestled with the torpor of the collective, championed individuality and the individual. Man was extolled as the 'measure and value' of all things. The human personality and its valuations, decisions and creative ego took the place of God, absolute truth and morality. The human spirit opposed the "spirit of the herd." The separation of the individual from the 'herd' and masses, therefore, became Nietzsche's most pressing concern. Part of this involved the *individual reflecting on his own values* and value judgments, – a very demanding task in view of the preponderantly materialistic outlook of contemporary socialism and militarism.

In *Zarathustra,* we read:

> "Only man placed values in things to preserve himself – he alone created a meaning for things, a human meaning. Therefore he calls himself 'man,' which means: the esteemer. ... To esteem is to create: hear this, you creators ... Through esteeming alone is there value: and without esteeming, the nut of existence would be hollow. Hear this, you creators! ... Change of values – that is change of creators. Whoever must be a creator always annihilates."[63]

63  Ges. W. vol. VI, p. 86; CM vol. 4, p. 75.

What first struck Zarathustra on his travels was man's confusion over a dominant value system. He discovered a colorful variety of evaluations, with each tribe and people holding onto its own so that "no neighbor understood the other." What seemed good to one was "evil" to another. What was the cause of this wide discrepancy in valuation? What could be put forward to balance out the absence of a supreme goal? Nietzsche was already beginning to hint at the possibility of the 'will to power' standing as the highest criterion of value.

The first reference to the *self as an inner authority providing man's goal* is an impressive one: Was it not possible, he asked himself, for the self, the inner friend, so to speak, to be responsible for uncovering a future aim and creating the overman? This is the meaning when Zarathustra stresses: "Let the friend be your festival of the earth and presentiment of the overman."[64] Such a friend was necessary when cutting oneself off from the spirit of the herd. Only loneliness smoothed the path to oneself, the self and the missing goal. Was the individual ready for this?

> "Is it your wish, my brother, to go into solitude? Is it your wish to seek the way to yourself? Then linger a moment, and listen to me."[65]

It is not clear what Nietzsche considered the 'self' to be. At first it seemed as if he thought of it as a cogent and powerful force in the instinctual sphere, which, like a 'rolling wheel,' corresponded to a primary movement of the soul. It was a view he was not able to retain.

He started by writing:

> "Are you a new strength and a new right? A first movement? A self-propelled wheel? Can you compel the very stars to revolve around you?"[66]

64  Ges. W. vol. VI, p. 89; CM vol. 4, p. 78.
65  Ges. W. vol. VI, p. 91; CM vol. 4, p. 80.
66  *Ibid.*

His call for treading the path to oneself may have made an impression, but not so the disappointing and exaggerated role attributed to the human ego in the aphorism that followed:

> "Can you give yourself your evil and your own good and hang your own will over yourself as a law? Can you be your own judge and avenger of your law?"[67]

We must pay due respect to his consideration of the self in a period of materialism and overheated collectivism in Germany; yet, by combining it with the ego in a concession to the scientific prejudices of his age, he trivialized his argument. Nevertheless, it was a novel thing to transfer the *function of the moral conscience* to the ego and dissociate it from the dominance of a general moral code. The next aphorism demonstrates that Nietzsche was not unaware of the critical inner situation that would result from overemphasizing the ego:

> "Terrible it is to be alone with the judge and avenger of one's own law. Thus is a star thrown out into the void and into the icy breath of solitude."[68]

In fact, Nietzsche was familiar with what it was like to feel the pain of desertion by God; whilst he also encountered the uncanny "seven devils" of the soul that arose from such pain. The following comment indicates the suffering such a path entailed:

> "Lonely one, you are going the way to yourself. And your way leads past yourself and your seven devils. You will be a heretic to yourself and a witch and a soothsayer and fool and doubter and unholy one and a villain."[69]

67  Ges. W. vol. VI, p. 92; CM vol. 4, p. 81.
68  *Ibid.*
69  Ges. W. vol. VI, p. 94; CM vol. 4, p. 82.

104

The confrontation with the seven devils mentioned here by Nietzsche would have been a wholly impossible venture for man, since its success would have called for the intervention of God Himself – the 'holy,' 'wise' and 'good.' Such a struggle would end up with the individual surrendering and immolating his self – a symbolic but accurate observation. The ancient alchemists were not wrong to stress that the great work demanded the whole man: *"Totum hominem requiret opus."*[70] Nietzsche put it this way:

> "You must wish to consume yourself in your own flame: how could you wish to become new unless you had first become ashes?"[71]

Despite the remarkable nature of his intuitive anticipation of the thought that *the process of man's self-realization* is a *mystery of death and rebirth,* his thinking lacked one important point: it failed to acknowledge the greater impersonal authority within the soul. Without an equalizing, regulative center to which the individual could entrust himself, the alchemical opus – in other words, the process of individuation – could not be brought to a conclusion.[72]

From his own suffering at the hands of traditional morality, Nietzsche knew only too well that the pathway to oneself was linked with the sacrifice and surrender of the self. He was not only familiar with the pain of being misunderstood and cut off, but also with the pain of the spirit.[73] However, what he knew too little about was the impossibility of finding the path to oneself without conducting an inner dialogue with a super-personal entity. He failed because he identified himself with the divine partner

70  See C.G. Jung, *Psychologie and Alchemie* [*Psychology and Alchemy*], Ges. W. vol. XII (C.W. vol. 12).
71  Ges. W. vol. VI, p. 94; CM vol. 4, p. 82.
72  See C.G. Jung, *Psychologie and Alchemie*, Ges.W. vol. XII (C.W. vol. 12).
73  See p. 116.

instead of acknowledging Him as his greater counterpart.

His conception of the creation of the overman necessarily fell victim to a similar misunderstanding. He was not able to realize such an idea in the form of an *inner mystery*. Nietzsche, however, made a fatal error in embodying this notion as a future legislator.

Nietzsche must have had an inkling of the difficulty and frequent failure of his efforts when he wrote:

> "Yes, I know from where I came:
> Ever hungry like a flame,
> I consume myself and glow.
> Light grows all that I conceive,
> Ashes everything I leave:
> Flame I am assuredly."[74]

The profound chapter on the 'Gift-Giving Virtue' was written with clear allusion to the *Christian mystery of sacrifice;* it portrays how Nietzsche envisaged the transformation, not only of mankind into what it was, but also of the individual into the overman; and , in addition, we see what he himself expected from his disciples. In a way comparable to his declaration that the creation of the overman necessitated the downfall of ordinary man, Zarathustra initially thought of dedicating himself to the greater power through suicide and leaving his spiritual legacy to his adherents. Beyond a shadow of a doubt he had in mind the Christian notion of the redeemer.

He chose a golden ball as the sign of his legacy, throwing it to his disciples with the words:

> "Verily, Zarathustra had a goal; he threw the ball: now you, my friends, are the heirs of my goal: to you I throw my golden ball."[75]

---

74 Ges. W. vol. V, p. 30; CM vol. 3/3, p. 367.
75 Ges. W. vol. VI, p. 108; CM vol. 4, p. 95.

106

As a symbol of highest value, the ball was to strengthen the tie between him and his followers, paralleled by the disciples, for their part, handing him a golden staff. The choice of symbols in both cases is worth noting, as each alluded to the *symbolism of the self*. Thus the staff was distinguishable by its golden handle depicting a snake coiled around the sun.[76] This gift was a symbol of the union of the sun and the snake, of light and chthonic wisdom, which represented a supreme cosmic value, binding Zarathustra and his adherents. In Nietzsche's eyes, such a spiritual bond heralded new creative energies that would help to complete the great work. The supreme 'virtue' is described thus:

> "… verily a new deep murmur and the voice of a new well."[77]

This symbol is derived from the Christian mystery of redemption whilst also signifying the devotion of the self to the highest form of meaning. But, unlike the Christian Gospel of devotion to a divine and afterworldly realm, Nietzsche was in search of an ultimate sacrifice of man to the meaning of the earth.

Moved by the numen of the moment, Zarathustra turned to his disciples and spoke the following words:

> "Remain faithful to the earth, my brothers, with the power of your virtue. Let your gift-giving love and your knowledge serve the meaning of the earth. Thus I beg and beseech you."[78]

He emphatically encouraged them to "give new value to all things" and to be prepared to fight for it in order to achieve the goal of a "resurrection of the body" and an "elevation of the spirit."

76 Ges. W. vol. VI, p. 109; CM vol. 4, p. 97.
77 Ges. W. vol. VI, p. 112; CM vol. 4, p. 99.
78 *Ibid.*

"There your body is elevated and resurrected; with its rapture it delights the spirit, so that it turns creator and esteemer and lover and benefactor of all things."[79]

Borne along by his prophetic vision, Zarathustra-Nietzsche warned of unknown dangers that threatened the discoverer of new values, and called for extreme watchfulness[80] and unity:

"You that are lonely today, you that are withdrawing, you shall one day be the people: out of you, who have chosen yourselves, there shall grow a chosen people – and out of them, the overman. Verily the earth shall yet become a site of recovery. And even now a new fragrance surrounds it, bringing salvation – and a new hope."[81]

With the prospect of the overman, he took leave of his disciples, giving them some useful pieces of advice, reminiscent of the Christian Gospel, to speed them on their way.[82]

*"Dead are all gods: now we want the overman to live – on that great noon, let this be our last will."*[83]

The first part of *Zarathustra* ends with the proclamation of a new high noon that for Nietzsche marked the supreme

79 Ges. W. vol. VI, p. 111; CM vol. 4, p. 99.
80 Ges. W. vol. VI, p. 113; CM vol. 4, p. 100f. "Wake and listen, you that are lonely.... Not only the reason of millennia, but their madness, too, breaks out in us. It is dangerous to be an heir."
81 Ges. W. vol. VI, p. 114; CM vol. 4, p. 100f.
82 Thus we read in Ges. W. vol. VI, p. 114f; CM vol. 4, p. 101:
"The man of knowledge must not only love his enemies, he must also be able to hate his friends. Or: One repays a teacher badly if one always remains nothing but a pupil. ... You had not yet sought yourselves: and you found me.... Now I bid you lose me and find yourselves; and only when you have all denied me will I return to you."
83 Ges. W. vol. VI, p. 115; CM vol. 4, p. 102.

moment of *the perfect completion of man and the world,* the revelation of a *worldly eternity*. It had become a spiritual fact that "man was secularized and deprived of God" (Loewith).

In spite of the compelling power of his words and the wisdom of his insight, Nietzsche's hope for redemption is a psychological disappointment. Both projections of the future into an *external reality* became exhausted: the projection of the reign of a godlike figure and his community of followers, as well as the expectation of an earthly empire. His visions were the inevitable consequence of proclaiming the death of God and transferring the highest values to this world. The image of a numinous, divine center was replaced by the hubris of the ego.

*Part Two*

The continuation of the tragedy was largely determined by the death of Richard Wagner,[84] which occurred between the writing of the first and second parts of the book.

This event was one of the most far-reaching of Nietzsche's life, in light of the fact that Wagner had for years been his idol in both a positive and negative sense. In order to come to terms with the sorrow he felt, Nietzsche was forced to reconsider all that Wagner had been to him: what it was that had excited his love, his disillusionment and finally, his desire to break free from this figure. From the start, he had been fascinated by the inexhaustible natural energy of Wagner's character, which was elemental and impetuous to the point of violence, and unbridled in its demand for power and recognition. Nietzsche's rejection of his pathos and artificial behavior during and over the construction of the Bayreuth *Festspielhaus* was just as categorical.[85] This whole complex of impressions, which in the search for

84 Wagner died on February 13th, 1883.
85 See p. 37.

himself Nietzsche had relegated to his unconscious, was now reawakened by Wagner's death, liberating him from the inhibitions he had once felt. It was mainly his own Dionysian inclinations,[86] represented by the wild and dark aspects of his nature, which freed him from an enormous weight and were allowed to emerge for all to see.

The apex of the next phase is, therefore, the emotion Nietzsche felt at his *own* creative *daimon*. This period is characterized by the glorification of willing and creating, by freedom from the pressure of a godlike authority, and also by the profound pain of loneliness. The intensification of the ecstatic side of his nature thus represents the motive force behind the second part of *Zarathustra,* with considerable dangers lurking within its poetic climaxes. As a result, it fosters a high degree of awareness, and the self-overcoming necessary to hold back his extravagant excesses.

Nietzsche's decisive turn from freethinking to a Dionysian attitude is introduced by a problematic dream prefiguring a disastrous end. In a mirror held up by a child, Zarathustra-Nietzsche perceived a dreadful image, which is described as follows:

"... For it was not myself I saw, but a devil's grimace and scornful laughter."[87]

What was this ghastly self-reflection? To all appearances, the *dark opponent* of the hitherto unchallenged concept of a God embracing both light and darkness – the devil – had come to life and was stepping forward. A hazardous situation developed, in which the dark, instinctual side, until now largely of theoretical import alone, was activated and threatened to rip the soul apart by opposing the 'divine' with the 'satanic.'

Instead of the expected outburst of fear and disquiet, Nietzsche was seized by a feeling of blessed and euphoric

86  See p. 28.
87  Ges. W. vol. VI, p. 119f; CM vol. 4, p. 105.

emotion,[88] indicating his tendency to suppress shock.

He was overwhelmed by a condition that possessed his soul like a raging storm. In repressing the emotional situation, his ego ran the risk of being overrun by the powerful, super-personal satanic complex, which revealed itself immediately afterwards as an exaggerated feeling of mission, described by Nietzsche thus: "Like a cry and a shout of joy I want to sweep over wide seas."

Possessed by the Dionysian fire of his soul he boldly remarked that God was a mere conjecture[89] and invention of man, thereby consciously rounding on the theological attitudes of his age and vindicating man's right to determine for himself. It appeared to him that such a right was the natural consequence of the death of God and included mankind breaking through to creativity. From then on, Nietzsche regarded the autonomous power of creating and shaping the self as the prerogative of man: his most noble task was the creation of the world, the transformation of himself and the procreation of a being that would surpass himself.[90]

It was from these and similar observations on the generation of a higher being that, encouraged by Nietzsche's sister, Elisabeth, misconceptions arose as to whether he was influenced by the Darwinist view of progressive biological development. Heinemann, Jaspers and Kaufmann have argued against such a connection. Although Nietzsche occasionally talks of "a higher formation of the whole body,"[91] of the "childbirth" of the overman and even of a "higher breeding of humanity,"[92] he did not think of it in a biological sense. On the contrary, he totally rejected the

88  Such a contrariwise running of inner states bears the psychological term 'enantiodromia.' See C.G. Jung, Ges. W. vol. VII, p. 77f (C.W. vol. 7, p. 71).

89  Ges. W. vol. VI, p. 123; CM vol. 4, p. 105.

90  In the literary bequest is written: "He who no longer finds greatness in God will no longer find it anywhere – he must deny or create it."
Ges. W. vol. XII, p. 329; CM vol. 10, p. 194.

91  CM vol. 10, p. 506.

92  Ges. W. vol. XV.

Darwinist idea of human development dependent on biological existence, hunger and nourishment, and particularly on the "development of humanity from a lower to a higher state,"[93] stressing in its place a *"form-creating force* working from within."[94] In contrast to Darwin, he underlined the importance of incorporating new value judgments with regard to the creation of higher types: it was necessary to "implant a will" in man so that he could become a tall tree.[95] The *"greatest elevation of power-consciousness* in man" was especially needed "to create the overman."[96] Nietzsche's 'will to power,' as the most essential impulse for developing force and strength in the individual, was a principle very different from Darwin's notion of selection. Nietzsche's battle cry was not the "domestication of man," but the "return to nature of the savage,"[97] so that man might cure himself of prevailing culture.

The renewal of culture required a creative impulse towards renewal, for it was on this that the deeper meaning of life was based. For Nietzsche, therefore, the very idea of an intensification of life and creativity meant an expression of strength with which to exhort the freedom of man. He was convinced that the creative will was vital to his own self-fulfillment as well as to that of the overman. It was not knowledge but willing that liberated man, a view that led him further and further away from the intellectualism of his times. He underpinned his doctrine of the primacy of willing without recourse to the metaphysical principle of a natural order, founding it instead on the freedom of man and his capacity for declaring 'I want.' In so doing, he diverged from the Schopenhauerian philosophy of willpower. In *Zarathustra*, we read:

---

93  Ges. W. vol. XVI, p. 147
94  *Ibid.* p. 120.
95  CM vol. 10, p. 612.
96  CM vol. 11, p. 225.
97  Ges. W. vol. XVI, p. 147.

"Willing liberates: that is the true teaching of will and liberty – thus Zarathustra teaches it."[98]

However, suffering was associated with creating, just as it was with every process of transformation. He who wished to propagate had to accept death. It was a realization forced upon Nietzsche at an early stage by his physical weakness, and that gradually became the deeper source of his knowledge.[99]
The aphorism stating that the self-transformer not only creates, but also gives birth, is impressive; he not only participates in his own birth, but in death as well:

"... Suffering is metamorphosis of the self, in every act of being lies death. One must not only be the child, but the giver of birth, too: as the creating one."[100]

Just as, from the start, Zarathustra contrasted light with darkness, he now emphasized the *polarity* of all actions and creations. To live meant also to die, to create, to give birth. He had already indicated the following in the *Gay Science:*

"*What is life?* – Life – that is: continually shedding something that wants to die. Life – that is: being cruel and inexorable against everything about us that is growing old and weak – and not only about us...."[101]

Yet, it also dawned on Zarathustra-Nietzsche that the true image envisaged by all creativity, the "image of images" (an analogy to God), did not lie in consciousness, but slept as if incarcerated deep down in the soul and its "hardest, ugliest stone."[102] Although it cannot be presumed

98  Ges. W. vol. VI, p. 125; CM vol. 4, p. 111.
99  See p. 196.
100  CM vol. 10, p. 213.
101  Ges. W. vol. V, p. 68; CM vol. 3/3, § 26, p. 400.
102  Ges. W. vol. VI, p. 126; CM vol. 4, p. 111.

that Nietzsche was aware of the similarity this figure of speech bore to the alchemical notion of a "Spirit in Matter,"[103] his vision of this image in all probability pointed towards the archetype of the *'lapis philosophorum'* [the philosopher's stone] inherent in the collective unconscious and, according to Jung, a symbol of the self. But Nietzsche did not grasp what "Zarathustra in himself" knew: namely, that it was a *god* which slept in his soul and that the secret of creation lay in bowing down before this divinity. It therefore remains equally doubtful if Nietzsche's mind, which so loved to explore the brightest spheres, could ever stoop before this "ugliness in matter," to this "image of images," and so bring it to life.

For the present, Nietzsche willfully ignored life's shadow, including one or two disagreeable things experienced by his contemporaries.[104] In his Dionysian enthusiasm for strength and power, he recklessly defied all the poisonous mendacity that crossed his path without looking into its unexplored meaning. The result was not only that he insulted priests for lolling "in fetters of false values and delusive words," but he also criticized the deceitful web of the virtuous, finally pouring out his anger on the rabble "which poisoned every well."[105] He also gave free rein to his frustration at his work being disregarded and ignored, a mode of behavior bound to cause compensatory reactions to rise from the unconscious.

In the image of the tarantula, an ancient symbol of vengefulness, and thus a metaphor of the dark side of the soul as it lies in wait in its cavern, Nietzsche's poetic imagination provided him with a profound piece of wisdom. It was perilous to get too close to the shadow realm

---

103   See C.G. Jung, *Psychologie und Alchemie,* Ges. W. vol. XII, p.340 (Quotation from the alchemist Ostanes) (C.W. vol. 12, p.103)
104   The continual interweaving of poetic and concrete reality makes it difficult to understand individual metaphors. This is also illustrated by the subject of the action constantly switching between Zarathustra and Nietzsche.
105   Ges. W. vol. VI, pp. 131-143; CM vol. 4, pp. 117-128.

114

of one's own conceit, its suppressed envy and "secret lusts of the tyrant" concealing the "madness of impotence"; it would inevitably lead to a boomerang effect and end up with the poisoned darts falling back on oneself. Nietzsche's provocative praise of lofty thoughts and an enhancement of the vital instincts in *Zarathustra* – "life wants to climb and overcome itself climbing" – summoned up the vengeance of the dark inhabitants of the cave. Similarly, his critical challenge to his era aroused the displeasure of the majority of his readers. In both cases, he was unexpectedly and perfidiously struck by his own shadow, symbolized as the "bite of the tarantula."[106] In the course of *Zarathustra,* it will be seen how this poison, popularly associated with tarantism or, more particularly, madness, concretely affected his life. The consequences were not just limited to physical suffering – migraine attacks, eye complaints, vomiting and fainting, – but also extended to the contemptuous disinterest with which the world greeted his work.

The first noticeable symptom was the deep gulf between his exaggerated sense of mission and an unconscious compensation for feelings of failure and inadequacy. Or, in other words: the conflict between the light of the male *logos* and the darkness of the female *eros* emerged more clearly than ever before. His blindness to the combative and challenging aspects of his writing would cause him many a gloomy hour. I would like to quote the following aphorism, which may account for certain elements of his behavior:

> "What was silent in the father speaks in the son; and often I found the son the unveiled secret of the father."[107]

Did Nietzsche's stance betray the secret wishes of a sickly country parson living the quiet life?

As if it were an analogy for the oscillation of Nietzsche's

106 Ges. W. vol. VI, p. 148; CM vol. 4, p. 131.
107 Ges. W. vol. VI, p. 145; CM vol. 4, p. 129.

being between the darkest and lightest instinctual drives, the sinister experience in the cavern of tarantulas was succeeded by its contrary, that is, the high excitement of Dionysian energy. In a similar, but more conscious, way to that of the "great vision of the eternal recurrence," Nietzsche was carried off to unimagined spiritual heights, where he came to know the unforgettable, but nevertheless painful, beauty and profundity of the spirit:

> "Spirit is the life that itself cuts into life: with its own agony it increases its own knowledge. Did you know that?"[108]

This provides a moving insight into the suffering of creative genius.

Unlike the mere intellect, the *action of the spirit* seized the entire human being in its *overpowering grasp,* releasing his instincts and placing all his forces at the disposal of creative life. In the light of this, the chapter on the 'Famous Wise Men' unleashed its scorn on the so-called wisdom of these men in practising idolatry rather than genuinely pursuing the truth. Their spirit was that of "well-fed draught animals" surrendering to the general will. They "remained the people who do not know what spirit is."[109]

The next aphorisms on the creative energy of the spirit are just as surprising:

> "You know only the spark of the spirit, but you do not see the anvil it is, nor the cruelty of its hammer.... And the happiness of the spirit is this: to be anointed and through tears to be consecrated as a sacrificial animal. Did you know that?"[110]

The plight of the creative human being caught in a distressing struggle between propagation and sacrifice is ex-

108 Ges. W. vol. VI, p. 151; CM vol. 4, p. 134.
109 *Ibid.*
110 *Ibid.*

cellently portrayed. To be and to will – both as a godlike creator and the resultant creation –, to act as hammer and anvil, thus experiencing spiritual passion at its most positive and negative: this was the unique demand of Nietzsche's spirit of creativity. It was his destiny to become the sacrificial offering of his own creative *daimon*.

His 'Night Song,' an indescribably beautiful musical rendition of the depth of experience, directly expresses his visionary exaltation. It bears testimony to the bliss and torment of the sweltering heat and freezing cold of his spiritual battle.

Below is an extract from the song:

> "Night has come: now all fountains speak more loudly. And my soul too is a fountain.
> Night has come: only now all the songs of lovers awaken. And my soul too is the song of a lover.
> Something unstilled, unstillable, is within me; it wants to be voiced. A craving for love is within me; it speaks the language of love.
> Light am I: ah, that I were night! But this is my loneliness that I am girt with light.
> Ah, that I were dark and nocturnal! How I would suck at the breasts of light!
> And even you would I bless, you little sparkling stars and glowworms up there, and be overjoyed with your gifts of light. But I live in my own light; I drink back into myself the flames that break out of me.
> I do not know the happiness of those who receive; and I often dreamed that even stealing must be more blessed than receiving...."

The last lines of the *Night Song* read thus:

> "Alas, ice is all around me, my hand is burned by the icy.
> Alas, thirst is within me that languishes after your thirst.

Night has come: alas, that I must be light! And thirst
for the nocturnal! And loneliness!
Night has come: now my craving breaks out of me
like a well; to speak I crave. Night has come; now all
fountains speak more loudly. And my soul too is a
fountain.
Night has come; now all the songs of the lovers
awaken. And my soul too is the song of a lover."[111]

Here, Nietzsche articulated the torment of the self and
his poignant inability to gain access to the sun and moon of
the brighter side of his nature:

"... the 'Night Song,' the immortal lament at being
condemned by the overabundance of light and power,
by his sun-nature, not to love."[112]

His longing for love was never satisfied in his lifetime.
His fear of being swallowed up by the "labyrinth of the
land of death" and of being captured by the carrier of the
*anima*[113] was always too great. More than one woman tried
to get close to him and was disappointed; but the tables
were turned with Lou v. Salomé, who rejected his proposal
of marriage. Even Cosima Wagner, the woman he adored
most of all and once described as the "nicest woman he had
met," remained unapproachable, despite mutual feelings of
friendship.[114] Her sacrificial devotion to the work of her

111 Ges. W. vol. VI, p. 153ff; CM vol. 4, p. 136ff.
112 Ges. W. vol. XV, p. 97; CM vol. 6, p. 345.
113 C.G. Jung sees the 'anima' as the mediator between consciousness and
the unconscious: vol. XIV/2, p. 390. On the one side, it reaches into
the realm of the conscious; on the other, into the maze of the
"labyrinthine land of death," as Nietzsche described the unconscious. It
also embodied the feminine side of man (C.W. vol. 14, p. 356).
114 In the context of his break with Wagner, his relationship with Cosima
also changed. After detaching himself from his friend, the woman *onto*
*whom he had projected his* anima remained associated with *a 'Yes' and*
*with a 'No,'* whilst she continued to have a great effect on him within
his inner fantasy.

husband, Richard, stood between them. What Cosima had meant to Nietzsche was clear only after his collapse. In his insane scribblings, she became Ariadne, the inscrutable symbol of an inner Dionysian world lost in the abyss.[115]

Karl Jaspers is not wrong in seeing the reason for Nietzsche's human failings in his inability to love; he "always loved himself alone, and in others only the vessel containing what was his own."[116] Nietzsche's profound mental problem is forcefully expressed in an aphorism written at the time *Zarathustra* was conceived (1882-83):

> "Now I am alone: I yearned for people – I searched for people – I only ever found *myself* – and nobody yearns for me anymore."[117]

It is tempting to consider Nietzsche in terms of typology. His one-sided nature prevented him from uniting body and spirit, the sun and the moon. The light of intuition outshone by far the two less distinct functions of feeling and emotion, which remained interwoven with the shadow side of the personality.[118] This explains his great difficulty in differentiating between imagination and reality and adequately translating his inner visions into realistic concepts. He lacked direct knowledge of mankind, as well as the capacity for evaluating how real the overpowering impressions of

---

115 See p. 266. In Greek mythology, Ariadne was the companion and transfigured wife of Dionysus (Kérenyi). She was also described as a labyrinth. Dionysus said: "Ariadne, you are a labyrinth."
   Ges. W. vol. XIV, p. 55; CM vol. 12, p. 402.
116 Karl Jaspers, *Nietzsche,* p. 86.
117 Ges. W. vol. XII, p. 324; CM vol. 10, p. 91. Cf. Ges. W. vol. XII, p. 324; CM vol. 10, p. 202: "Nobody comes to my any more. And I myself: I went to all, but got to *no one.*"
118 See C.G. Jung, *Die Psychologie der Typen* [*The Psychological Types*], Ges. W. vol. VI, p. 433f and p. 413f (C.W. vol. 4, p. 380 and p. 398f).

his soul, including his erotic drives, actually were[119] – all this, in spite of his remarkable intuitive understanding for characterological coherence.

The creative fulfillment and spiritual power of the Dionysian afforded Nietzsche further insights that were of enormous importance to him in establishing his 'great philosophy.' The proclamation of the death of God and the glorification of life and the earth cleared the way for the complete formulation of thoughts with which he had already been sporadically concerned before *Zarathustra*. They culminated in the 'revaluation of values,' a break with conventional morality that opened the door to wholly new concepts of good and evil.

The starting point for his new-found understanding was the *process of transformation* that formed the central core of *Zarathustra*. In it he discerned the constant progression of the generative drive inherent in all creative life towards ever higher life-forms. Fundamental to this was the knowledge that accession to a new form involves destruction of the old. Creation and annihilation were two aspects of one and the same creative process of life, something that was impossible without sacrificing cherished values. Nietzsche repeatedly stressed that self-mastery was the vital prerequisite for creativity of the spirit.[120] This mode of behavior, practised since earliest childhood, mirrored the urgency of giving up previous values and ties in order to make room for the creation of new and higher ones. It also laid bare the manner in which the Zarathustra's overman called for the sacrifice of existing mankind:

---

119 In the 'Dancing Song,' Nietzsche movingly portrays his difficulty in coming to terms with his erotic desires. Although he is enchanted by the seductive dance of young girls, he cannot spontaneously give himself up to his feelings and emotions. He retreated into a noncommittal game that, as a result of his disloyalty to himself, left him in a depressive and even suicidal state of mind: "Why, what for? by what? Whither? Where? How? Is it not folly to be alive?" Ges. W. vol. VI, p. 159; CM vol. 4, p. 141.

120 Ges. W. vol. VI, p. 167; CM vol. 4, p. 148.

"Man is something to be overcome: that is the doctrine of life as the great act of self-overcoming."[121]

This was the rather impossible condition for self-realization that the iron will of Nietzsche was prepared to undergo in his search for truth.

This radically new perspective on creativity, life and overcoming oneself was, in principle, derived from vital considerations. It brought Nietzsche alongside Bergson and Dilthey as a fellow founder of a philosophy of life that set about confronting the intellectual spirit and 'bourgeois' morality of then current times with the fundamental *irrationality of life.*

Before even getting to the problem of creatively shaping life, which was to be intensified and transformed by a process of creation, destruction and self-conquest, Nietzsche was first and foremost concerned with ascertaining the fundamental driving forces behind the process itself. His now famous answer was that the primordial motive resided in the *will to power,* the essential will for self-creation.

In his early work, *Fate and History* (1862), he had already intuitively admired the strong will as one of the most effective motives man possessed.[122] Some twenty years later, in *The Dawn,* Nietzsche observed the epitome of healthy instinct in the "striving for excellence" and the "craving for power."[123] Finally, in *Zarathustra,* the 'will to power' emerged as the *leitmotif* of all living things, so that life itself came to be synonymous with "the will to grow stronger."[124]

"Where I found the living, there I found the will to power; and even in the will of those who serve I found the will to be master."[125]

121  CM vol. 10, p. 579.
122  See p. 8.
123  Ges. W. vol. XVI, p. 153/155; CM vol. XIII, p. 310/262.
124  Ges. W. vol. VI, p. 168; CM vol. 4, p. 147f.
125  Ges. W. vol. VI, p. 167; CM vol. 4, p. 147f.

Life, self-mastery and the 'will to power' now formed a coherent, indivisible core incorporating all vital phenomena.

Yet these concepts by no means covered the whole of the problematic field occupied by the creative formation of life. The need to reconsider the roles of good and evil in the context of a 'revaluation of values' presented Zarathustra-Nietzsche with a fundamental dilemma.

In Nietzsche's opinion, the values of good and evil, whose absolute character he had already vigorously denied in *The Dawn,* were themselves an expression of human creativity and, as such, also determined by the 'will to power.'

> "That is your whole will, you who are wisest: a will to power – when you speak of good and evil, too, and of valuations."[126]

Being themselves the result of self-overcoming, they, too, were subject to transformation:

> "Verily, I say unto you: good and evil that are not transitory do not exist. Driven on by themselves, they must overcome themselves again and again."[127]

He noted above all that the very creation of new moral values, as with all created things, submitted to the transforming process of creation and annihilation. Even the new value attributed to good presupposed the destruction of the previous one, setting in motion the hazardous reappraisal of all existing values.

> "And whoever must be a creator in good and evil, verily, he must first be an annihilator and break

---

126 Ges. W. vol. VI, p. 165; CM vol. 4, p. 146.
127 Ges. W. vol. VI, p. 169; CM vol. 4, p. 149.

values. Thus the highest evil belongs to the highest goodness: but this is creative."[128]

It was and is necessary to substitute this with a new way of thinking opposed to a Christian morality bent on preserving the universal values of good and evil. Nietzsche envisaged the repeated reordering of value as essentially comprising the total reversal of values hitherto held, and thus as being derived not only from the annihilation of previous conceptions of good, but equally from *the constant reshaping of what until then had been regarded as evil*.

He saw the need for a view diametrically opposed to the Christian tenet of the preponderance of good. All spiritual progress was based on the transformation of moral values, and therefore, it was what had hitherto been 'evil' that would best serve the creative process in man. It was important that he realized the part played by collective 'evil' in every individual act of creation, but he rendered this untimely assumption untenable by *combining evil with the striving for power*. At first only hinting at this, Nietzsche later developed his idea of connecting evil and the striving for power in *Beyond Good and Evil*.

This opening attempt at revaluing Christian values showed Nietzsche treading new ground and tending in the direction of a radically new estimation of morality. In spite of the sharply polemic tone of such comments attacking Christian morals, the fundamentally ethical strain in Nietzsche's efforts should not be overlooked.[129] What constituted his primary target was the 'ancient' Judaeo-Christian moral code, which, from the onset of his speeches, Zarathustra intended to replace with a new and inward one; he demanded the surrender of 'thou shalt' and the slaying

---

128 Ges. W. vol. VI, p. 169; CM vol. 4, p. 149.
129 In a letter of Nov. 1882 to Lou v. Salomé it can be seen how, at that time, Nietzsche recognized the "desire for a holy selfishness, i.e., the desire for obedience towards the highest of things" as the highest moral worth. *Dokumente der Begegnung*, p. 262.

of the "Old Testament dragon."[130] The bequest states:

"Morality died from moralizing."[131]

And similarly:

"God killed God."[132]

Such statements were not the product of immorality but designed to prepare for a new ethic that would possibly be more responsible than the previous one. This Nietzsche demonstrates in an aphorism written at the time:

"I had to *abolish* morality in order to assert my moral will."[133]

And:

"But now comes the redemptive criticism of morals and morality: *They are killing themselves.*"[134]

Although Nietzsche emphasized that it was Zarathustra's most difficult sacrificial act to break away from the 'old morality,'[135] it is astonishing how unaware he seems to have been of the perils involved in the abolition of traditional morality. Was it so certain that new morals would arise out of the annihilation of the old? Was there not a greater risk of the individual falling victim to his own instincts?

His renewed pleas for overcoming the self make it obvious that Nietzsche had not considered this a threat as such,

130 "We want to be the *heirs* of hitherto existing morality: and *not* start anew. All our activity is nothing but morality that turns towards its previous form." Ges. W. vol XIII, p. 125.
131 CM vol. 10, p. 30.
132 *Ibid.*
133 Ges. W. vol. XIII, p. 176; CM vol. 10, p. 359.
134 Ges. W. vol. XIV, p. 308; CM vol. 10, p. 16.
135 CM vol. 10, p. 180.

124

since for him, self-overcoming was not only a precondition for creative success but, at the same time, the strongest counterbalance to any possible excess of the 'will to power.' In his view, it had nothing to do with stoic self-control or with the suppression of vices, let alone with self-castigation. Instead it comprised the ability to refine and *sublimate*[136] the *instincts*, thereby elevating them to a higher plane. It was, therefore, highly moral in motivation and, according to one of the leading experts on Nietzsche, Walter Kaufmann, fundamental to grasping his moral temperament.[137] For Nietzsche, sublimation represented a process of leading to "the purification of our opinions and valuations"[138] and requiring a subtle sense of the 'style' of character.[139] The procedure was equally dependent on an immutable inner core of feeling, on 'probity' and 'noble-mindedness,' and finally, on a certain temerity in the treatment of others and discipline towards oneself.

In the *Gay Science*, Nietzsche had regarded the ultimate ambition of morality as *creative self-formation*, a process that would be consummated through the endless conflict between the will to have more from life and the desire to overcome oneself. We read:

> "We, however, *want to become those we are* – human beings who are new, unique, incomparable, who give themselves laws, who create themselves."[140]

136 Ges. W. vol. II, p. 18, § 1; CM vol. 2/1, p. 23, § 1.
   There is a similar passage in the bequest: "*My task:* to sublimate all instincts so that the perception of the strange is extensive and yet still associated with enjoyment...." Ges. W. vol. XI, p. 262; CM vol. 9, p. 211.
   In his *concept of sublimation,* so important to the metamorphosis of the instincts, Nietzsche anticipated the corresponding term used by Freud, who attached to it the meaning of transferring the libido onto an instinctual social goal.
137 W. Kaufmann, *Nietzsche,* p. 228ff, ch. 7 & 8.
138 Ges. W. vol. V, p. 257; CM vol. 3/3, p. 563, § 335.
139 Ges. W. vol. V, p. 219; CM vol. 3/3, p. 530, § 290.
140 Ges. W. vol. V, p. 257; CM vol. 3/3, p. 563, § 335.

However attractive this aim may have sounded, it had a double edge, and was largely unsuccessful. On the one hand, it demanded the strength to shape oneself, and so ran the risk of unbridled self-assertion; on the other, it called for a painful sacrifice,[141] the ultimate renunciation of greatness and demise of mankind's hitherto banal existence. Such was the subliminal echo of Zarathustra's sinister prophecy and prediction of the *downfall of man with the creation of the overman*. It was impossible to resolve the craving for power and longing for self-conquest without the necessary spiritual principle to guide and regulate them.

The dream of the devil's grimace led, as expected, to the gradual emergence of a more gloomy picture of the world. Nietzsche could no longer withdraw from the demonic engagement of his soul. By identifying with the satanic adversary, he became increasingly alienated from himself. He felt urged to reorder values on the basis of his *fascination for the phantom of power* that resided both in the spirit and the creative will, and Christian truths were invalidated as a consequence. But there was an inner toll to be paid, in the form of profound feelings of inferiority alternating with excessive delusions of grandeur.

After boasting that he was the revaluer of values, he began to be plagued by doubts about his mission. He vented his anger over his unfulfilled fantasies of greatness on his contemporaries, and the sublime pillars of virtue whose souls "shudder with godlike desires."[142] He also arraigned the power-lust of those at home in the "land of culture," who to him were the "dappled and motley" paintings of all that had ever been believed.[143] He arrogantly branded scholars as being identical to the workings of a clock, and was bitingly critical of poets, whose spirits he described as "the peacock of peacocks" and a "sea of vanity."[144] What

---

141 See p. 116: "And the happiness of the spirit is this: to be anointed and through tears to be consecrated as a sacrificial animal."
142 Ges. W. vol. IV, p. 173; CM vol. 4, p. 152.
143 Ges. W. vol. IV, p. 176; CM vol. 4, p. 154.
144 Ges. W. vol. IV, p. 190; CM vol. 4, p. 166.

else could these assaults have been but the projections of his own unfulfilled delusions of power? They isolated him from his contemporaries, clouded his instinct and self-esteem and buried his natural sense of good, evil and life's worth.

He did not have to wait long before his unconscious compensated for such overbearing fantasies. Events in *Zarathustra* continued in rapid succession: Zarathustra-Nietzsche fell into a mountain of fire and then had a terrible dream leading him into the castle of death. Finally came an encounter with the deplorable figure of the hunchback,[145] an uncanny presentiment of the future.

In a bold act of self-assertion, Zarathustra-Nietzsche defied the dark omens of his fate again and again. He ignored all the warning signs after descending into the jaws of hell and shook his head at a ghostly voice that called, "It is time! It is high time!"[146] A fire-spitting hound, a sort of *memento mortis,* approached him spitting fire and, through the steam, it was snorting, bragging with its subversive ideas. Instead of sarcastically dismissing this fire hound as the "earth's ventriloquist," Zarathustra-Nietzsche would have done better to have recognized in it his own boastful counterpart. He did contrast it with the fictional existence of another fire hound that spoke "from the heart of the earth," but he overlooked the significance of his own words when he retrospectively renounced the whole episode as shadowy and unreal – namely, that "the heart of the earth is of gold."

145 Parallel to these inner developments, Nietzsche's own personal life was becoming difficult to bear. He was suffering a good deal from loneliness, worsened by the break with his long-standing friend, Paul Rée. He missed both Rée and his many fruitful flashes of philosophical inspiration. Their parting company was the result of jealousy over Lou von Salomé. He was also under pressure in his relationship with his sister Elisabeth, who had been an ugly party to that conflict. Her planned marriage to the "notorious" anti-Semite, Dr. Bernhard Förster, troubled Nietzsche deeply and unleashed a vehement desire for revenge. He wrote to his friend Overbeck that his secret hatred of his sister brought him to the brink of madness.

146 Ges. W. vol. IV, p. 191; CM vol. 4, p. 167.

Only the observation, "It is time," caused him to reflect: "High time for *what* ?" Though deeply saddened and regarding everything as empty, he still had not realized that it was high time to abandon the shadow of power he had projected onto the fire-spitting hound, giving it up in favor of the other.

A further sign seemed to be necessary, and it came in a terrible dream of the castle of death, which impressed upon him the measure of the danger he was in.

It was not only the castle of death,[147] the roaring wind (a symbol for Odin and analogy to Dionysus), the dark vault or the black coffin that signalled insanity, but above all, the sinister laughter. Though Nietzsche – according to his bequest – 'knew'[148] how threatening the situation was, he could not understand the message sent to him from the depth of his soul. He held onto the image of his own greatness and refused to give up his superhuman and overly-demanding mission, despite his secret knowledge that he was tempting fate, death and madness.

Hardly had he recovered from the terrors held by the vision of death than his unconscious was sending him another compensatory signal, this time in the shape of a wretched, slender hunchback,[149] gruesome to behold and looking more like a collection of "fragments from limbs"

147 Amid the "death-rattle silence," he tried in vain to open the gates to the castle, until suddenly something happened that shook him: "Thrice, strokes struck at the gate like thunder; the vaults echoed and howled thrice.... Then a roaring wind tore its wings apart; whistling, shrilling and piercing, it cast up a black coffin before me. And amid the roaring and whistling and shrilling the coffin burst and spewed out a thousandfold laughter.... And I cried in horror as I never had cried before."
Ges. W. vol. VI, p. 199f; CM vol. 4, p. 174.

148 In the bequest is written (vol. 10, p. 368):
"I myself am the wind that breaks in the gates to the tombs of the dead. I myself am the coffin full of colorful maliciousness and angelic grimaces, I myself am the laughter of life in the midnight tombs of the dead."

149 Ges. W. vol. VI, p. 203; CM vol. 4, p. 177.

than a man. This meeting would have been an opportunity to bring to account the "cripple in himself," representing the sickness and imperfection of his nature. In place of gaining such an insight into his shadow world, he was overrun by the fear and hopelessness of a human existence enslaved to the past and without prospect of a liveable future. He asked himself whether it would ever be possible to liberate the will, imprisoned as it was in the past and the unconscious, from the burden of time. In view of this dependency, how could humanity ever attempt to free itself from the control of the past? In the end, Nietzsche was able to shake off this fit of depression. Flying in the face of all reason, he tried to save himself by audaciously commending himself to the creative will.

> "All 'it was' is a fragment, a riddle, a dreadful accident – until the creative will says to it: 'But thus do I will it ... thus shall I will it.' "[150]

This decision deceived the others, and perhaps even Zarathustra himself, into believing that he had pulled himself together again. The pathological concept of the greatness of a free and independent will had triumphed over his fear of the crippled and shadowlike nature of the human being.

Yet there remained in him a deep-rooted inner dichotomy over this encounter with the hunchback that made him doubt in his mission as the herald of truth. It was also difficult for him to pursue the path of loneliness, since he depended on friends to help prepare his work for publication and, at the same time, was anxious not to be misunderstood. His frightened question was whether they would not call his overman a 'devil.'[151] And would they ever understand Zarathustra's gospel of the reality of evil? These fears apart, Nietzsche knew deep down that he must continue along the path he had already set out on. "Men must become *more evil* ... this is my greatest pain – I must

150  Ges. W. vol. VI, p. 208; CM vol. 4, p. 181.
151  Ges. W. vol. VI, p. 213; CM vol. 4, p. 186.

*make* them more evil."[152] What he probably had in mind was to make them stronger and rougher.

Zarathustra-Nietzsche's tortured conflict between love for his disciples and an inner obligation to proclaim the 'truth' was divulged in the ensuing conversation with his soul – the central symbol of his inner world. Ghostly and insinuating was the way his "angry mistress," an interesting variant on Spitteler's 'mistress soul,'[153] sought, with half-irate whispers, to rouse him to complete his work. Equally spectral was her urgent reminder: "You know it, Zarathustra, but you do not say it,"[154] and with it, his fear-

---

152  CM vol. 10, p. 539.

153  Carl Spitteler (1845-1924) was known to Nietzsche through a written controversy they had had over a charge of plagiarism.

154  The penetrating urgency of this vision appears to me to justify a full quotation: "Yesterday, in the stillest hour, the ground gave way under me, the dream began ... the clock of my life drew a breath. Never had I heard such stillness around me: my heart took fright. Then it spoke to me without voice: 'You know it, Zarathustra.' And I cried with fright at this whispering, and the blood left my face; but I remained silent.
Then it spoke again without voice: 'You know it, Zarathustra, but you do not say it.'
And at last I answered defiantly: 'Yes, I know it, but I do not want to say it.'
Then it spoke again without voice: 'You do not *want* to, Zarathustra? Is this really true? Do not hide behind your defiance.'
And I cried and trembled like a child and spoke: 'Alas, I would like to, but how can I? Release me from this! It is beyond my strength!'
Then it spoke to me again without voice: 'What does it matter to you, Zarathustra? Speak your word and break!
And I answered: 'Alas, is it *my* word? Who am I? I await the worthier one; I am not worthy even of being broken by it.'
Then it spoke to me again without voice: 'O Zarathustra, he who has to move mountains also moves valleys and hollows ... ' And I answered: 'They mocked me when I found and went my own way...'
Then it spoke to me again without voice: 'What matters their mockery? You are one who has forgotten how to obey: now you shall command...'
And I answered: 'I lack the lion's voice for commanding.' Then it spoke to me again as a whisper: 'It is the stillest words that bring on the storm. Thoughts that come on doves' feet guide the world...'
Then it spoke to me again without voice: 'You must yet become as a child and without shame.'

...

130

ful silence and struggle to achieve the task she had set. He met her call for hardness, domination and command with a trembling voice: "I do not want to." The exchange with himself, set in the "stillest hour," ended in a burst of horrible laughter that "tore his entrails" and "split open his heart."

Laughter is characteristic of Zarathustra-Nietzsche, as we see from Nietzsche's notes:

> "Destiny and laughter are Zarathustra's mother and father ... "[155]

In other words, Nietzsche, in triumphantly attempting to overcome his fate, bled to death in the process.[156] This he had already indicated in the words, "annointed and consecrated with tears as a sacrificial animal." For the time being, we can only guess at what startled him about his conversation with himself, and it probably had to do with the notion of the 'eternal recurrence.' But his decision to leave his friends behind and go on alone at least makes it clear that he emerged from this battle the vanquished victor. His inner demon, embodied in the 'mistress soul,' had proved itself the stronger in wrestling with his timid ego. After a dubious victory over the strongest of his obstacles, the road was now open for him to enter the last section of his journey.

And I reflected for a long time and trembled. But at last I said what I had said at first: 'I do not want to.'
Then laughter surrounded me. Alas, how this laughter tore my entrails and slit open my heart!
And it spoke to me for the last time: 'O Zarathustra, your fruit is ripe, but you are not ripe for your fruit. Thus you must return to your solitude again: for you must yet become mellow.'
And again it laughed and fled; then it became still around me as with a twofold stillness. But I lay on the ground and sweat poured from my limbs." Ges. W. vol. VI, p. 215ff; CM vol. 4, p. 187ff.
155   CM vol. 10, p. 546.
156   Lou Andreas-Salomé's *Friedrich Nietzsche in seinen Werken* contains a masterly portrayal of this conflict within himself.

*Part Three*

In the third part of *Zarathustra,* originally conceived as its last, the tragedy gains momentum. In his diaries, Nietzsche called this section '*Zarathustra's self-overcoming,*' occasionally also a "model for mankind's self-overcoming,"[157] both of which pointed towards an heroic test of courage. Naturally, the question arises as to whether he would have the necessary resiliance to realize his concept of greatness and whether he could openly commit himself to his *reappraisal of morality,* that is to say, acknowledge a *mysterium iniquitatis* [mystery of evil] and the secretly nurtured conviction of the 'eternal recurrence.' Nietzsche was indeed in need of a few more unconscious thrusts to acquire the strength to accept the fate he believed to be marked out for him.

In the introduction to the third part, his pathway to greatness is described in terms of "the loneliest wandering" on the coldest of nights. It was identical to his being torn apart by the clash of the highest heights and deepest abysses in him:

> "You are going your way to greatness: Peak and abyss – they are now joined together! ... Before my highest mountain I stand and before my longest wandering: to that end I must first go down deeper than ever I descended."[158]

His soul was filled with depression and bitterness, occasionally interrupted by his laughing at himself. Evil memories and hopes weighed heavily upon him. Because mental torment often produced physical effects with Nietzsche, he began to suffer from more than his usual sensitiv-

---

157 CM vol. 10, p. 522. The third part of *Zarathustra* is also described by Nietzsche as the book of "seven solitudes," CM vol. 10, p. 498.
158 Ges. W. vol. VI, p. 224; CM vol. 4, p. 194.

132

ity to the cold, to the rigors of his chosen path, and to physical exhaustion. "And soon it happened that he who had laughed wept: from wrath and longing Zarathustra wept bitterly"[159] – a confusing mixture of concrete and poetic truth informs the pages of *Zarathustra*.

During his wanderings, his self-doubt was symbolized by the unforeseen mockery of a dwarf, who sat on his back and hindered his climb. As the *bearer of secret knowledge* and the 'spirit of gravity,' the latter could stand for Nietzsche's ever-present presentiments and fears, simultaneously compensating for his immoderate aspirations to spiritual greatness. This mysterious inner conflict between darkness and light is revealed in the derisive attack of the dwarf:

> " 'O Zarathustra,' he whispered mockingly, syllable by syllable, 'you philosopher's stone! You threw yourself up high, but every stone that is thrown must fall ... far indeed have you thrown the stone, but it will fall back on yourself.' "[160]

This violent *breaking out of the shadow* necessarily had to jar the timid and hesitant wanderer into a reaction. Like an invalid tired of the martyrdom of his mission, Nietzsche gathered himself for the counterattack.

> "Courage, however, is the best slayer – courage which attacks: which slays even death itself, for it says, 'Was *that* life? Well then! Once more!' "[161]

He challenged his hard-pressed adversary to do battle:

> " 'Stop, dwarf!' I said. 'It is I or you! But I am the stronger of us two: you did not know my abysmal thought. *That* you could not bear!' "[162]

159  Ges. W. vol. VI, p. 227; CM vol. 4, p. 196.
160  Ges. W. vol. VI, p. 229; CM vol. 4, p. 198.
161  Ges. W. vol. VI, p. 230; CM vol. 4, p. 199.
162  Ges. W. vol. VI, p. 231; CM vol. 4, p. 199.

Taking up the gauntlet, the dwarf threw these profound words at him:

> "All that is straight lies," the dwarf murmured contemptuously. "All truth is crooked; time itself is a circle."[163]

Half in wrath and half in fright at the exposure of his most carefully guarded secret, Nietzsche could no longer hold back a growing awareness of his inner truth:

> "'Behold,' I continued, 'this moment! From this gateway, Moment, a long eternal lane leads *backward:* behind us lies an eternity. Must not whatever can walk have walked on this lane before? Must not whatever can happen have happened, have been done, have passed by before? ... and I and you in the gateway, whispering together, whispering of eternal things – must not all of us have been there before?'"[164]

This was the heart of the matter: he was oppressed by the idea of the 'eternal recurrence' of all events as it forced its way into his consciousness! It may be surprising to learn that Nietzsche could be so disquieted by the full realization of this thought. However, for him it represented much more than a mere abstract notion, being instead a *mystical image that touched deep emotions.* The concept of a repetitious cycle of events not only pulled back the mat from under any reassurance of ultimate redemption or of life after death, it also discouraged any thought of the individual's progress.

Nietzsche's battle with the dwarf exhibits the entire spectrum of tensions within the 'eternal recurrence,' stretching from a defiant 'Yes' to a timid 'No.' The huge

163  Ges. W. vol. VI, p. 231; CM vol. 4, p. 200.
164  *Ibid.*

excitement he felt at the very mention of it is evinced by the gruesome chain of occurrences accompanying the idea.

At the precise moment of its manifestation, a dog began to whine more terribly than Nietzsche had known since his childhood. Was it all a dream? Was what followed just an inner vision, a premonition? What had happened? We read:

> "*But there lay a man.* And there – the dog, jumping, bristling, whining ... had I ever heard a dog cry like this for help? And verily what I saw – I had never before seen the like. A young shepherd I saw, writhing, gagging, in spasms, his face distorted, and a heavy black snake hung out of his mouth ... the snake crawled into his throat, and there bit itself fast. My hand tore at the snake and tore in vain: it did not tear the snake out of his throat. Then out of me came the cry: 'Bite! Bite its head off! Bite! – ' The shepherd, however, bit as my cry counseled him: he bit with a good bite. Far away he spewed the head of the snake – and he jumped up. No longer shepherd, no longer human – one changed, radiant, *laughing* ! Never yet on earth has a human being laughed as he laughed."[165]

Nietzsche never stopped yearning for this laughter, which remained "a longing" that "never grew still."

Why was it that this uncanny laughter should give the impression of insanity?[166] What inner conflict was it indicating? What was the connection between the notion of recurrence and the bitten-off head of the snake? The black snake – archetypal symbol of the nullity of life and inscrutability of fate – stood for the deep sense of helplessness that had assailed Nietzsche in the face of his trivialization of experience. Everything he consciously suppressed but

---

165  Ges. W. vol. VI, p. 233f; CM vol. 4, p. 201f.
166  Lou v. Salomé makes the most effective reference to this laughter in *Nietzsche in seinen Werken.*

secretly 'knew' – the threat of sinking into the earth's chasm and of being fragmentized by the bursting coffin – found its crowning image in the strangulating snake and its head. Nietzsche's command to the shepherd to bite off the head, with its disturbing connotations of 'abysmal thought,'[167] displayed his renewed attempt to escape his destiny. As can be seen in the bequest, he regarded spitting out the head in terms of redemption.[168]

Viewed psychologically, it must be admitted that the liberation envisaged is a deeply problematic one, an opinion further supported by the infernal laughter of the shepherd. It may be said that the act of severing the snake's head can be understood in terms of rejecting the shadow[169]; it was thus a *failed endeavor* to resolve the dichotomy between a fear of living, that is, of ending a meaningless existence, and a defiantly self-assertive attitude. The deed unequivocally expresses his despair at facing death. What is more: Nietzsche's dismissal of the dwarf, the 'spirit of gravity,' and of the 'eternal recurrence' of the world had the questionable effect of clearing the way for his inflationary notions of greatness and his craving for power.

After going through the terrifying events which brought him face to face with a fear of the *yawning chasm of nothingness* (Jaspers) and death, Nietzsche had to find the courage to continue believing in his mission, that very mission mentioned in Zarathustra's initial proclamation. The overman wanted to create, and mankind had to be raised to this end. The only complication was whether or not man had to destroy himself in doing so.

Nietzsche's mental state was next reflected in a situation reminiscent of a condemned man fighting to escape his fate

---

167  CM vol. 10, p. 585
168  *Ibid.* p. 578: "Redemption ... I spit out the snake's head!"
169  On rejecting the 4th function, C.G. Jung wrote: "Nietzsche in his *Zarathustra* decided to reject the 'snake' and the 'ugliest man,' thus exposing himself to an heroic convulsion of consciousness which led, logically enough, to the collapse foretold in the same book." Ges. W. vol. XII, p. 184 (C.W. 12, pp. 14-18).

with what little strength he had left. He lacked the inner vigor needed to comply with Zarathustra's monstrously unreasonable demands. Powerless to accede to the stringency of heroic greatness, Nietzsche's ego took refuge in identifying himself with the concept of greatness alone. By presenting this transformation in a new perspective, Nietzsche demonstrated his subtle sense of psychology. Everything that took place around him seemed to have grown smaller, things as well as people,[170] which betrayed how exacting he had become in what he expected from greatness. In *Zarathustra,* we read:

"Curse all cowardly devils in you who like to whine and fold their hands and pray."[171]

His boundless contempt for the servile and false reached the point where he virtually had to get it out of his system by shouting it aloud:

"I am Zarathustra, the godless: where shall I find my equal? And all those are my equals who give themselves their own will and reject all resignation. I am Zarathustra, the godless: I still cook every chance in my pot. And only when it has been cooked through there do I welcome it as *my* food."[172]

An outburst displaying such audacious self-glorification, with Nietzsche actually identifying himself with the

170  Ges. W. vol. VI, p. 245f; CM vol. 4, p. 211f.
171  Ges. W. vol. VI, p. 250; CM vol. 4, p. 215.
172  Ges. W. vol. VI, p. 250; CM vol. 4, p. 215.
   A little later, he writes: "I am my own precursor among this people, my own cock's crow through dark lanes. But *their* hour will come. And mine will come too. Hourly they are becoming smaller, poorer, more sterile – poor herbs! poor soil!... O blessed hour of lightning! O secret before noon! I yet hope to turn them into galloping fires and heralds with fiery tongues – they shall proclaim with fiery tongues: It is coming, it is near – *the great noon!"*
   Ges. W. vol. VI, p. 252; CM vol. 4, p. 217.

archetype, shows Nietzsche to be a man with nothing more to lose. The high emotion indicated a vulnerable spot in his personality that can be characterized as a deep-rooted *self-valuation disorder* (narcissism). He no longer felt secure in a world whose essential values had lost all their credibility. His God was dead, and he could do no more than project the numinous image of a superior power onto a future overman. Even this hope was tinged and dulled by the sinister prophecy of Zarathustra, to the effect that the end of man must precede the creation of the overman. What troubled Nietzsche is made clear in a passage from the bequest:

> "Beyond the center of life – irrevocably sacrificed – never to return."[173]

One cannot overestimate what it cost him in suffering to grapple with this realization. He was overwhelmed by a feeling of intense loneliness....

Psychologically speaking, Nietzsche was probably the victim of a fatal misunderstanding. His identification with Zarathustra, the godless god of creation, demonstrates – as we have just seen – how overpowering the archetype had been. To put it another way, this meant that he was no longer in a position to relate properly to Zarathustra's messages – verbal, dreamlike or figurative – since he himself had claimed the mantle of the prophet. He had robbed himself of the chance to contact the greater part of his soul and replaced it with his ego. The tragedy of Nietzsche's life begins *when he regards himself and the archetype of the man-god as one.* It is obvious that Nietzsche has been subjected to too much pressure by the task lodged in his unconscious. Despite becoming one of the founding fathers of depth psychology by virtue of his astounding discoveries of the unconscious, he foundered on the problem of isolating the ego from the archetype. Instead of establishing a *relationship* with the latter and thus objectifying it, he actu-

173  CM vol. 10, p. 526.

ally counted himself and his ego as constituent parts of the archetype. It was left to later research on the process of individuation and the connection between the ego, the self and the archetype to find ways of objectifying over-powerful archetypes.[174]

Meanwhile the inner tension mounted – by analogy – in a series of dramatic events. Zarathustra-Nietzsche[175] was led in the course of a dream to "the foothills beyond the world," where he "held scales and weighed the world."[176] In the dream he took three of the "most evil" and "best cursed" traits – voluptuousness, the desire to dominate and selfishness – in order to weigh them and test their moral worth. It is hardly surprising that in his presumptuous and self-assertive desire to sit in judgment on the world he should praise those characteristics dubbed "evil" vices by the collective.[177] He saw them as virtues with the major aim of creating the image of the overman. Essential to the realization of this purpose was the possession not only of a strong will but also of an attitude despising the lower part of the personality. Unlike conventional morality he desig-nated selfishness the indispensable prerequisite for man's perfection,[178] as it instilled the necessary stringency and capacity to bear disappointment and sacrifice friends. Self-ishness, far from being contemptible, bore witness to man's loyal love of himself; a dangerous statement that, unchecked, could lead to frequent misinterpretations:

174  In Jung, we read (Ges. W. vol. XI, p. 344; C.W. vol. 11, p. 315):
     "It is a psychological rule that when the archetype has lost its metaphysical hypostasis, it becomes identified with the conscious mind of the individual, which it influences and refashions in its own form. And since an archetype always possesses a certain numinosity, the integration of the numen generally produces an inflation of the subject." See Jung's work on the individuation process in: Ges. W. vol. VII (C.W. vol. 7).

175  See p. 114 on the convergence of Zarathustra-Nietzsche.

176  Ges. W. vol. VI, p. 274; CM vol. 4, p. 235.

177  CM vol. 10, p. 529: "All *virtue and self-overcoming* is only meaningful in preparing for the *ruler*."

178  Ges. W. vol. VI, p. 278f; CM vol. 4, p. 238f.

"One must learn to love oneself – thus I teach – with a wholesome and healthy love, so that one can bear to be with oneself and need not roam."[179]

Seductive as this thought may have been, it had a catch. Although Nietzsche was right to refer to the necessity of sacrifice and self-loyalty, his further view that moral responsibility was in the final analysis subordinate to the ego was very questionable. The next aphorism has an arrogant ring:

"He, however, has discovered himself, who says, 'This is *my* good and evil': with that he has reduced to silence the mole and dwarf, who say: 'Good for all, evil for all!'"[180]

This outrageous act of capricious identification with the image of God culminated in the famous section on the 'Old and New Tablets.'[181] Obsessed by the thought of making new laws as ruler and legislator of the world, Zarathustra-Nietzsche successively *smashed the old tablets to set up new ones.* He envisaged the task of the new tablets as abolishing the law of Moses and preparing for a new future in which the individual would be released from the errors and pressures of the past, of the repeated utterance 'it was.' He was concerned with raising a strong aristocracy which allowed one to breathe freely and use willpower in an entirely new way. To this end ordinary man had to move aside and the "old idolater of the law" be overcome. Nietz-

179 Ges. W. vol. VI, p. 282; CM vol. 4, p. 242.
180 Ges. W. vol. VI, p. 284; CM vol. 4, p. 243.
  See also the bequest: CM vol. 10, p. 562: "That is something that wants to give me *orders* (said the old dragon). Why are we wrestling with one another. Let us see who is the stronger. This is how *evil* comes about." In *Beyond Good and Evil,* Nietzsche's conception of evil becomes increasingly problematical, inasmuch as he associated power and strength with cruelty and the desire to appropriate (p. 221).
181 Ges. W. vol. VI, p. 287ff; CM vol. 4, p. 246ff.

sche proclaimed with Dionysian extremity the approach of a new human type who, like Zarathustra, "[had] the highest soul, which reached deepest"[182] and could best endure the inscrutable abyss of life. From now on the soft mentality of goodness, justice and love would be replaced by boldness, readiness to fight, decisiveness and especially the inexorability of the will – that is to say, by a healthy and victorious "I want."[183] The quintessence of the new tablets can be summed up in the imperative: "Become hard."

"This new tablet, o my brother, I place over you: *become hard.*"[184]

By hoping for a hard and steely humankind, Nietzsche diverged furthest from the opposite side of his being, from his sensitivity and his need for affection and support. The camel was as much a part of his nature as the lion, to put it in the words of Zarathustra's opening speeches. The more severe he was with himself, the more prey he was to fear and melancholy; the higher his strivings took him, the more he surrendered himself to the underworld.[185]

Had it not been for this *rupture of opposites,* he confessed that he would never have had the requisite elasticity to complete his creative mission. It was this that produced the hectic, overwrought irritability and diseased exaltation

182 This highest of types he portrayed as the one who had: "the most comprehending soul ... the soul which, having being, dives into becoming; the soul which *has,* but *wants* to want and will: ... the soul which loves itself most in which all things have their sweep and countersweep...." Ges. W. vol. VI, p. 304; CM vol. 4, p. 261.
183 See p. 92f.
184 Ges. W. vol. VI, p. 312; CM vol. 4, p. 268.
185 CM vol. 10, p. 538. Nietzsche wrote: "Oh, Zarathustra said, I cannot release myself from hell – the underworld, where everything dead rises up against me and even the shadows still speak: Life is a torture." Anxieties, the fear of fate, the fear of bad dreams and bad thoughts, these are the things that deny him sleep. But also the "affection towards all living things could" become a danger to him and paralyze his will, he also wrote in the bequest.

that helped him carry his mission through. The aphorisms that follow unveil Nietzsche's pathological self-assurance:

"Thou destination of my soul, which I call destiny. Thou in me! Over me! Keep me and save me for a great destiny! ... That I may one day be ready and ripe in the great noon ... – a sun itself and an inexorable will, ready to annihilate in victory!"[186]

The letters of this period are also striking:

"I have things on my soul that are a hundred times heavier to bear than *la bêtise humaine*. It is possible that I spell doom for all future races, that I shall be their undoing, – and it is therefore highly probable that, one day, I shall turn dumb out of love for mankind."[187]

The enantiodromic law of the meeting of opposites, which states that sooner or later an overly one-sided attitude turns into its opposite,[188] points to his strength giving way as a consequence of his megalomaniac act of self-glorification. Nietzsche fell into a stupor of despair that did not lift for some seven days, leaving him lying in his cave as if dead. Nietzsche's path was the way of suffering. This is shown by his retrospective notes describing the "contents of the third Zarathustra as divine suffering." In a condition comparable to the temple incubation of the ancients, Nietzsche's 'ultimate depth' became activated – we later read in *Zarathustra* – and his "abyss began to speak ..." His inner demon will not let go of him.

Two thoughts burst out, articulated by his two animals, the eagle and the serpent: firstly, that of the *'eternal recurrence,'* and secondly, the notion that *evil is man's best*

186  Ges. W. vol. VI, p. 312f; CM vol. 4, p. 268f.
187  To Malvida von Meysenburg, February 1884, in: Nietzsche, *Briefe,* p. 278.
188  Cf. C.G. Jung vol. VII, p. 77f (C.W. vol. 7, p. 71).

*power*. What he had hitherto hardly dared think now appeared in the full glare of light:

> "Everything goes, everything comes back; eternally rolls the wheel of being. Everything dies, everything blossoms again; eternally runs the year of being."[189]

In a manner less violent than in the case of the strangulating snake, Nietzsche was moved to disgust by renewed mention of the 'eternal recurrence,' yet still torn by the choice of either accepting or rejecting this 'abysmal thought.' Apart from his resistance to the concept that even the smallest of men would always return, it was his disgust at the smallness of mankind in general that mauled and choked him.

> "All-too-small, the greatest! – that was my disgust with man. And the eternal recurrence even of the smallest – that was my disgust with all existence."[190]

With the words "all is the same, nothing is worthwhile, knowledge chokes" he reached the rock bottom of despair, after which his mood began to change. From deep within a violent excitement arose, giving vent to all the things he had struggled to suppress:

> "My torture was not the knowledge that man is evil – but I cried as no one has yet cried: 'Alas, that his greatest evil is so very small! Alas, that his best is so very small!"[191]

The emotional shaking he received also helped him to gain a sense of himself. He was now given the full and wholesome strength to stand by his fateful idea and the truth he felt within. The pressure exerted on him even lent

189  Ges. W. vol. VI, p. 317; CM vol. 4, p. 272.
190  Ges. W. vol. VI, p. 320; CM vol. 4, p. 274.
191  Ges. W. vol. VI, p. 319; CM vol. 4, p. 274.

him the courage to describe the power of evil as the best force at mankind's disposal:

> "... only this have I learned so far, that man needs what is most evil in him for what is best in him – that whatever is his best power and the hardest stone for the highest creator; and that man must become better and more evil."[192]

Despite the fact that such a thought posed problems of misinterpretation, Nietzsche was content merely to present it and suspend any more detailed commentary. He was satisfied to have overcome his inner uncertainty and found the grit to express this monstrous and highly controversial idea. His most urgent question was how such a crippling notion could be rendered bearable. The notes in his bequest illustrate that only by lifting oneself above existing morality and overcoming within oneself dearly-held thoughts could an inner balance be reached. We read:

> "Solution Zarathustra III:
> You must raise yourself above morality, you have seen through it – all your *misery* is a consequence of *it* ... there is no other way for man to *overcome himself*. The *slightest* concealment nullifies all his strength: he feels that he has *avoided* a thought that now comes tumbling down on him with all its might! It is a wrestling match: who is *strong* enough, Zarathustra or the thought? (Meaning: the instinct for truth or prevailing morality) Why truth? Zarathustra *cannot* do anything else!"[193]

What he goes on to say is also of interest:

> "*Overcoming the past in us* ... very difficult! It is by no means the evil impulses alone that should be over-

192 *Ibid.*
193 CM vol. 10, p. 521 (partly my emphasis).

144

come – the so-called good impulses must be over-powered and consecrated anew!"[194]

In order to be capable of overcoming the self to such a degree, Nietzsche also stated in the bequest that "loneliness in eternity, beyond morality" was called for: the strength to sacrifice existing friendships, the courage and the will to suffer, and above all the courage of the lion to say 'I want' (an allusion to Zarathustra's three metamorphoses).

This moving confession slowly bestowed on Nietzsche the audacity to express his most concealed thought and unconditionally admit to a great mystical experience which presented time and eternity as one. In it he discovered a "substitute for the belief in immortality" of the Christian Gospel. Nietzsche put the following words into the mouths of his animals, the mouthpieces of his unconscious:

> "I come again, with this sun, with this earth, with this eagle, with this serpent – not to a new life or a better life or a similar life: I come back eternally to this same, selfsame life, in what is greatest as in what is smallest, to teach again the eternal recurrence of all things, to speak again the word of the great noon of earth and man, to proclaim the overman again to men. I spoke my word, I break with my word: thus my eternal lot wants it: a proclaimer I perish."[195]

In the ensuing quiet and silence of his heart Zarathustra-Nietzsche communed with his soul. Like the 'Night Song,' the one 'On the Great Longing' also testifies to his endur-ing poetic gift. Not only is it enchantingly beautiful, but it reveals the deepest ultimate wisdom, as well. This was the first occasion Nietzsche was granted direct perception of and full participation in the mystery of the *coincidence of opposites*. The gist of what we read is as follows: is not taking the same as giving, the future identical with the past?

194  *Ibid.* p. 519.
195  Ges. W. vol. VI, p. 322; CM vol. 4, p. 276.

Are not 'Yes' and 'No' concordant, contempt and love indivisible? Does not understanding become the same as singing and reach beyond the naming of names?[196]

This dialogue reawakened in him a sense of mission and reminded him of the transfiguring beauty of life, allowing him once more to feel love for the impenetrability of all life, much as Faust had done. At that point, he whispered to his soul that life was dearer to him than all his wisdom.

The third part ends with a full "Yes to lust and eternity," as well as to the *apotheosis of the ring of recurrence*. As if in a dream or trance Nietzsche heard an old, heavy bell ponderously booming out the hours from the sleep of midnight, through the awakening of dawn to the noon of eternity.

> *"One:*      O man, take care!
> *Two:*       What does the deep midnight declare?
> *Three:*     'I was asleep.
> *Four:*      'From a deep dream I woke and swear:
> *Five:*      'The world is deep.
> *Six:*       'Deeper than day has been aware.
> *Seven:*     'Deep is its woe.
> *Eight:*     'Joy – deeper yet than agony.
> *Nine:*      'Woe implores: Go!
> *Ten:*       'But all joy wants eternity.
> *Eleven*:    'Wants deep, wants deep eternity.'
> *Twelve!* ..." [197]

In the 'ring of recurrence,' everything that until now had been no more than an intellectual idea reverted to the immediate experience of reality. An earlier aphorism demonstrates what the ring meant to Nietzsche as he describes it in terms of the highest virtue of the self:

> *"The thirst of the ring lives in you: every ring strives and turns to reach itself again."* [198]

196  Ges. W. vol. VI, p. 324f; CM vol. 4, p. 278f.
197  Ges. W. vol. VI, p. 332f; CM vol. 4, p. 285f.
198  Ges. W. vol. VI, p. 136; CM vol. 4, p. 121 (my emphasis).

It is not only Nietzsche's deep thirst to *realize his self* that the ring of recurrence displays, but also his additional yearning for the *mystery of eternity*.

The seventh and final seal of his magnificent poetic vision of the ring goes like this:

"If ever I spread tranquil skies over myself and soared on my own wings into my own skies: if I swam playfully in the deep light-distances, and the bird-wisdom of my freedom came – but bird-wisdom speaks thus: 'Behold there is no above, no below! Throw yourself around, out, back, you, who are light! Sing, speak no more! Are not all words made for the grave and heavy? Are not all words lies to those who are light? Sing! Speak no more!' Oh should I not lust after eternity and after the nuptial ring of recurrence? Never did I find any other woman to bear my children but this woman, whom I love: *For I love you, oh eternity!*" [199]

Such passages dispel all doubt about Nietzsche having a deeply *religious* personality and revealing a passionate longing for *eternity and the super-temporal.* The noble end to his quest was releasing the mystery of the 'ring of recurrence' from its prison of stone and thereby freeing the overman.

After completing the third part of *Zarathustra,* he wrote to his friend Erwin Rohde:

"My Zarathustra is finished ... Everything in it is my own and is without model, comparison or predecessors; whoever has once lived in it will return to the world wearing another face." [200]

199  Ges. W. vol. VI, p. 338f; CM vol. 4, p. 291.
200  *Nietzsches Register*, ed. Richard Oehler, p. 280. Letter of 4 February 1884.

## Part Four

Nietzsche was wrong: these three parts were followed a year later by a fourth; but one which, admittedly, was much more loosely connected to the previous parts. Striking is the absence of that Dionysian spark which had so enlivened the work before; it made room for a spirit of pessimism close to nihilism. Resignation and melancholy weighed heavily on Nietzsche's soul; disappointment at the indifferent reception of his previous three books is constantly present as an undertone. Hope was also fading in him that a 'higher' type of humanity, unifying the spirit and the will, would be born.

He concretized his bitter experiences in eight figures – all 'higher' examples of humanity – who, close to drowning and despair, sought out Nietzsche for a cure.

In *Zarathustra,* he wrote: "It is *the highest man* that cries for you."[201]

All of them lacked something, were disillusioned in spirit and languished in their own dissatisfaction. Like masks, so to speak, they demonstrated Nietzsche's pain both at his own unfulfilled expectations and the respective *compensatory reactions of the shadow.* Crushed ideals and crushed hopes were met with feelings of disgust, contempt and vengeance; but the delusion of grandeur also reared its head.

Thus, the soothsayer represents that aspect of Nietzsche's personality that *"froze to death" from intellectual conscience,* that had lost life's meaning and been "choked by knowledge." Inwardly tired and despairing, he disappointedly taught:

> "But all is the same, nothing is worthwhile, no seeking avails, nor are there any blessed isles anymore."[202]

201 Ges. W. vol. VI, p. 351; CM vol. 4, p. 302.
202 Ges. W. vol. VI, p. 352; CM vol. 4, p. 302.

The 'conscientious in spirit' that Nietzsche found covered in blood in the swamp was similarly branded. He, too, embodied an aspect of Nietzsche, namely his *intellectual doggedness* and hatred of intellectual shortcomings:

> "Rather know nothing than half-know much! Rather be a fool on one's own than a sage according to the opinion of others! I go to the ground – ..."[203]

> "That you, O Zarathustra, once said, 'spirit is the life that itself cuts into life,' that introduced and seduced me to your doctrine. And verily with my own blood I increased my own knowledge."[204]

There was further masquerading by two kings in the company of a donkey who, *obsessed with power*, bemoaned the decline of the world and the deceitfulness of society. Tired of political cunning, they were fed up with:

> " ... representing the first among the rabble."[205]

The conversation with the old pope, a man "in black with a gaunt, pale face" who was "retired" after the death of God and had lost his way, went deeper. He represented the pious side of Nietzsche's personality, a side *now disillusioned with God* and with nothing left to do but either become godless, or else become God Himself.

The pope referred to his disillusionment in the following manner:

> "He who loved and possessed him most has also lost him most now."[206]

> "He was a concealed god, addicted to secrecy. Verily,

203 Ges. W. vol. VI, p. 363; CM vol. 4, p. 311.
204 Ges. W. vol. VI, p. 364; CM vol. 4, p. 312.
205 Ges. W. vol. VI, p. 357; CM vol. 4, p. 305.
206 Ges. W. vol. VI, p. 377; CM vol. 4, p. 323.

even to his son he came in a sneak way. At the door
of his faith stands adultery."[207]

"Eventually, however, he became old and soft and
mellow and pitying ... and one day, he choked on his
all-too-great-pity."[208]

At this moment, he was interrupted by a vexed Nietzsche, who sharply retorted:

"There is good taste in piety too; and it was this that
said in the end, 'Away with *such* a god! Rather no
god, make a destiny on one's own; rather be a fool,
rather be a god oneself!'"[209]

The pope's reply was thoughtful:

"O Zarathustra ... You are more pious than you believe. Some god in you must have converted you to
your godlessness. Is it not your piety itself that no
longer lets you believe in a god? And your overgreat
honesty will yet lead you beyond good and evil
too."[210]

Was the pope, Nietzsche's 'pious' shadow figure, perhaps right? Might Nietzsche have been a secret seeker of
God?

The figure of the 'ugliest man,' the murderer of God, is
ambiguous, awakening Nietzsche's most violent emotions.
He is branded the inexpressible scum of mankind and
bearer of the gruesome fate of being "without God, without
goodness, without spirit."[211] The abysmal suffering of
Nietzsche at the hands of his destiny, his inner compulsion

207  Ges. W. vol. VI, p. 378; CM vol. 4, p. 323.
208  Ges. W. vol. VI, p. 378f; CM vol. 4, p. 324.
209  Ges. W. vol. VI, p. 380; CM vol. 4, p. 324f.
210  Ges. W. vol. VI, p. 380; CM vol. 4, p. 325.
211  CM vol. 11, p. 382.

to oppose the collectively ingrained values of truth and goodness and to always represent the cause of *evil,* is abundantly obvious here. As the murderer of God, he was the psychological embodiment of the 'ugliest man,' that shadow figure that stood in sharpest contrast to the 'good' one required by the moral code. As the *opponent of collective interpretations of worth,* he was the representative of all that was viewed as bad, outrageous and evil, in other words, the personification of the collective shadow. One cannot therefore wonder at the fact that his appearance stirred the most contradictory of feelings in Nietzsche. The comments that follow attempt to justify the murderous deed of the 'ugliest man,' with Nietzsche attributing these words to him:

> "The god who saw everything, *even man* – this god had to die! Man cannot bear it that such a witness should live ..."
> "His pity knew no shame: he crawled into my obscurest nooks. This most curious, overobstrusive, overpitying one had to die."[212]

The profound pity Zarathustra felt in the face of this man, destined to be God's murderer, finds expression in the aphorism below:

> " 'How poor man is, after all,' he thought in his heart; 'How ugly, how wheezing, how full of hidden shame. I have been told that man loves himself: ah, how great must this self-love be! How much contempt stands against it.' "[213]

> "None have I found yet who despised himself more deeply: that, too, is a kind of height. Alas, was he perhaps the higher man whose cry I heard?"[214]

212  Ges. W. vol. VI, p. 387; CM vol. 4, p. 331.
213  Ges. W. vol. VI, p. 388; CM vol. 4, p. 332.
214  *Ibid.*

It is highly significant that Nietzsche should bow down before the shadow figure collectively despised for his lack of piety and spirit. He thereby pointed to the fact that the oppositions light and dark, Redeemer and Satan, belonged together. This secret reaction in the unconscious could never be suppressed, as Nietzsche pertinently showed; instead it remained constantly active, though largely unconscious, within the individual. Nietzsche's question about whether the 'ugliest man' could possibly be regarded as a 'higher man' feeds speculation over Nietzsche's knowledge of the secret that *a light may be hidden* in the *abysmal* part of the psyche, in its 'ugliest man.'

The 'magician' may also be counted as one of the 'higher men,' and be seen to belong to the company of the profound but inscrutable shadow figures. In him, Nietzsche movingly invests *the suffering his creative mission* cost him in the shape of doubts about his greatness. He wears the mask of an actor, betraying, on the one hand, the desire for greatness, but at the same time, cleverly concealing that wish. It is not unlikely that Richard Wagner was the godfather of this figure, himself one of the most fateful characters in Nietzsche's life.

Here is an abridged version of the text spoken by the magician:

> "Stretched out, shuddering,
> Like something half-dead whose feet one warms –
> Shaken, alas, by unknown fevers,
> Shivering with piercing icy frost-arrows,
> Hunted by thee, O thought![215]
> Unnameable, shrouded, terrible one!
> . . . .

215 The "great thought" was described in the bequest as "the head of Medusa, petrifying the world." CM vol. 10, p. 360, says: "... open your eyes, see the *whole* truth: *to be or not to be the higher man!*" This thought could be just as much about the 'eternal recurrence' as the overman.

What wouldst thou gain by listening?[216]
What wouldst thou gain by torture,
Thou torturer!
Thou hangman-god!
. . . .
Cruellest hunter!
Thy proudest prisoner,
Thou robber behind clouds!
Speak at last!
What wouldst thou, waylayer, from me?
Thou lightning-shrouded one! Unknown one! Speak,
What wilt thou, unknown-god
. . . .
Me thou wilt have?
Me – entirely?
Hah, hah!
And are torturing me, fool that thou art,
torturing my pride?[217]
. . . .
Away!
He himself fled,
. . . .
No! Do come back
With all thy tortures!
To the last of all that are lonely,
O, come back!
All my tear-streams run
Their course to thee?
And my heart's final flame –
Flares up for *thee* !
O, come back,
My unknown god!
My *pain* ! My last happiness."[218]

---

216  In the bequest, the magician asks the sensitive question: "Where is the
     creative in me?"
217  CM vol. 11, p. 310.
218  Ges. W. vol. VI, pp. 366-370; CM vol. 4, pp. 313-317.

This poem reflects the depth of the plight Nietzsche's soul found itself in. In it, the distress of the "disenchanted magician" destroying himself, of the "enchanter of all,"[219] comes to light; so, too, the torment of the creator[220] caused by suffering from the diminishing of his creative force and awareness of how false his behavior had been. His talk with the magician reveals his constant effort to *disguise himself and pretend he is great* [221] – a distressing acknowledgment of his shadow. What had already been hinted at by the grimace of the devil now takes on a clearer form: Nietzsche perceives himself as the tragic victim of his fascination for the god Dionysus, who – according to *Beyond Good and Evil* – reflects the contrast between the philosopher and redeemer, on the one hand, and the sorcerer, faker and devil on the other. Although his posture right up to his collapse tended rather towards the positive and affirmative side that the Dionysian stood for, the other also became increasingly apparent, both in the *demonic determination of a zealot* and the *cynicism of his despair*. Hand in hand with his inner disintegration went the loss of the creative spark and intellectual vivacity that was once his: despite the fact that he maintained his razor-sharp thinking in the works that followed, this loss was unmistakable.

It is surprising to note the striking similarity between the 'Magician's Song' and a hymn he composed when he was twenty to the 'Unknown God,'[222] who was strongly reminiscent of the god Odin. An indelible experience when he was fifteen years of age gives an indication of what this wild and stormy god meant to his innermost soul. His

219 CM vol. 11, p. 355
220 *Ibid.* p. 310.
221 *Ibid.* p. 349. The precise formulation is: "I am a maker of words: What do words matter? What do I matter?"
222 The third stanza of this poem reads (*Der werdende Nietzsche*, p. 23):
"I want to know Thee, unknown one,
Who reaches deep into my soul,
Roams through my life like a storm,
Thou ineffable one, my kin!
I want to know Thee and serve Thee myself." See p. 9.

notes make it clear that he fainted as a result of a fit of anxiety brought on by a particularly threatening dream.

In this dream, Nietzsche found himself in a "wonderfully lovely evening landscape" walking with his friend Wilhelm,[223] when they were both suddenly startled by a piercing cry. Shortly afterwards, when night had fallen with a sinister veil, they came upon a dark figure and his barking dog in the woods who suddenly placed his whistle to his mouth and blew, whereupon Nietzsche fell unconscious.[224]

Just as the whistle had then disconcerted Nietzsche, so thirty years later the 'hunter' frightened him again with his mockery and his ice-cold aim. In both cases, an uncanny figure appeared out of the darkness of the soul's background, a sort of warning cry that shook him to the core. In the trauma of his youth it was the archetypal figure of Odin, the storm god of passion, death and madness,[225] who, as the wild huntsman, had made him start; now, in the 'Magician's Song', it was the god Dionysus who excited his lament, his pain and his love.[226] Not only was his relationship with Dionysus accentuated by this god, a streak of lightning emerging at the poem's end as "of an emerald beauty,"[227] it was further reinforced by his renaming the song the 'Lament of Ariadne,' a mythological figure carried off by Dionysus.[228] In his work, he often mentioned the unfathomable Ariadne, which hints at a secret – aired only after Nietzsche's breakdown – his affection for Cosima Wagner, namely. Only in the very last of his letters, written during his insanity, does her full significance as the *carrier of an image of the soul* of Nietzsche and as the embodiment

223 The friend is Nietzsche's adolescent companion Wilhelm Pindar.
224 From Nietzsche's notes, p. 85f.
225 See Martin Ninck, *Der germanische Schicksalsglaube.*
226 The transformation of the Odin figure into Dionysus is not surprising, since both are related by the shared archetypal content of death and madness.
227 Ges. W. vol. VIII, p. 432; CM vol. 6, p. 401.
228 Ges. W. vol. VIII, p. 429; CM vol. 6, p. 398.

of his ideal become clear.[229] Inside Nietzsche, Dionysus and Ariadne belonged together.

The last figure to appear was the one he called the 'shadow,' whose ghostlike, dim and antiquated form was always close behind. It incorporated in a ghastly way the *pain, the 'vanity of life' and of nihilism.* Thus the shadow lamented:

> "With you I strove to penetrate everything that is forbidden, worst, remotest.... With you, I broke whatever my heart revered; I overthrew all boundary stones and images; I pursued the most dangerous wishes: verily over every crime I have passed once. With you I unlearned faith in words and values and great names.... Nothing is true, all is permitted: thus I spoke to myself.... Alas, where has all that is good gone from me – and all shame, and all faith in those who are good? Alas, where is that mendacious innocence I once possessed, the innocence of the good their noble lies? ... Too much has become clear to me: now it no longer concerns me. Nothing is alive anymore that I love; how should I still love myself?"[230]

His further confession of having not only lost his aim, but also his home, is a moving one:

229 Curt Janz writes on the insane scribblings: "... three manifestos were sent to Cosima Wagner at the start of January 1889. In one is written: 'Ariadne, I love you.' But it was not only to her that he aired his dire secret; he also did so in two letters to the only living person he placed alongside her and above himself, Jacob Burckhardt. On the 4th of January, he wrote to him: 'Now you are – my friend – our greatest teacher: for I, together with Ariadne, have only to be the golden balance of things, in every part of us we have those who are above us ... Dionysus,' and on the 5th of January we read: 'The rest is for Frau Cosima ... Ariadne.... From time to time a spell is cast....' Ariadne is not only this sole Frau Cosima, she represents an entire spiritual world, a whole world of culture at the very least, the essence of life, she is a canon." Curt Janz, *Nietzsche,* vol. 3, p. 28.
230 Ges. W. vol. VI, p. 397f; CM vol. 4, p. 339f.

" 'Where is my home?' I ask and search and have searched for it, but I have not found it. O eternal everywhere, O eternal nowhere, O eternal – in vain!"[231]

Nietzsche's soul was being ripped apart, with the shadow figure appearing in the guise of a hollow-cheeked ghost as nihilistic compensation for his hungry pursuit of greatness and truth.

After the oppressive meeting with the 'higher man,' who reflected himself by showing not only his own doubts about his greatness, but also revealing his disgust and hatred, Nietzsche fled into solitude. What depressed him most was the excessive weakness of his nature, the shadow of impotence that compensated for his godlike ambitions.

Alone with himself he rediscovered himself, albeit in a dimension removed from the human and the earthly and beyond the opposition of good and evil, light and dark, a dimension pointing forward to the mystical oblivion he later experienced. Buoyed up by an unfathomable feeling of happiness, he thought that the world – at *noon* – had become round and perfect, indeed that he himself was falling into the "timelessness of eternity."[232]

"When will you drink this drop of dew which has fallen upon all earthly things? When will you drink this strange soul? When, well of eternity? Cheerful, dreadful abyss of noon! When will you drink my soul back into yourself?"[233]

We do not know what now happened to Nietzsche at this

231  Ges. W. vol. VI, p. 398; CM vol. 4, p. 341.
232  See also the mystery of immortality, p. 76.
233  Ges. W. vol. VI, p. 403f; CM vol. 4, p. 345. In *The Wanderer and his Shadow,* he had already described noon as a time when all things sleep, but with the expression of eternity on their faces, a time when everything is caught up in a net of light. Ges. W. vol. III/2, p. 358, and CM vol. 2/II,2, p. 690, § 308.

moment of *deepest emotion at the archetype of the self,* at the noonday hour when death and eternity converge as one. Was it the presentiment of madness, which, as a condition existing beyond good and evil, could signify the highest fulfillment as well as the deepest abyss? This deeply moving experience of oneness transformed him. What before he had scarcely dared to think he now regarded as certain: the 'higher men' were not strong enough to accompany him on his path. Returning to his cave, he addressed the following words to his guest, fully aware of his new-found strength:

" 'You may indeed all be higher men ... but for me you are not high and strong enough.... You are mere bridges: may men higher than you stride over you. You signify steps: therefore do not be angry with him who climbs over you to *his* height.... It is not for you that I wait in these mountains ... no, no, and thrice no. It is for others that I wait here ... for those who are higher, stronger, more triumphant and more cheerful, such as are built perpendicular in body and soul: *laughing lions* must come!' "[234]

Was this not also a realization that the 'higher man' in himself needed to mature? Yet, instead of turning towards the suffering shadow figures in himself, Nietzsche – psychologically speaking – did exactly the opposite: he proclaimed his liberation from them! This decision completed a perilous step in the direction of a *dissociation between his spirit's upward striving and the chthonic, earthy side of his being.* This not only threatened to uproot his spirit, but also to overwhelm his instincts with aimless chaos.

Carried along by his vision of laughing lions, Zarathustra-Nietzsche and his disciples sat together to take supper – one of the many allusions to the Gospels, in this case, to Christ's 'Last Supper.' We see a transformed Zarathustra passionately outline his picture of the higher man. He

234  Ges. W. vol. VI, p. 410f; CM vol. 4, p. 350f.

praises sensuousness and the rights of the body more boldly than ever before, turning against any form of asceticism and declaring himself prepared for battle and war in defense of the right of the master race. He valued the higher man's ability to despise,[235] to embrace the abyss and, above all, to know "that the greatest evil is necessary for the overman's best."[236] Now fully given over to the Dionysian spirit, he appealed to his guests to overcome the small-mindedness, the "little virtues," to allow the overman – his "first and only concern" – to be resurrected.

> "Well then, you higher men! Only now is the mountain of man's future in labor. God died: now *we* want the overman to live."[237]

In his view, both the will to life and to power, as well as selfishness and the love of work, were necessary to attain this high aim: not only the courage of the eagle to fear no abyss, but also the strength to bear failure and to learn how to laugh!

> "The higher its type, the more rarely a thing succeeds.... Is it any wonder that you failed and only half succeeded, being half-broken? Is not something thronging and pushing in you – man's *future* ? Man's greatest distance and depth and what in him is lofty to the stars, his tremendous strength – are not all these frothing against each other in your pot? Is it any wonder that many a pot breaks? Learn to laugh at yourselves as one must laugh! You higher men, how much is still possible!"[238]

He continued: "Avoid all such unconditional people," all who belong to the plebeian, "have heavy feet" and do not

235 Ges. W. vol. VI, p. 418; CM vol. 4, p. 357.
236 Ges. W. vol. VI, p. 420; CM vol. 4, p. 359.
237 Ges. W. vol. VI, p. 418; CM vol. 4, p. 357.
238 Ges. W. vol. VI, p. 426; CM vol. 4, p. 364.

know how to dance! In contrast to his archenemy – the spirit of gravity, the earthbound shadow – he praised the pure air of the heights:

> "Lift up your hearts, my brothers, high, higher! And do not forget your legs either. Lift up your legs, too, you good dancers; and better yet, stand on your heads."[239]

Convinced that he alone lived up to this image of the overman who could laugh and dance, Nietzsche enthusiastically seized the crown of roses and set it upon his head, finally throwing it to those present and exclaiming:

> "This crown of him who laughs, this rose-wreath crown: to you, my brothers, I throw this crown. Laughter I have pronounced holy: you higher men, *learn* to laugh!"[240]

This Dionysian outburst, which betrayed signs of the *excesses of self-conceit as well as the laughter of decline*,[241] was followed by Nietzsche's worst depression. His fragile nature prevented him from indulging in such transgressions, oscillating as they did between self-adoration and self-destruction and displaying his impending insanity for all to see.

239  Ges. W. vol. VI, p. 428; CM vol. 4, p. 366.
240  Ges. W. vol. VI, p. 430; CM vol. 4, p. 368.
241  Lou Andreas-Salomé, who had the good fortune of knowing Nietzsche personally, sensitively described this situation: "The great thing is that he knew he was declining, but departed with laughter on his lips, his intellectual life coming to an end 'in a wreath of roses' and in Dionysian dithyrambs as he excused, justified and glorified life. And what their joyful music was meant to drown out was a cry of pain. They are the final violation of Nietzsche at the hands of Zarathustra." Lou Andreas-Salomé, *Nietzsche*, p. 229.
    She ends her book – one of the best written about Nietzsche – with the words: "His laughter reverberates with an ambiguity that is unsettling, even to us: the laughter of him who errs, and the smile of him who overcomes."

The poems that followed show exactly what was going on within Nietzsche's soul, songs of 'higher men' sung during his brief absence. Whilst one song delivered by the 'sorcerer' culminated in the mockery of his poetry, the song of 'the conscientious man' attacked Nietzsche's love of science, whose "only motive was to ward off danger." The climax of Nietzsche's blackout is reached by the 'Desert Song' played by the mask of the 'shadow,' which contains hidden erotic feelings. It is a song full of steamy eroticism and biting criticism of the dignity of the European.[242] Although the decline of all previous values held by Nietzsche to the level of mere lustfulness may seem rather embarrassing, its effect upon those present was overpowering! As if they had been struck by lightning, those who had been in despair jumped up and were cured! It was the 'Desert Song' rather than the request for laughter that worked the miracle of reviving the spirits of life. Like children, they lay on the ground and prayed. A litany ensued, inducing the 'ugliest man' to praise God. But the one to whom they prayed was an ass, whose patience, brotherly love and hidden wisdom they glorified – a startling allusion to the Christian God. However, when the speech about the love of the ass for its mates began, Zarathustra-Nietzsche could no longer contain himself; jumping amongst his now mad guests and shouting Yea-Yuh.[243] It would have been hard to have imagined a more grotesque image for a *descent into the animality of the world of the shadow,* the abyss of existence. The monstrous dimensions of what was happening can only be fully grasped when one considers that, in mythology, the ass not only symbolizes bestial sexuality but also the dark, opposing sun of Lucifer.[244] The glorification of God in the form of the ass is a clear example of Nietzsche's soul succumbing to the instinctual aspect of the image of God: it represents the most forceful expression of compensation for Nietzsche identi-

242 Ges. W. vol. VI, p. 448; CM vol. 4, p. 348. See p. 15.
243 Ges. W. vol. VI, p. 455; CM vol. 4, p. 390.
244 In mythology, the ass is also a symbol of the devil.

fying himself with the aspect of God's light. What he had frequently prophesied as the destiny of modern man was now his own: namely, God gradually becoming an animal.[245] The splitting of his being into the light and dark aspects of the image of God had now come about; in other words, what he suffered was the fate of Dionysus-Zagreus: *that of being ripped apart by the contrasts within human nature.*

In *Zarathustra,* the ass festival was followed by each individual guest being asked about the motives for his praying to the ass. Their answers reveal the 'real' truth of man hungry for God and the spirit; *their adherence to the 'old god' of childhood, the world of light and of the 'truth.'* Thus the pope confesses:

"Better to adore God in this form than in no form at all!"[246]

Whilst 'the shadow' admits:

"The old god lives again, Zarathustra, you may say what you will."[247]

After which the 'conscientious in spirit' emphasizes:

" ... but it is certain that God seems relatively most credible to me in this form."[248]

And finally, the 'ugliest man' answers Zarathustra's question as to whether the old god is still alive with:

"Whether that one *still* lives or lives again or is thoroughly dead – which of the two of us knows that best? I ask you. But one thing I do know; it was from

245  Ges. W. vol. VII, p. 99; CM vol. 5, p. 91.
246  Ges. W. vol. VI, p. 455; CM vol. 4, p. 390.
247  Ges. W. vol. VI, p. 456; CM vol. 4, p. 391.
248  Ges. W. vol. VI, p. 457; CM vol. 4, p. 391.

you yourself that I learned it once, O Zarathustra: whoever would kill most thoroughly, laughs."[249]

What the sarcastic reply was driving at was the dubious knowledge that cynical mockery was in the best position to dispense with all things holy.

The ass festival, with its parody of the Christian God, unmasks the full extent of Nietzsche's complex behavior. On the one hand, the joyousness of his guests led him to venerate God in the form of the ass; on the other, his actions bordered on the absurd, demonstrating that the *longing for the unknown god* was still alive deep within his soul. The adoration of the ass embodied an enduring childhood wish to have a God watching over him, one to pray to and honor.[250] Since the death of his father and the activation of the archetypal paternal image, a constant readiness existed to project the image of the father, of God, onto appropriate figures (Jacob Burckhardt, Richard Wagner, Arthur Schopenhauer). Nietzsche's projections continually defeated both the cynicism of his intellect and the excessive will to self-assertion that had dogged him since earliest childhood.[251] By proclaiming, '*I want,*' he was compensating just as much for his considerable dependency as for the Old Testament command: 'Thou shalt!' – which had been beaten into him. Let me remind the reader of the 'Three Metamorphoses of the Spirit,' in which Zarathustra

249  Ges. W. vol. VI, p. 458; CM vol. 4, p. 392.
250  In the *Gay Science,* we read: "You will never pray again, never adore again ... you renounce to it ... you resist any ultimate peace...." Ges. W. vol. V, p. 216; CM vol. 3/3, p. 527, § 285.
     The later passages that concern Nietzsche's problems with reversion to the old faith point towards inner regressive tendencies. Instead of reflecting on the symbolic significance of each relapse, he brusquely pushed them aside.
251  Nietzsche's will to assert himself was already apparent in his early conviction that he was something quite special. The aphorism from *Zarathustra* : "If there were gods, how could I endure not to be a god! *Hence* there are no gods," points in the same direction, not to mention the many inflated observations of his final years.

revealed his new spirit. He called the last and highest stage the "transformation into the self-rolling wheel," which was intended to indicate the autonomy of the individual. I will return to the religious problem later.

Returning, after this digression, to the dramatic core of *Zarathustra,* we note that Nietzsche's descent into the brutish unconscious had, in addition to its blasphemous side, a religious one: not only was becoming God and becoming an animal regarded as one, but Nietzsche himself *reestablished contact* with his *earthly roots* and thus regained the strength to remain true to his inner necessity – the pressing secret of the 'eternal recurrence.'

Nietzsche's next poetic flash of inspiration may seem paradoxical, since it ascribed the realization of the profundity of life and fate to the 'ugliest man,' that is, to a character who most forcefully compensated for the traditional values of consciousness. As such, this figure possessed neither "spirit, nor God, nor goodness," and was, furthermore, highly problematical as the "murderer of God."

Nevertheless, Nietzsche reported that, in the secrecy of night, "in which all men come closer to each other," this symbol of archetypal evil began to speak loudly and clearly:

> "For the sake of this day, I am for the first time satisfied that I have lived my whole life ... 'Was *that* life?' I want to say to death. 'Well then! Once more!' "252

How do we interpret the deep, electrifying effect that these words exerted upon Nietzsche? Psychologically speaking, they touched a secret hidden within the archetypal shadow. Thanks to his familiarity with the collective unconscious and access to the knowledge it contained, it was precisely this sort of shadow figure that was capable of becoming the mouthpiece of *the most hidden primordial knowledge,* an inscrutable mythical wisdom that – as was the case with the concept of the 'eternal recurrence' – had been in existence since Heraclitus' time. Therefore, if such

252 Ges. W. vol. VI, p. 462; CM vol. 4, p. 395f.

a twilight figure as 'the ugliest man' could declare his sympathy with the beauty of life, and concomitantly to this, its repeated recurrence, then the proclamation of such a thought could not really cause offence to the world!

Thus, later on, we also read in *Zarathustra:* "Zarathustra stood there like a drunkard, his eyes grew dim." "Thoughts running over his soul" – "wandering like a heavy cloud between past and future," he gradually regained his senses. Enraptured by the midnight hour, he was able to become one with himself and fully confess his closely guarded secret of the 'eternal recurrence,' which, for him, signified the immortality of the worldly. In this trance-like state, and unimpaired by his sceptical intellect, he drew the 'higher men' into the enchantment of the night and the "well of timelessness."

What, to start with, had only been communicated to his soul and articulated by his animal spokesmen[253] was now to be announced to everyone. In this condition of ecstatic rapture, Nietzsche began the 'Drunken Song,' a song of eternity, in which noon and midnight flowed into each other, pain equalled desire, and wisdom resembled foolishness. For this brief moment of *mystical immersion "beyond all opposites,"* he had the chance to embrace, with his whole being, the 'eternal recurrence' and the unity of all opposites – of the worldly and the eternal, above and below, male and female. The tenth stanza of this song reads:

"You higher men, what do you think? Am I a soothsayer? A dreamer? A drunkard? A midnight bell? A drop of dew? A haze and fragrance of eternity? Do you not hear it? Do you not smell it? Just now my world became perfect; midnight, too, is noon; pain, too, is joy; curses, too, are a blessing; night, too, is a sun. – Go away or you will learn: a sage, too, is a fool.

Have you ever said 'Yes' to a single joy? O my

253 CM vol. 10, p. 568: "He did not find himself in *any man* – and so he looked for the *animals*."

friends, then you said Yes to *all* woe. All things are entangled, ensnared, enamored.... Eternal ones, love it eternally and evermore; and to woe, too, say: 'Go – but return! 'For all joy wants eternity."[254]

Liberated from the oppressive burden of this secret and, at the same time, strengthened by it, Nietzsche perceived once more the light of his mission on the very next day. In the brilliance of the rising sun and surrounded by a flurry of birds, he reflected upon recent events. Happy and unencumbered, he awaited the guests, who were already bidding him good morning as doves settled upon his shoulder and, to his surprise, a powerful and shaggy lion lay down at his feet, rubbing its head on his knee. Everything appeared to be building up towards a sign, and indeed, the lion unexpectedly sprang to its feet and, roaring, drove back the approaching 'higher men': Nietzsche could not but interpret this strange behavior as an omen of fate, an unmistakable message that these men were not his true companions. Was he not a victim of his own pity for their plight, and was he not deceived in his expectations? These higher men embodied only one side of his being, his love for man and for the world, but they had no ultimate understanding of his spiritual undertaking. His duty became clear to him:

"My suffering and my pity for suffering – what does it matter? Am I concerned with *happiness*? I am concerned with my *work*. Well, then! The lion came, my children are near, Zarathustra has ripened, my hour has come: this is *my* morning, *my* day is breaking: *rise now, rise, thou great noon*!"[255]

He recognized as the task apportioned to him by fate that he should be the *proclaimer of light*, thus bringing mankind

254  Ges. W. vol. VI, p. 469f; CM vol. 4, p. 402.
255  Ges. W. vol. VI, p. 476; CM vol. 4, p. 408.

166

closer to the *'great noon,'* the consciousness and completion of man's innermost being.

The book ends with the words:

> "Thus spoke Zarathustra, and he left his cave, glowing and strong as a morning sun that comes out of dark mountains."[256]

Zarathustra-Nietzsche will now travel his path alone, accompanied solely by the two animals that symbolize spirit and strength[257] – the eagle and the lion – whilst the serpent that belongs to the dark aspect of life is left behind. The parting from his companions completes the *separation of his conscious personality from the shadow side.* It is not stated where this path to the 'great noon' – constituted by the moment of fundamental decision for the individual either for or against the 'eternal recurrence' – will lead. It could equally mean new life or spiritual death.

It is, therefore, uncertain whether Zarathustra-Nietzsche's high aims can be realized. It is true that he showed men the way to create a new image of God, the image of the overman, just as he opened our eyes to the immortality of worldly existence. But could the aims that formed the basis of this new view of the world, those of "lighting the flame of the future" and leading mankind to a new 'morality' and a new order be achieved without the support of the 'higher men'? Does not his separation from them endanger his work, since these concrete carriers of his ideas and his message represent nothing less than the earthbound bridge to both the outer and the inner Zarathustra-Nietzsche? As a lone man, will he not miss the healing, regulative effect of the 'spirit of gravity,' which would keep him in touch with the chthonic background of the soul, as well as with external reality?

256 *Ibid.*
257 As often before, Nietzsche is half-consciously, half-unconsciously referring to the Holy Scripture, since the two animals mentioned – the lion and the eagle – are also those of the Evangelists John and Mark.

What marks the end of *Zarathustra,* the tragedy of Nietzsche's life, is more than just the danger presented by the fading of his spirit in the "well of eternity"; it is also the way his ego is totally overwhelmed by the demonic devil's grimace. The gloomy prophecy that, "your soul will die more quickly than your body," has yet to come to pass.

In Nietzsche's following works, the author's alienation from life and from the world, the strengthening of his mystical personality and a corresponding blindness with regard to the power of evil do indeed become increasingly apparent, with the result that their 'untimely' character predominates. The inexorability of his search for truth and for God, which made him doubt more and more the presence of any sort of value, would finally lead him to the *brink of nothingness* before which only the *reality of the will to exist* could assert itself.[258] In glorifying himself and his becoming one with the image of the redeemer, he brought about his own end.

The dithyramb, 'Amid Birds of Prey,' quoted in part below and written at the time of *Zarathustra,* bears eloquent witness to his mental distress:

" ... O Zarathustra,
cruellest Nimrod!
Lately God's huntsman,
net to net all virtue,
arrow of the wicked! –
Now –
hunted down by yourself,
your own booty,
burrowed into yourself ...

You sought the heaviest burden
and you found *yourself* –
its is a burden you cannot cast off ...

258  See p. 215.

Now –
contorted
between two nothings,
a question-mark,
a weary riddle –
a riddle for *birds of prey* ...
– they will soon 'resolve' you,
already they thirst for your 'resolution,'
already they flutter about you, their riddle,
about you, hanged man! ...
O Zarathustra! ...
*Self-knower* ! ...
*Self-hangman* ! ... [259]

A letter to Franz Overbeck further evinces the inner plight of Nietzsche after he had finished *Zarathustra* :

" ... I hold up before myself the images of Dante and Spinoza, who were better at accepting the lot of solitude. Of course their way of thinking, compared to mine, was one which made solitude bearable; and in the end, for all those who somehow still had a 'God' for company, what I experience as 'solitude' really did not yet exist. My life now consists in the wish that it might be otherwise with all things than I comprehend, and that somebody might make *my* 'truths' appear incredible to me...." [260]

259  Ges. W. vol. VIII, p. 421ff; CM vol. 6, p. 389ff.
260  Letter to Overbeck of 2 July 1885,

# C. The Period after *Zarathustra*

## *I. Beyond Good and Evil*

After the gloomy anticipation of his fate in *Zarathustra*, Nietzsche was granted three full years before his mental collapse. They were years in which he suffered terribly from being ignored and misunderstood by his contemporaries, increasing his feelings of isolation and alienation until they became virtually unbearable. In a letter to Overbeck, he stated:

> "If only I could give you an idea of how *lonely* I feel! There are as few living beings as there are dead ones to whom I am close. This is indescribably painful; and I can only put it down to experience in, and a lifelong, step-by-step development of, my capacity to endure this feeling that I have not yet been destroyed by it."[1]

The mental confrontation within was all the more active. His imagination was preoccupied with the bold plan to create a "philosophy of the future," something he intended as the crowning glory of his insights, but which never materialized.

First to appear was the work, *Beyond Good and Evil,* conceived over many years and partly written at the same time as *Zarathustra*. Repetition was unavoidable, although the focus of *Beyond Good and Evil* was, in contrast to *Zarathustra,* a philosophical and reflective one. In *Ecce homo,* he later described the central problem of the book as:

1 Letter to Overbeck of 5 August 1886.

" ... the revaluation of our values so far, the great war...."[2]

Guided by an unshakable desire for the truth, his goal was to test the objectivity and tenability of hitherto held values. More courageous than ever before was his radical questioning of the supposedly incontestable tenets of traditional morality. To him, nothing was certain any longer, neither belief in reality nor in the 'old god' and the 'immortal soul.'[3] His questions tended in one direction: *What was truth?* Were there true and false judgments? What was the current state of the assumptions, prevalent since Plato, of a 'pure spirit in itself' and of 'goodness in itself'? The doubts he cast upon morality, his acknowledgement of the reality of evil and finally his justification of the 'will to power' as the general motivation behind actions and as the fundamental key to the world: all these things were radically new and dangerous.

He was, above all, concerned with fighting a moral law based on transcendental concepts, in spite of the advantages that accrued from having faith in the universality of the moral order. Thus he noted:

" ... it [the moral hypothesis] granted man an absolute value. It conceded to the world, in spite of suffering and evil,the character of perfection ... evil appeared full of meaning ... it posited that man had ... an adequate knowledge precisely regarding what is most important ... morality was the great *antidote* against ... *nihilism.*"[4]

Yet all of these high values came to grief, he gathered from examining his own times, as a consequence of the demands imposed by reality. What was really happening was that the mentality of the herd was on the increase as

2 Ges. W. vol. XV, p. 102; CM vol. 6, p. 350.
3 Ges. W. vol. VII/1, p. 19; CM vol. 5/1, p. 23, § 10.
4 Ges. W. vol. XV, p. 145f; CM vol. 12, p. 211.

171

habits became automated, the truth was being concealed and mankind was inclining more and more towards mendacity and self-deception. In short: the old ideals derived from faith in a super-personal meaning had lost their ability to convince. Nietzsche increasingly came to regard all hope in possible meaning as redundant. It was indispensable that a radical reconsideration of the validity of Western morality should take place. Nietzsche's categorical mind, which constantly thought in terms of an 'either-or,' found itself having to deal with a hypothesis directly opposed to historical morality: was it not obvious that *immorality* had won the day, that doubts about the meaning of existence and with it, the tendency towards the *dissolution of values* had become dominant? Was not all in vain?[5] Was the age not slipping into nihilism?

For the time being, he felt it was essential to fight concepts of *the absolute*, whether in terms of *truth* or *morality*, with more energy than ever before. Allied to his criticism of the generality of values was the further and still more important goal of finally breaking apart the *Christian foundations of morality*. For Nietzsche, there was no possible doubt that belief in truth was dependent on faith in the Christian God: undermining the truth inevitably did the same for the Christian faith – a consequence he was very thorough about drawing in his ensuing works. He was well aware of the offence his new thoughts would give, knowing that, with his philosophy, he was taking up a position "beyond good and evil."[6]

Although Nietzsche was falling back on thoughts already developed in *Human All-Too-Human*, the radicalism of his criticism and the boldness of what he was doing were something new. In attacking the universality of basic Western principles of knowledge, he first and foremost aimed to undermine the 'sacrosanct' validity of intellectual categories taught by Kant. He was as vexed by the

5 Ges. W. vol. XV, p. 182; CM vol. 12, p. 213.
6 Ges. W. vol. VII/1, p. 13; CM vol. 5/1, p. 18, § 4.

postulation of objective meaning in the table of categories,[7] of the demonstrable forms of space and time, as he was by that of any timeless, transcendental subject of knowledge based on pure reason. He was equally critical of materialistic atomism[8] and its presupposition of an absolute concept of substance, whilst he also questioned the scientific principle of causality and thereby intuitively anticipated the results of modern atomic research. He seemed to reject the materialistic concept of an "atomism of the soul," which regarded the soul as an "indelible, eternal and indivisible" monad. Schopenhauer's teachings were also put in doubt, despite the fact that Nietzsche held him in high esteem as a thinker and educator. What he objected to was Schopenhauer's hypothesis of the 'directness' of pure knowledge and of the 'thing in itself' on the basis of a constant ego. In Nietzsche's view, both the notions of 'I think' and of 'I wish'[9] rested on the false premise of an *immutable subject of thought:* "A thought comes when 'it' wishes" and not when "I wish"; the very argument that "it thinks in us" was going too far.[10] From the viewpoint of the theory of knowledge, the concept of an 'I' was as unlikely as a binding subject of knowledge. "The subject was only a fiction" to him.[11] All knowledge was merely interpretation, the subject "not anything given," but "something added and invented and projected behind that which exists."[12] In psychological terms, the ego was some kind of reflector or mirror of events in the unconscious and represented neither something that was unified nor that remained identical.

By denying a general, binding subject of knowledge Nietzsche also invalidated a direct and secure *faith in truth.* Was it possible to reach the reality of truth through

7 Ges. W. vol. VII/1, p. 19; CM vol. 5/1, p. 24, § 11.
8 Ges. W. vol. VII/1, p. 22; CM vol. 5/1, p. 26, § 12.
9 In his bequest, Nietzsche complements this thought by stating that there are no direct certainties. He was principally thinking of Descartes' basic idea of *cogito, ergo sum.* Ges. W. vol. XIV, p. 4f; CM vol. 11, p. 640f.
10 Ges. W. vol. VII/1, p. 27; CM vol. 5/1, p. 31, § 17.
11 Ges. W. vol. XV, p. 407; CM vol. 12, p. 398.
12 Ges. W. vol. XVI, p. 12.

thought? The very concept of truth was a questionable one. But his bequest shows how unclear his notion of truth in fact was. At certain times, it meant something which "was direct and certain" and that "did not deceive," at others, something "free of emotions and instincts" – both of which made demands difficult to realize. The problems surrounding a concept of truth forced him to ask the heretical question:

"What in us really wants truth? ... Why not rather untruth? and uncertainty? even ignorance?"[13]

It was a question he never answered.

In his struggle against the tendency to conceive basic ideas of philosophy as universal and absolute concepts, Nietzsche struck at the heart of the prevailing theory of knowledge. His criticism of those who presupposed the immutability of basic principles such as space, time, causality, substance and the ego would not only be confirmed by the results of research in the natural sciences (the relativity of space and time in atomic physics) but also by the psychology of the unconscious.

Nietzsche's criticism of truth and the pursuit of it was, as we have seen in *Human All-Too-Human,* also related to human motivations. What at that time he had intuitively recognized to be true now gained in conviction: whenever the individual believed he was acting truthfully, honestly and decently, he was making the mistake of deceiving himself. His everyday decisions about morality and truth were not, as he supposed, the reflection of a need for objectivity and universality but something completely different, namely desire and passion! Truth did not indicate an object existing 'in itself' as traditional theories of knowledge would have it; instead it derived in principle from man, the knowing subject, and his instinctual drives – a viewpoint representing a total reversal of that hitherto held. As *Zara-*

13  Ges. W. vol. VII/1, p. 9; CM vol. 5/1, p. 15, § 1.

174

*thustra* had already implied, man and the values that living forced upon him now moved into the foreground. In the place of pure reason came the *facts of life* – the desires of the heart, the condition of one's health (so important to Nietzsche), indeed the whole of man's instinctual life – and these formed the basis of knowledge, action and consciousness in general. "Most of the conscious thinking of a philosopher is secretly guided ... by his instincts."[14] By thus reducing thought and consciousness to instinctual situations in a way that was more decisive than ever before, Nietzsche created a new means of looking at things, preparing the ground for an even deeper psychological perspective.

Yet, for the time being, we will content ourselves with the fact that all thought and growing awareness rested on relative and "subjective sensibilities." Just as he saw in thought no more than the "behavior of the instincts," so he regarded consciousness as a passive registration of unconscious impressions, serving as a "means of communication."[15] What follows shows that, in contrast to the philosophical assumption of categories of reason (Kant), Nietzsche stressed the biological usefulness of knowledge.

Nietzsche's departure from the traditional concept of knowledge and truth is unmistakable. He not only denied the objectivity of knowledge and the fact that a statement of truth could be made independent of instinctual desire, but he went even further in undermining contemporary conceptions and even questioned the adequacy of logical criteria of what was 'true' and 'false.' Existential yardsticks replaced logical ones. This meant, above all, that judgments should be tested according to their *suitability for life*. In the same way as so-called 'true judgments' did not always lead to the advancement of life, 'false judgments' could not always be seen as inimical to existence. In direct opposition to the dominant theory of knowledge, 'false judgments' could obviously also be beneficial to the individual insofar

14  Ges. W. vol. VII/1, p. 12; CM vol. 5/1, p. 17, § 3.
15  Ges. W. vol. XVI, p. 37.

as they *served life,* with the same applying to pronounce-
ments built on guile and lies.

> "The falseness of judgment is for us not necessarily
> an objection to a judgment; in this respect our new
> language may sound strangest. The question is to
> what extent it is life-promoting, life-preserving, per-
> haps even species-cultivating."[16]

The substitution of a logical viewpoint with a purely *vital*
one was rather disturbing and represented a decisive,
though lone, step towards the complete *relativization* of
knowledge. It would reach its climax two years later in the
contestable assertion that it was impossible to know anything of what is 'true' or 'false.' It was from this same
spirit of relativity that we read in *Zarathustra:* "Nothing is
true, everything is allowed" – an assumption that *sus-
pended all certainty about our understanding of the world*
and led straight to anarchy. The bequest contains the following statement on the significance of truth:

> "*Truth is the sort of error* without which a certain type
> of living being could not exist. Value for life is what
> finally counts ..."[17]

Whereas in the *Gay Science* Nietzsche had bemoaned the
relativity of knowledge, in *Beyond Good and Evil* that very
subjectivity was the force behind his pioneering discovery
of the *perspectivism of knowledge.*[18] On the basis that all
individual knowledge was conditioned by the instincts, he
was able to draw conclusions about the general subjectivity
and relativity of the intellectual processes. He was moving

16 Ges. W. vol. VII/1, p. 122; CM vol. 5/1, p. 18, § 4.
17 CM vol. 11, p. 506.
18 Nietzsche was not alone in his theory of perspectivism. Sören Kierkegaard had developed a similar viewpoint years before, although he
   preferred as his starting point the concept of individual existence to the
   notion of instinct.

towards a full-scale revaluation of the theory of knowledge: as a result of viewing the truth perspectivistically, the Christian interpretation of existence, resting as it did on transcendental values, underwent a fundamental transformation. What, up to now, had enjoyed the status of objective statement revealed itself to Nietzsche as an *individual interpretation of meaning* derived from the particular condition of the human being's instincts.[19] Disappointing though a perspectivistic approach to contemporary theory of knowledge might have been, it represented a remarkable discovery in terms of psychological understanding. In effect, it laid open the fact that the process of knowledge principally rested on *individual projections.*

Nietzsche himself felt deeply ambivalent about discovering the perspectivistic approach to meaning, for, on the one hand, he regretted losing the remaining objectivity and knowledge, whilst on the other, he welcomed the new opportunities that a *more realistic* mode of understanding presented.

In *The Dawn,* Nietzsche had written:

> "Never to be able to see into things out of any other eyes but *these?* ... And that perhaps means: the impossibility of knowledge! Misery and disgust!"[20]

His note of the same period sounds more positive:

> "Task: *to see things as they are!* Means: to be able to look at them through a hundred eyes, through *many* persons!"[21]

There were just as few moral phenomena as there were true ones:

19  "Ultimately, man finds in things nothing but what he himself has imported into them." Ges. W. vol. XVI, p. 97.
20  Ges. W. vol. IV, p. 322; CM vol. §/1, p. 287, § 483.
21  Ges. W. vol. XII, p. 13; CM vol. 9, p. 466.

"... [even] good and evil ... [were] only interpretations and not factual, nothing in themselves ... "[22]

"There are no moral phenomena, there is only a moral interpretation of these phenomena...."[23]

The closer Nietzsche came to the insight that there was *no meaning in itself* – let alone an objective world order –, the more vigorously he denied the existence of objective truth and thus the more committed he was to an interpretation of events based on the perspective of the individual: *the more eyes that saw, the more complete the view.*

In a way similar to the physiologically based judgments of *The Dawn,* Nietzsche made it even more clear in *Beyond Good and Evil* that it was the *body* that was fundamental to all valuation and interpretation, since it represented the basis of the instinctual processes. His opinion was unmistakable – namely that:

"...our thought and evaluations ... [were] only the expression of desires that lay behind them."[24]

Accordingly, it was the bodily needs of the individual that interpreted the world.[25]

He was even more obvious in his diary:

"The exegesis itself is a *symptom* of certain physiological conditions, likewise of a particular spiritual level of prevalent judgments: *Who interprets? –* Our affects."[26]

In the final analysis all judgments could be attributed to

22 CM vol. 12, p. 131.
23 Ges. W. vol. VII, p. 100; CM vol. 5, p. 92, § 108, Ges. W. vol. XV, p. 335; CM vol. 12, p. 149.
24 Ges. W. vol. XIII, p. 66; CM vol. 12, p. 17.
25 CM vol. 12, p. 315.
26 Ges. W. vol. XV, p. 333f; CM vol. 12, p. 161.

the organs, to the muscles! – an observation that must be taken with a pinch of salt, but which, nevertheless, expresses Nietzsche's preference for exaggerations.

Nietzsche regarded it as more problematical than it at first appears to trace the individual's act of giving meaning back to the impulses of the instincts. The immediate question was, 'who or what interprets?' Who was the subject of the exegesis? In view of his denial that any stabilizing influence of a central ego existed, such an ego could hardly assume this function. If this fact alone called into question the reliability of the interpretation of meaning, then the effect was redoubled by the constant fluctuation of the emotional and instinctual impulses. Did not everything end up in a bottomless chaos? Nietzsche saved himself from this worrying situation by unexpectedly discovering a regulative authority deep down at the very bottom of the human soul. Insofar as this stood as an immutable feeling that "this is what I am," it could be said to form the center that Nietzsche was seeking.[27] He assigned to it the role of a signpost that would lead the individual to his own personal identity.

> "But at the bottom of us, really deep down, there is, of course, something unteachable, some granite of spiritual *fatum,* of predetermined decision and answer to predetermined selected questions. Whenever a cardinal problem is at stake there speaks an unchangeable 'this is I'... At times we find certain solutions of problems that inspire strong faith in *us;* some call them henceforth their 'convictions.' Later – we see them only as steps to self-knowledge, signposts to the problem we *are....*"[28]

This unteachable element had nothing to do with the conscious ego of logic; it was rather 'something' provided by the emotions to draw attention to the self that resided in

27 Ges. W. vol. VII, p. 191; CM vol. 5, p. 170, § 231.
28 *Ibid.*

the body.[29] In spite of the irrational character of the feeling of selfhood, the psychological significance of the fateful factor that existed 'deep down' should not be underestimated. It kept the human being from total destruction and from being swallowed up by the void. Its effectiveness may well have been the reason for Nietzsche retaining the *continuity of his thought* and his intellectual consistency to the very last days of his mental awareness, in spite of a disappearing concept of truth, a relativization of knowledge and a nihilistic tendency of his own world-view. The deeply rooted feeling that 'I am,' that 'I myself' existed, was the springboard from which Nietzsche launched his affirmation of life, holding in check the inclination of his being towards self-disintegration.

Yet such *stable self-awareness* could not disguise the fact that his personality was still in the process of falling apart. By replacing his person with a variety of roles and masks, as he did in *Zarathustra,* Nietzsche presented the separate aspects of the human personality in the form of eight shadow figures. He loved to let a mask speak instead of himself, whether it was the mask of the philosopher – as in *Beyond Good and Evil* – or that of the 'Immoralist,' or even that of the 'Antichrist.'

Returning to the theme of perspectivism, Nietzsche's discovery that all knowledge and valuation was perspectivistic in nature proved particularly fruitful for the interpretation of unconscious processes. Inasmuch as the methods of interpretation had hitherto assumed the primacy of the conscious ego and had thus hardly come close to an understanding of dreams, fantasies or creativity – let alone of neurotic phenomena, such as complexes, obsessions, etc. – the focus of attention now shifted to the unconscious. I am thinking in particular of the methods of depth psychology that were being developed by Freud even before Nietzsche's breakdown as a means of understanding neurotic symptoms. It became clear that the curing of neurosis required a careful penetration of the meaning of the symp-

29  See p. 96.

180

toms, something only possible through a method that relied on *insight into the unconscious mind.* Methods of interpretation that attempted to grasp the relationship between symptoms and unconscious reminiscences, complexes and archetypal figures, in other words, those methods that looked for the *projection-mechanisms* behind the symptoms, now became indispensable.[30] It must also be mentioned, in conclusion, that the perspectivistic approach, as practised by C.G. Jung, demanded a consideration of unconscious modes of attitude (extraversion and introversion) as well as of the habitual functional modes (feeling, thinking, intuition, sense), so that interpretations would avoid leading nowhere.[31]

Looking back to Nietzsche's rejection of an objective knowledge of truth,[32] we must not ignore how depressing and agonizing it must have been for him to come to this conclusion. It represented the crushing result of an inner necessity and the final link in the chain of ideas concerning the death of God, the failure of metaphysics and the vanity of all postulations of universal and absolute truths. Despite the philosophical and religious tradition he grew up in, Nietzsche felt an inner compulsion to increasingly question the concept of truth that had originated in antiquity and since then had virtually come to signify a divine absolute. At the time of *Beyond Good and Evil,* he recorded a confession of the classical origin of his spirit and its transformation from a metaphysical mode of thought to one that was godless and nihilistic:

> "But you will have gathered what I am driving at, namely, that it is still a *metaphysical faith* upon which

30 Sigmund Freud, Ges. W. vol. I (S.E. vol. I), and C.G. Jung, Ges. W. vol. IV (C.W. vol. IV).
31 C.G. Jung, Ges. W. vol. VI (C.W. vol. VI).
32 After finishing *Zarathustra,* he noted down: "There are many kinds of eyes. Even the sphinx has eyes – and consequently there are many kinds of 'truths,' and consequently there is no truth." Ges. W. vol. XVI, p. 47; CM vol. 11, p. 498.

our faith in science rests – that even we seekers after knowledge today, we godless anti-metaphysicians, still take *our* fire, too, from the flame lit by a faith that is thousands of years old, that Christian faith which was also the faith of Plato, that God is the truth, that truth is divine. But what if this should become more and more incredible, if nothing should prove to be divine anymore unless it were error, blindness, the lie – if God Himself should prove to be our most enduring lie?"[33]

Nietzsche did not know moderation. His path finally led him from the extreme of metaphysical belief to the opposite extreme of nihilism and the rejection of all values.

Just as destructive as his denial of the classical concept of truth was Nietzsche's *abolition of the occidental concept of morality*. We have already seen how he confronted traditional morality, which could be reduced to an essence of laws and rules following the pattern of the statement 'thou shalt,' with a moral outlook based on subjective criteria. Whilst the former aimed at suppressing the passions and was, above all, intended as a strengthening of the spirit of the herd, Nietzsche constructed the foundations necessary for the realization of his own goal on an "enhancement of the type 'man' " and on the reinforced sense of responsibility to oneself that went with it. What he had in mind was:

"... the enhancement of the type 'man,' the continual 'self-overcoming of man' to use a moral formula in a supra-moral sense,"[34]

– in effect, a meaning that lay *beyond good and evil*.

The development of the concept of morality was a step-by-step procedure initiated by his criticism of moral preju-

33 Ges. W. vol. V, p. 275; CM vol. 3/3, p. 577, § 344. The fifth book of the *Gay Science* was written and published some five years after the previous four, but was later issued together with them.
34 Ges. W. vol. VII/1, p. 235; CM vol. 5/1, p. 205, § 257.

dices and his positive evaluation of attitudes that stressed the instincts. In thus referring morality back to irrational mental factors, he had already been emphasizing the significance of remaining loyal to one's conscience of oneself. The comments below originated in this period:

> "They will call you the destroyers of morality: but you are the discoverers of yourselves."[35]

And:

> "We must free ourselves from morality in order *to be able to live morally.*"[36]

The expression, 'morality,' is here used in two ways: on the one hand, to indicate conventional rules based on laws and regulations, and on the other, to allude to a subjective responsibility to oneself. The latter attitude, described as the "new morality,"[37] concerned Nietzsche's view of the "embodiment of evaluations" and derived from the individual experience of man and the conditions of his personal existence. In accordance with the importance he placed on the body, it included feelings, emotions and the human being's physiological states. Thus we read in the bequest:

> "The spiritual is to be understood as the sign-language of the body."[38]

This new outlook required man to learn a new moral viewpoint no less responsible than the one hitherto held. Its prerequisite was that the messages transmitted by the body should be *listened to* and taken seriously.

Nietzsche had already established truth as dependent on organic functions; now morality acquired meaning from *the*

35 Ges. W. vol. XII, p. 266; CM vol. 10, p. 212.
36 Ges. W. vol. XIII, p. 124; CM vol. 10, p. 17.
37 See p. 123f.
38 Ges. W. vol. XIII, p. 165; CM vol. 10, p. 285.

*organic perspective.* This view of things also received its specific, supreme character through the inclusion of the *creative dimension* of life. Only by freeing morality from the primacy of the intellect and by placing it within the context of the *Dionysian whole* was Nietzsche able to achieve a thoroughgoing revaluation of morality. From here, he gained totally new criteria, which included, above all, a re-estimation of the traditional concepts of evil and power. Although Nietzsche had already pointed to the transformation of the moral view in *Zarathustra,* relating it to the creative process of propagation and annihilation,[39] it was only in *Beyond Good and Evil* that he had tried then to demonstrate that everything tradition regarded as 'good' meant nothing but the *stagnation* of the process of development and of living; whilst higher values resided in the as yet unformed and forward-looking things collectively judged to be 'evil.' As we have tried to show, this reversal of valuations led to the paradoxical assertion that the *best strength of man lay in what the collective saw as 'evil.'* [40]

Nietzsche was well aware that this new and eminently misunderstandable appreciation of evil demanded strong individuals who could stand up to the prevailing conceptions of morality. He emphasized more strongly than ever the advancement of a 'higher type of man' who was conscious of his task and who not only versed himself in continual overcoming of the self,[41] but was also cognizant of his power, rank and position.[42] The knowledge that the fundamental striving of the individual rested on the acquisition of power and that the *leitmotif* of all living things was the 'will to power' had already been alluded to in *Zarathustra,*[43] and this prepared the ground for further more or less questionable interpretations. It was principally the importance assigned to the strong will that was able to

39 See p. 120.
40 See p. 122f.
41 See p. 120.
42 Ges. W. vol. VII/1, p. 235; CM vol. 5/1, p. 206.
43 See p. 121.

command and to control mankind, which contained the germ of evil. Nietzsche's own reduction of all purpose and meaning[44] to the 'will to power' was a dangerous generalization of the power-hypothesis. According to him, the essential motive behind all thought and action – including creativity and self-development – was the *expansion of power,* the 'accumulation of strength.' It was this that determined both economic and political interests and the need for respect and esteem.

By underlining the tendency to exert ever greater power and strength and extend one's effective radius, Nietzsche touched on a very recalcitrant problem. Since power indisputably included hardness, violence, the desire to dominate and tyranny – all affects that the collective regards as evil, – any intensification of the 'will to power' could develop in a dangerous way, threatening the life of the community. Although Nietzsche knew about this danger, he still saw the fullest extension of the 'will to power' as desirable. Indeed, his opinion viewed the enhancement of the very tendencies and affects evaluated as 'evil':

"... the affects of hatred, envy, covetousness ... [all] conditions of life – as factors which, fundamentally and essentially, must be present in the general economy of life and must, therefore, be further enhanced if life is to be further enhanced."[45]

It was primarily this uncanny *amalgamation of the will live with the reality of evil* that left Nietzsche's psychology open to condemnation as destructive. Thus we read:

"We think that hardness, forcefulness, slavery, danger in the alley and the heart ... the art of experiment and devilry of every kind, that everything evil, terrible, tyrannical in man, everything in him that is kin to

44  Ges. W. vol. XVI, p. 92; CM vol. 12, p. 97.
45  Ges. W. vol. VII/1, p. 36; CM vol. 5/1, p. 38f, § 23.

beasts of prey and serpents, serves the enhancement of the species 'man' as much as its opposite does."[46]

These and similar statements were responsible for the uneasiness with which Nietzsche's name was, and continued to be, met. He spoke out clearly for the fact that the power drives considered 'evil' by the collective were indispensable to the enhancement and development of the "species 'man'."

Nietzsche was understandably aware of the embarrassment caused by the shadow side of his assertions, which he described as the expression of a 'refined immorality,'[47] but he undoubtedly lacked insight into the emotional consequences he was thereby engendering. The following lines appear as malicious, unfeeling and irresponsible, the more so since they come from the pen of a philosopher who was extremely careful in the conduct of his own life, who emphasized self-conquest and who was very concerned to maintain a mask:

> "– we sail right *over* morality, we crush, we destroy perhaps the remains of our own morality ... – what matter are *we*!"[48]

Nietzsche fell totally prey to the suggestive force of evil, in spite of his awareness that the values the collective condemned as 'evil' should not be underestimated. Seen from a psychological angle, the fascination of evil relied on the fact that the very evil which excited collective rejection was capable of showing the individual back to the possibilities he had blocked out until then.[49] By this, I mean hitherto repressed, suppressed, forbidden and pathological contents whose integration into the human consciousness can bring about an expansion of the personality. Life is often so ster-

46 Ges. W. vol. VII/1, p. 65; CM vol. 5/1, p. 61f, § 44.
47 Ges. W. vol. VII/1, p. 36; CM vol. 5/1, p. 38, § 23.
48 *Ibid.*
49 L. Frey-Rohn, *Das Böse,* p. 194.

186

ile and empty that evil, springing from deep within the unconscious, becomes the only means of rejuvenating and renewing the pattern of existence. In this respect, the most beneficial elements are the impulses springing from the as yet unformed, archetypal layers of the soul. My example is the extraordinary stimulus the natural sciences received from the access they gained in the 17th century to knowledge which, until then, had been forbidden, such as the rotation of the earth around the sun. I would also remind the reader of the improbable development of economics once mercantile thought had been allowed to come into its own and the limitations imposed on the spirit of liberalism had been relaxed after the French Revolution. What we regard as a release of creative inclinations in the individual within the context of the process of self-realization (the process of individuation) is, in the larger framework of culture and humanity, the equivalent of those stimuli that cause the renewal of historical epochs.

Nietzsche's interest was strongest in the question of advancing the creative processes of life, but his way was barred by a fanatical overestimation of power and strength. He fell more and more under the spell of an unreal glorification of resilience, cruelty and exploitation, increasingly affording his works the air of destructiveness. In *Beyond Good and Evil* he writes:

"... life itself is essentially appropriation, injury, overpowering of what is alien and weaker ... incorporation and at least, at its mildest, exploitation...."[50]

And:

"'Exploitation' does not belong to a corrupt or imperfect and primitive society: it belongs to the *essence* of what lives, as a basic organic function; it is a consequence of the will to power, which is, after all, the

50 Ges. W. vol. VII/1, p. 237f; CM vol. 5/1, p. 207, § 259.

will of life. If this should be an innovation as a theory – as a reality it is the *primordial fact* of all history...."[51]

It is doubtful whether Nietzsche was ever fully conscious of the explosive character of his idea that 'will to power' was the deeper meaning behind all life, values and actions. His call for humanity "to become the embodiment of the will to power" – not out of "morality or immorality," but for the preservation of life and the extension of power – was equally unrelated to reality. His constant goal in all this was to produce strong men on whom he could build his *philosophy of the future,* in other words, that of the *overman.*

Blinded by the myth of strength and power and seduced by the ever present Dionysus-archetype, Nietzsche's conception of greatness could find no satisfaction in the assumption held up to then that various power interests were competing with each other. He was taken with the idea that a unified conception of the world would lead to a greater understanding of its essential nature. Setting aside his continual rejection of a metaphysical justification of his philosophy, it was an inner force that determined his presupposition that only *one* basic form of the will existed and that all functions, desires and passions were derived from that single will to power. He even went so far as to conceive of the mechanical prerequisite for life in terms of an elaboration of the will. Accordingly, we read in *Beyond Good and Evil* :

"... to determine *all* efficient force univocally as – *will to power*. The world viewed from inside, the world defined and determined according to its 'intelligible character' – it would be 'will to power' and nothing else."[52]

51  Ges. W. vol. VII/1, p. 238; CM vol. 5/1, p. 208.
52  Ges. W. vol. VII/1, p. 58; CM vol. 5/1, p. 55, § 36.

The oft-quoted 'original' of this passage in the bequest is as follows:

"And do you know what 'the world' is to me? ... This world: a monster of energy, without beginning, without end; a firm, iron magnitude of force ... a sea of forces flowing and rushing together, eternally changing, eternally flooding back, with tremendous years of recurrence ... blessing itself as that which must return eternally, as a becoming that knows no satiety, no disgust, no weariness: this my *Dionysian* world of the eternally self-destroying ... my 'beyond good and evil without goal, unless the joy of the circle is itself a goal ... *This world is the world of power –* and nothing *besides* ! And you yourselves are also this will to power – and nothing besides."[53]

We greet this grandiose and imposing conception of the world with uneasy astonishment. Can mankind bear this insight? Here, the world is presented as an all-embracing monstrosity, a vast, expanding force. Just as power induced the individual to increase his strength and the will to power was the underlying characteristic of all becoming, so Nietzsche saw in the world as a whole nothing but the 'will to power' – the will to intensify strength. He was careful to stress that this view was essentially determined by the inner perspective of the individual human being. What the world outside the individual looked like remained uncertain.[54]

The essence of this cosmic will to power was underlined by Nietzsche designating it 'Dionysian' and thereby returning to his former enchantment at the hands of the god Dio-

---

53 Ges. W. vol. XVI, p. 401f; CM vol. 11, p. 610.
54 I will ignore the fact that elsewhere the world is depicted as a mechanical game of forces, which, among other things, was intended to corroborate the concept of the 'eternal recurrence,' and leave it to the philosophers to explain this contradiction. See Karl Loewith and Karl Jaspers!

nysus in *The Birth of Tragedy*. In the intervening period, however, the face of this god had undergone considerable changes: the tragic figure suffering at the facts of existence had become one who affirmed life and fate. As the principle of self-creation and self-destruction, he signified both creating anew and destroying, both order and chaos.

Great though Nietzsche's apotheosis of the will to power was, the same slide into metaphysics befell him that he had condemned in Christianity. He was urged to go beyond empirical reality in search of a principle that permitted him to see the world as a whole. By extending its significance to that of the quintessence of being, Nietzsche lost its specific meaning and fell into generalizations.

Nietzsche's tendency to make a *cosmic world principle* of the 'will to power' is the main difference between between his and Alfred Adler's psychological conception of power. In the craving for power, the latter identified compensation for an inferiority complex. Its positive goal was the integration of this need for esteem within the human community by therapeutic means. Nietzsche, on the other hand, viewed the 'will to power' as a force that lay behind all events. Within the human being, it aimed at making an overman of him; within the context of the world as a whole, it succeeded in portraying nothing less than an anonymous, mystical being (monster!) responsible for the fate of mankind.

Nietzsche's exaltation of the will to power not only expresses his search for a principle justifying the world, but also his search for a *position diametrically opposed to Christianity*. By alluding to the Dionysian element in power, he therefore believed he would be able to replace morality with *an attitude towards good and evil that went beyond established values*. He was convinced that "morality was a white lie," the much-praised spirit a deception, and God himself "the longest lie"; Christian morality even had on its conscience the fact that it had awakened Satanic powers. As far as he was concerned, God's existence had been abolished, but what about that of his opponent, the

190

devil? In the following aphorism, Nietzsche articulates the thought:

> "What? Doesn't this mean, to speak with the vulgar: God is refuted, but the devil is not?"[55]

He was obviously aware of how terrible such an idea was, which cleared the way for the absolute rule of the devil. Thus it became crucial for him to establish the extent to which the instincts, inevitably longing for release, could be sublimated. Could they, in any way, be rendered beneficial? His optimistic assertion is a surprising one:

> "My yardstick is how far a man, a people, can let loose the most terrible instincts and use them to its advantage without being ruined by them: or rather to increase the fertility of its deeds and works."[56]

Yet, if here he had in mind a sanctification or even a deification the devil, then he was undermining all his own efforts.

> "Goal: the sanctification of the most powerful, most fertile and most excellently infamous forces, to use the old image: the deification of the devil."[57]

Did Nietzsche believe that he could substantiate a morality beyond good and evil with such a flippant dismissal of Christian theology? The concept of a sanctified devil was much more likely to deliver the individual directly into the hands of evil. Who could guarantee that an individual free of all constraint would stay within his domestic limits?

Whatever the case may be, the fact remains that Nietzsche's glorification of power and the devil had a fatal effect on his life. His attitude inexorably conjured up the dark

55 Ges. W. vol. VII/1, p. 58; CM vol. 5/1, p. 56, § 37.
56 CM vol. 12, p. 11.
57 *Ibid.*

internal and external powers that, in the end, would turn against him. The high-flown identification of his person with the godless one concluded with Nietzsche totally idolizing himself, clearing the way for his own destruction.

Nevertheless, it is surprising that Nietzsche should at the same time have confessed to a "fear which never let him rest," the fear that everything which Europe designated "humanity, humaneness, pity and justice"[58] could lower standards to meet the mediocrity of the herd. Borne along by this anxiety, he predicted the necessary appearance of a *new type of man,*[59] an *aristocratic man* still able to recognize the value of the 'pathos of distance.' This new type, in contrast to 'moral man,' embodied the 'noble man' who, conscious of the differences in rank between men, stood up for the morality of the rulers, in other words, for a morality founded on esteem for the strong and powerful. In him, Nietzsche saw the prototype of man living beyond good and evil.

His bitter struggle for a new morality that included the characteristics of evil rejected by the collective was therefore followed by his wrestling with the problem of the hierarchy amongst men. His aristocratic soul found nothing more repulsive than bringing all men down to the same level through equal rights, to the level of the "happily grazing herd," by which he meant a brotherly love embracing all mankind. He confronted the general ideal of well-being with what we think of as a dangerous demand for a hierarchy of power and creativity, pitting man against man.[60] *Rank was decided on the basis of the quantity of power possessed* : an attitude that could only be squared with his aristocratic outlook with immense difficulty. In the bequest, he wrote:

58  CM vol. 12, p. 72.
59  CM vol. 12, p. 73.
60  CM vol. 13, p. 20.

"Is rank decided by the power quantum that is you? The rest is cowardice."[61]

His notes contain the same:

"By what is *value* objectively measured? By the quantum of *increased and organized power* alone, by the will for more in all that happens...."[62]

Such a celebration of power was not only suspect for giving too much attention to the strong individual, but also for its corresponding disregard of the weak and most ugly of men. Nietzsche's imagination was first and foremost captured by the "great man's" ability to "engage in his service" those good and evil drives he himself shared in. It afforded the highest rank to those capable of determining values.

"Order of rank: He who *determines* values and directs the will of millennia by giving direction to the highest natures is the *highest* man."[63]

His goal was a morality to lead *"man to the heights"* and create a ruling caste. Nietzsche expected such *"lords of the earth" ultimately to "replace God"* [64] – a presumptuous demand that betrays the ambivalence of his valuations. This inner imbalance is also revealed in the contrast he drew between the man of power and violence on the one side, and the guiding man of wisdom on the other. In *Beyond Good and Evil,* he sought to elaborate the *figure of the philosopher* who would combine both strength and spirituality as one, whom Nietzsche increasingly envisaged in

61 *Ibid.*
62 CM vol. 13, p. 40. There is a similar remark in CM vol. 11, p. 289: "The highest man would possess the greatest variety of instincts and in the greatest strength bearable in relative terms."
63 Ges. W. vol. XVI, p. 359; CM vol. 11, p. 106.
64 Ges. W. vol. XII, p. 418; CM vol. 11, p. 620.

terms of his Dionysian model.

As far as Nietzsche was concerned, the philosopher had nothing to do with the academic scholar, who saw himself as the representative of intellectual objectivity and who ironed out all problems, yet who lacked the essential characteristic of manliness. By way of complete contrast, Nietzsche assigned him the role that extended from the "lord of the earth to the overman." His most important feature was his capacity for creating and implementing new values. Afraid of modern man's becoming emasculated, and worried by increasing democratization and the cult of the small state, Nietzsche invested all his hopes in him. He expected in return a broad sense of responsibility and conscience for the development of the whole, as well as the ability to take on the role of a leader of men. These philosophers thus had the task of initiating the revaluation of values, creating a new type of man and pushing the future in a new direction. The comment below is a concise summary of Nietzsche's ideal:

> "Their 'knowing' is *creating,* their creating is a legislation, their will to truth is – *will to power.*"[65]

Even if Nietzsche did not associate his *ideal of the philosophical leader* with boundless despotism but with men of the future capable of carrying the greatest of responsibilities,[66] his thoughts nevertheless concealed extraordinary dangers. How easily this hierarchical idea lent itself to abuse by tyrannies and dictatorships seeking to make mere slaves of others is a lesson taught us by the 20th century.[67]

65 Ges. W. vol. VII/1, p. 162; CM vol. 5/1, p. 145, § 211.
66 CM vol. 12, p. 24.
67 I would not like to give the appearance here of making Nietzsche's writings responsible for what happened under *National Socialism.* Virtually nothing is known about any direct influences. Still, his prophetic mind was sensitive to the *archetypal constellations in the unconscious* present in the spirit of his age, which also determined what later rulers would do. See p. 89ff.

He was, however, aware that his picture of a future given over to a commanding and legislating ruler was so alien to the present historical reality and had been discredited to such an extent that it was highly doubtful whether it could ever be realized. The consequence of the events he designated the "triumphal procession of the herd," in other words, the tendency to postulate equal rights for all, made the very idea of a ruler so unpopular in the modern Europe he knew that the great man, the philosopher (himself included) was compelled to *wear a mask.* Although he had always been characterized by a noble reticence, this, his first mention of the mask as a guarantee of distance, still takes us by surprise. Increasing isolation, the suffering at being misunderstood, together with a loosening grip on reality – all these factors may well have been the cause of his increased caution, in addition to the gradual emergence in him of a mystical Dionysian streak that was already cutting him off from the world.

Unlike the situation in the times of Plato, when Socratic irony embodied the ideal of greatness, Nietzsche regarded the *mask of nobility* as the appropriate reflection of the great man in his own age, to which both the pathos of distance and the instinct for reverence belonged. Nietzsche was writing of himself when he stressed:

> "... He shall be greatest who can be loneliest, the most concealed, the most different, the human being beyond good and evil, the master of his virtues, he that is overrich in will. Precisely this shall be called *greatness:* being capable of being as manifold as whole, as ample as full."[68]

He was still referring to himself when he praised the subtle sense the noble-minded had for "self-limitation and justice." His allusions to the "spiritual haughtiness" of every man "who has suffered profoundly" bear witness to his own experiences.

68 Ges. W. vol. VII/1, p. 164; CM vol. 5/1, p. 147, § 212.

"The spiritual haughtiness and nausea of every man who has suffered profoundly – it almost determines the order of rank *how* profoundly human beings can suffer – his shuddering certainty, which permeates and colors him through and through, that by virtue of his suffering he *knows more* than the cleverest and wisest could possibly know, and that he knows his way and has once been 'at home' in many distant, terrifying worlds of which '*you* know nothing' – this spiritual and silent haughtiness of the sufferer, this pride of the elect of knowledge, of the 'initiated,' of the almost sacrificed, finds all kinds of disguises necessary to protect itself against contact with obtrusive and pitying hands and altogether against everything that is not its equal in suffering. Profound suffering renders noble; it separates."[69]

Such passages show that Nietzsche was not just a one-sided herald of power and strength; he also had another side, that of deep suffering resulting not only from the lonely seclusion of the spiritual human being, but also from pride at having been chosen. It is impressive that he should have recognized *in suffering the irrefutable pre-condition for man to mature and deepen his identity,* he, who since earliest childhood, had been dogged by physical and mental pain.

"… and whatever has been granted to it of profundity, secret, mask, spirit, cunning, greatness – was it not granted to it through suffering, through the discipline of great suffering?"[70]

Nietzsche's attempt to see the positive side of this suffering is moving: despite being "dirt, nonsense, chaos," man also possesses the power and strength of the sculptor who "knows how to form something from the clay." What

69  Ges. W. vol. VII/1, p. 258; CM vol. 5/1, p. 225, § 270.
70  Ges. W. vol. VII/1, p. 181; CM vol. 5/1, p. 161, § 225.

he had already come to realize as the wisdom of life in *Zarathustra* – to be the 'anvil' as well as the 'hammer' – he now restated with the words:

"In man, *creature* and *creator* are united."[71]

He was painfully conscious of the fact that he was both the *'sacrificial animal' and the 'sacrificer'* – a secret that forced him into "keeping silent and concealing" his innermost nature.[72] As the creator, he was cruel to himself; as the creature, he suffered the torment of metamorphosis. Such passages belong to the most unnerving of Nietzsche's confessions and are a much better indication of innermost being than his philosophical debate. One of his greatest achievements was this acknowledgement that creativity is inseparable from suffering.

His repeated dialogues with his 'soul,' however, also reveal the fear his 'new mode of thought' might arouse in the world and among his friends. In addition, therefore, he recognized the immense value his mask had in protecting and preserving himself. He was not only afraid of articulating the 'truths' he had sensed all too early, but equally of becoming fully aware of what he knew. In the bequest, he wrote:

"... we have a knowledge we fear, we do not wish to be alone with.... We do want to take nothing more to heart, we want to pray to the *mask*."[73]

"Whatever is profound loves masks; what is most profound even hates image and parable.... There are occurrences of such a delicate nature that one does well to cover them up with some rudeness to conceal them; ... Such a concealed man who instinctively

71 *Ibid.*
72 See also Lou von Salomé and Ernst Bertram, both of whom have made impressive studies of the sacrificial animal.
73 CM vol. 12, p. 80.

needs speech for silence ... wants and sees to it that a mask of him roams in his place through the hearts and heads of his friends.... Every profound spirit needs a mask: even more, around every profound spirit a mask is growing continually...."[74]

Nietzsche repeatedly emphasized respect for the masks of others; it was a mask that encouraged his reverence for pupils:

"An educator never says what he himself thinks, but always only what he thinks of a thing in relation to the requirements of those he educates.... Such an educator is beyond good and evil; but no one must know it."[75]

Since Nietzsche's acute sense of shame was closely allied to his reluctance to betray secrets, he concealed a good deal of what troubled him.

"Whoever has a lot to proclaim keeps much of it locked up inside: He who is called upon to light the fuse must long remain – a cloud."[76]

But he also saw the mask as "the hardest test of independence,"[77] helping us "not to remain stuck to a person," nor "to remain stuck to our own virtues." C.G. Jung's concept of the persona touches on a similar case. By this, he meant a protective shell affording security against the world around. On the one hand, it projected outwards the way an individual wanted to appear; on the other, it hid his inner being from the prying eyes of the world. He wrote on this:

74  Ges. W. vol. VII/1, p. 60; CM vol. 5/1, p. 57, § 40.
75  Ges. W. vol. XVI, p. 352; CM vol. 11, p. 580.
76  Ernst Bertram, *Nietzsche*, p. 364.
77  Ges. W. vol. VII/1, p. 62; CM vol. 5/1, p. 59, § 41.

"Through the persona a man tries to appear as this or that, or he hides behind a mask, or he may even build up a definite persona as a barricade...."[78]

Nietzsche was tormented by having no friends with whom he could hold a lively conversation. Fear of the world, fear of his own knowledge and of being alone with his thoughts may well have contributed to the stress he laid on the mask, at the same time awakening the mystical side in him. Whatever the case may be, towards the end of *Beyond Good and Evil,* he fiercely advocated the beneficial effect of mystical experience, something that would again become apparent in the most aggressive of his works, the *Twilight of the Idols.* The primordial archetypal image of the philosopher – of himself – that he held up was that of Dionysus, "that great ambiguous one and tempter god."[79] As in the *Birth of Tragedy,* he praised the transformational power of this god, who, thanks to the experience of the most profound opposites, could guide men from the dark depths of existence to the light.[80] Dionysus was to Nietzsche both the "most terrible, ambiguous and mendacious one,"[81] and the "genius of the heart" who "knows how to descend into the netherworld of every soul" and who "is a divining rod for every grain of gold"; and who also knows how to make man "stronger, more evil and more profound; more beautiful."[82]

The 'Aftersong' to *Beyond Good and Evil,* which portrays a never-dying, constantly disappointed longing for a friend, ends with the mystical experience of the 'great noon.' In this 'Feast of feasts,' Nietzsche experiences the completeness engendered by a meeting with his friend

78  C.G. Jung, Ges. W. vol. VII, p. 192 (C.W. vol. VII, p. 172f).
79  Ges. W. vol. VII/1, p. 272; CM vol. 5/1, p.238, § 295.
80  For Nietzsche, Dionysus was another name for Zarathustra, to whom he was grateful for – as he himself underlined – initiating him into the mystery of evil, the philosophical expression of which *Beyond Good and Evil* was.
81  Ges. W. vol. XVI, p. 362; CM vol. 12, p. 354f.
82  Ges. W. vol. VII/1, p. 273; CM vol. 5/1, p. 239, § 295.

Zarathustra: "The wedding of dark and light"! – the coincidence of opposites beyond good and evil. The text is memorable:

> "Youth's longing misconceived inconstancy.
> Those whom I deemed
> Changed to my skin, the friends of whom
> I dreamed
> have aged and lost our old affinity:
> One has to change to stay akin to me.
> ...
> The song is over – longing's dulcet cry
> Died in my mouth:
> A wizard did it, friend in time of drought,
> The friend of noon – no, do not ask me who –
> At noon it was that we turned into two –
> Sure of our victory, we celebrate
> The Feast of feasts:
> Friend Zarathustra came, the Guest of guests!
> The world now laughs, rent are the drapes of fright,
> The wedding is at hand of dark and light.[83]

This vision of the 'inner companion' may seem overwhelming, but it was dangerous at the same time to be a "disciple and initiate" of this god, whether he be Zarathustra or Dionysus.[84] This experience inevitably led to disintegration. Through his studies of Greek philosophy Nietzsche knew only too well that Dionysus was a god of disruption and madness as well as of blissfulness. Those swept along by the Dionysian archetype could not help but have to face all that both the light and satanic darkness entailed.[85] This was why, in *Zarathustra*, Nietzsche had al-

---

83 Ges. W. vol. VII/1, p. 279; CM vol. 5/1, p. 243 ('From High Mountains').
84 Ges. W. vol. VII/1, p. 272; CM vol. 5/1, p. 238, § 295.
85 Ges. W. vol. XVI, p. 386; CM vol. 13, p. 224. The word 'Dionysian' expresses: "... an urge to unity, a reaching out beyond a personality, the

...

ready surrendered with reckless contempt to the flame of the demon consuming him within and, in a burst of infernal laughter, had set the rose-wreath crown upon his head. No less challenging was his current panegyric to golden laughter, which, in *Beyond Good and Evil,* he praised not only as the Olympian vice itself, but also as the highest rank a philosopher could attain.[86]

Predictably, he became even more courageous and *more obstinate in his attempt to come to terms with destiny.* The abyss represented by the Dionysian will to create, the tension between light and dark and between the longing to be like God and the dark impulse towards destruction, these things took hold of him and drove him more and more into impassable and untimely terrain. His desire to know the impossible and receive mystical enlightenment finally tipped him over into insanity.

## II.  On the Genealogy of Morals (1887)

This book is, as Nietzsche wrote in *Ecce homo,* the darkest and most uncanny of his writings.[87] As the record of a series of reversals experienced after the publication of *Beyond Good and Evil*, it betrayed signs of disillusionment and an instinct for vengeance he was unable to completely suppress, in spite of his highly-developed art of self-mastery.

As Curt Janz relates, his friends' reactions to the publication of *Beyond Good and Evil* were crushing. Nietzsche felt particularly offended about the incomprehension shown

everyday, society, reality, across the abyss of transitoriness: a passionate-painful overflowing into darker, fuller, more floating states; an ecstatic affirmation of the total character of life which remains the same, just as powerful, just as blissful, through all change; the great pantheistic sharing of joy and sorrow that sanctifies and calls good even the most terrible and questionable qualities of life; the eternal will to procreation, to fruitfulness, to recurrence; the feeling of the necessary unity of creation and destruction."

86  Ges. W. vol. VII, p. 270; CM vol. 5, p. 236, § 294.
87  Ges. W. vol. XV, p. 104; CM vol. 6, p. 352.

201

by his friend Erwin Rohde, who criticized the work as exemplifying "the visions of a hermit and soap-bubbles of thought." He rejected, above all, the relativization of all value-judgments and the interpretation of all philosophy from the viewpoint of power. Though Jacob Burckhardt's warm-hearted and sensitive reply and Widmann's respect for a book he described as 'dynamite' went some way towards soothing the pain, Nietzsche remained deeply wounded. In the very next year, his long empty friendship with Rohde came to an end.[88] It is therefore self-explanatory that Nietzsche should have given full vent to his anger in this work, which is permeated with an irritating and "hot breath" (Janz). Despite the emotional tenor, however, it is a remarkable testament to his intellectual clarity. It is no exaggeration to designate the *Genealogy of Morals* his "final *reckoning with morality.*" Nietzsche prided himself in having brought to light three revolutionary truths in this work, which together originated in the basic conception of the 'will to power.'

*First Essay:* 'Good and Evil,' 'Good and Bad'

In the first essay, Nietzsche attempts to illuminate Judaeo-Christian morals from the perspective of resentment *[Ressentiment]*. In the second, he establishes that the psychology of conscience is grounded in the instinct for cruelty, and in the third essay, uncovers the aspect of power in the ascetic ideal of the priest.

The picture of man at the heart of Nietzsche's argument that the origin of morality lay in a hierarchical order of power is an aggressive and negative one. He was uncompromising in his proclamation that it was a 'quantum of power' that decided the rank held by the various social strata. To have power meant to him "to be strong, to be

88  A strained relationship with his sister's husband, Dr. Förster, the engagement of Lou Salomé and the death of his close friend, Heinrich von Stein, did nothing to improve the mood of Nietzsche, who was already depressed by headaches, colds and bouts of weakness.

powerful, to be a ruler,"[89] whilst the weak man, incapable of resisting strong stimuli, thereby proved himself helpless. Using the perspective of *power and impotence,* superiority and inferiority, Nietzsche unfolded a wholly new concept of 'good and evil.' An entry of 1886 shows what these values signified for him:

> "What is good? Everything that heightens the feeling of power in man, the will to power, power itself. What is bad? Everything that is born of weakness. What is happiness? The feeling that power is growing, that resistance is overcome...."[90]

The clashing conceptions of good and evil were, according to Nietzsche, the result of the social group in which the valuations concerned were framed. The attitude held by the warrior towards power was different from that of the priest, that held by the 'man of the herd' at odds with the view of the leader figure, and – needless to add – the slave's perspective incompatible with his lord's. The problems posed by the various hierarchical relationships had, at root, the factor of whether one belonged to the class that ruled or the one that obeyed. In either case, it was an aspect of the central notion of power that was at work, albeit opposing ones.

Nietzsche himself was principally interested in the *perspectivistic vision of the slave and master,* and for him, the tension between the Judaeo-Christian and Roman worldviews were paradigmatic of this dichotomy – Judaea and Rome. According to him, the Roman 'masters' regarded

89 Ges.W. vol. XV, p. 187; CM vol. 12, p. 217, refers to: "... human beings who are sure of their power and represent the attained strength of humanity with conscious pride." By contrast, the weak are instinctually unwarlike, and, whilst the strong man reworks his experiences and incorporates them into his destiny, the weak man is prematurely destroyed by minor experiences. Whereas the "aggressive pathos" is a part of strength, the weak man feels "vengefulness and rancor." Ges. W. vol. XV, p. 21; CM vol. 6, p. 274.
90 Ges. W. vol. VIII, p. 218; CM vol. 13, p. 192.

goodness as related to the powerful and to those defiant of strength, whereas evil they linked with weakness and impotence. In the opposite way, the 'slave' of Judaea saw the characteristics of justice, pity and humility as good, indeed all the values associated with the ascetic morality of the caste of priests, whilst power and oppression represented evil, as far as he was concerned.

The confrontation of the two was the starting point of Nietzsche's famous doctrine of resentment, on which would be founded not only the psychology of the 'slave' but also of asceticism and bad conscience. The 'master' drew all his worth from spontaneous manifestations of strength and force, whilst typical of the over-sensitive legal morality adhered to by the 'slaves' of Judaea was the feeling of resentment and "monstrous and uncanny" hatred towards all powerful affirmers of life. Yet despite the fact that they were suppressed and not adapted to life, these feelings of hatred were not ineffective: Quite the contrary, in fact!

Though Nietzsche's description of the slaves is a worrying one, for him it above all had the importance of a paradigm; a paradigm of how dangerous it was to suppress feelings of hatred within oneself. It cannot be denied that the discovery he made as a result of this greatly benefitted psychological research, that is to say, his recognition that *all affects denying the opportunity to be discharged as an action* would *work their way further inside* and from there become more intensively active on both a creative and destructive level. In the form of spiritual vengeance – either as sophisticated cleverness or as priestly morality – the inhibited emotions created their own kind of 'satisfaction.'[91] It may have been abstruse to apply the doctrine of resentment to the morality of the Jewish people, yet the notion of suppressed emotional discharge operating from the unconscious was to acquire unexpected credibility

91 Nietzsche created the expression, "the slave revolt of morality," to cover this radical revaluation of suppressed affects as spiritual vengeance. Ges. W. vol. VII/2a, p. 131, 317; CM vol. 5/2a, p. 268, 270, § 7 and 10.

through Freud's doctrine of repression, developed wholly independently of Nietzsche.

Nietzsche himself identified spiritually with the concept of the ruling caste, which, thanks to its esteem of all living things, was able to translate all its powerful impulses directly into actions. The epitome of such a moral attitude Nietzsche saw in Napoleon, *"the noble ideal as such* made flesh" ... "the synthesis of the *inhuman* and *superhuman.*"[92] What particularly fascinated him about these 'noble' races was the residue of a barbaric, natural brutality and unbroken force of what once had been the wild manifestation of life.

Thus he wrote in the *Genealogy of Morals:*

> "One cannot fail to see at the bottom of all these noble races the beast of prey, the splendid *blond beast* prowling about avidly in search of spoil and victory; this hidden core needs to erupt from time to time, the animal has to get out again and go back to the wilderness: – the Roman, Arabian, Germanic, Japanese nobility, the Homeric heroes, the Scandinavian Vikings – they all shared this need. It is the noble races that have left behind them the concept 'barbarian' wherever they have gone; even their highest culture betrays a consciousness of it and even a pride in it ... all this came together in the minds of those who suffered from it, in the image of the 'barbarian,' 'the evil enemy,' perhaps as the 'Goths,' the 'Vandals.' The deep and icy mistrust the German still arouses today, whenever he gets into a position of power, is an echo of that inextinguishable horror with which Europe observed for centuries that raging of the blond German beast (although between the old Germanic tribes and us Germans there exists hardly a conceptual relationship, let alone one of the blood)."[93]

92  Ges. W. vol. VII/2a, p. 337; CM vol. 5/2a, p. 288, § 16.
93  Ges. W. vol. VII/2a, p. 322; CM vol. 5/2a, p. 275, § 11.

This now famous and infamous passage on the raging of the "blond beast" has been repeatedly interpreted as a criticism of the German people. Although one cannot avoid seeing a note of rancor and even repugnance on Nietzsche's part here, the actual motivation behind the statement is probably his glorification of the barbarian's closeness to nature and to the depths of life.

Nietzsche's utopian and unrealistic enthusiasm for power and naturalness evoked images of men to be both admired and feared, men whose elasticity and resilience made them the carriers of the future, predestined to prepare the coming of the overman. In spite of his realization of how terrible and dangerous such 'barbaric men' could be, still they elicited great admiration from Nietzsche for their wickedness and wantonness. This is why he could write the sentence below, grotesque in its misconception of reality:

> "Almost everything we call 'higher culture' is based on the spiritualization of *cruelty,* on its becoming more profound: this is my proposition. That 'savage animal' has not really been 'mortified,' it lives and flourishes, it has merely become – divine."[94]

Nietzsche may have totally exaggerated his assertion that the creative force of life was based on the sensation of cruelty and the demonic side of nature; nevertheless, he did touch on something in which he was correct, namely, the value of the primordial creativity and purity of nature. But in doing so, he went far too far, leaving behind those spiritual aspects indispensable to any sort of cultivation.

94 Ges. W. vol. VII/1, p. 186; CM vol. 5/1, p. 166, § 229. An interesting assertion is that, unlike the impression left by such fulminant statements, Nietzsche possessed in his personal life a pronounced *ethical sense*. He demanded of himself an attitude of obedience towards himself and his destiny. This he also asked of his friends and acquaintances. His comment that "the man of knowledge might well feel like God become animal" alludes to the same thought. Ges. W. vol. VII/1, p. 99; CM vol. 5/1, p. 91, § 101.

Obsessed by the idea of renewing culture at the primordial root of all life and shaping it with new impulses, Nietzsche virtually ignored the dangers inherent in what he was saying. This is why he did not shrink from interpreting the general fear of barbarity and unpredictability as nothing but an indication that man was ensnared by the security his own bourgeois order offered him. The dilemma the world faced left it with the choice of either being destroyed by too much morality or asserting itself with elemental brutality and violence; Nietzsche chose to follow with the latter course. From the excess of untamed strength, he hoped to create a new form of life that satisfied the desire for ever more life and ever more power. His immoderate over-valuation of strength and the demonic urge to live was primarily directed against the predominance of Christian doctrine, from whose torpid morals he wished to rescue the world. In doing so, he was probably unaware that the motivation behind this bid for ethical freedom arose from his personal *adhesion* to Christian ideals, whether they consisted of brotherly love, pity or asceticism itself. In battling with the Christian disavowal of our instinctual nature, he became its victim. The increase in his activity could also justifiably be attributed to his emerging illness.

The parts of his bequest written in these years (1885-87) demonstrate how Nietzsche was increasingly occupied by the dark side of morality, by the demonic abyss. We read:

"Terribleness is part of greatness: let us not deceive ourselves."[95]

At approximately the same time, he wrote in the pages of his diary:

"Man is beast and super-beast, the higher man is inhuman and superhuman: these belong together. With every increase of greatness and height in man, there is also an increase in depth and terribleness: one ought

95  Ges. W. vol. XVI, p. 377; CM vol. 12, p. 388.

not to desire the one without the other – or rather: the more radically one desires the one, the more radically one achieves precisely the other."[96]

Below, he aims a cutting remark at Christianity:

"Neither has one dared to grasp that an increase in the terribleness of man is an accompaniment of every increase in culture; in this, one is still subject to the Christian ideal and takes *its* side against paganism."[97]

As Heraclitus had once done, so also Nietzsche underlined the *antithetical character of being,* which consisted of the coexistence as well as the enantiodromic confrontation of these opposites.[98] Although the recognition that the light and dark side functioned together in shaping events and actions was one that proved highly significant to psychology, the conclusions Nietzsche himself drew from this were perilous indeed. For he went on to require the *realization of the dark side of morality* – an attitude that, put in such absolute terms, could cause great harm:

"What is mediocre in the typical man? That he does not understand the necessity for the reverse side of things: that he combats evils as if one could dispense with them; that he will not take the one with the other.... Our insight is the opposite of this: that with every growth of man, his other side must grow too: that the highest man, if such a concept be allowed, would be the man who represented the antithetical character of existence most strongly.... That man must grow better *and* more evil is my formula for this inevitability."[99]

96 Ges. W. vol. XVI, p. 377; CM vol. 12, p. 426.
97 Ges. W. vol. XVI, p. 368; CM vol. 12, p. 456.
98 See C.G. Jung: Ges. W. vol. VII, p. 78 (C.W. vol. 7, p. 71).
99 Ges. W. vol. XVI, p. 295f; CM vol. 12, p. 519f.
See p. 144 concerning the final sentence.

With bizarre vehemence, he made the following demands, perhaps a sign that he was trying to compensate for the increasing doubts he was having:

> "It is part of this state to perceive not merely the necessity of those sides of existence hitherto denied, but their desirability; and not only their desirability in relation to the sides hitherto affirmed (perhaps as their complement or precondition), but for their own sake, as the more powerful, more fruitful, *truer* sides of existence."[100]

Nietzsche was now alarmingly clear about what he had previously been tempted to obscure,[101] committing the unforgivable mistake of confusing the actual existence of evil with its right to be lived through. He overlooked the fact that what mainly counted in facing repressed aggressions, in facing evil, was how one could come to terms with such a threatening power.[102] Beckoned on by his ideal of a future, godlike overman, he expected that, by trusting the regulative forces of creativity residing in mankind, things would take a positive turn. These were all utopian expectations that could become dangerously explosive when not anchored to any fundamental psychological or religious conception. Nietzsche was carried away by his myth of the strong man to the extent that he had become ignorant of the world, remaining totally unaware of how destructively violent these instincts could be once released. What or who could guarantee that the individual possessed by dark powers would be in a position to find his way back to an ordered way of life? In view of his denial of positive,

100 Ges. W. vol. XVI, p. 383; CM vol. 12, p. 455.
101 Although the above passages relating to evil all come from the bequest and were therefore unpublished, the spirit they convey coincides with comments made in *Zarathustra, Beyond Good and Evil*, and *The Genealogy of Morals* on the amalgamation of power and 'evil.' The repetitive remarks that "evil is man's best part," and that "man must become better and more evil!" go very much in the same direction.
102 See also L. Frey-Rohn, *Das Böse,* p. 202.

regulatory, ethical forces within the individual, Nietzsche's hypothesis that man could break through to a 'truer existence,' to an existence equal to Dionysian affirmation, was nothing more than wishful thinking. In the bequest, he wrote on this matter:

> "It [his philosophy] wants rather to cross over to the opposite of this – to a Dionysian affirmation of the world as it is, without subtraction, exception or selection – it wants the eternal circulation: – the same things, the same logic and illogic of entanglements. The highest state a philosopher can attain: to stand in a Dionysian relationship to existence – my formula for this is *amor fati*."[103]

Much more likely is the assumption that man, in pursuing his "dark impulse" towards this divine 'Yes,' does not "become aware of the right path," but will instead find himself on the directest way to the "devil" and his "own hell."

Nietzsche's psychology of evil belongs to the most dangerous of his ideas. Evil remains, in fact, nothing other than something potentially good, the "liberation" of which demands a subtle knowledge of the psychical connections between the "conscious and the unconscious."[104] He clearly perceived that the "savage animal" living on in man's unconscious was in touch with the deeper layers of the soul and its creative possibilities. But what he ignored was the fact that to deal with the dark powers required the highest degree of prudence and caution on the part of the individual if he was to avoid losing control. Psychologically speaking, there is nothing to insure that the individual case can endure the risk, nor do any objective criteria exist as to what would be right in each situation. In the final analysis, the encounter with evil – whether as a form of

103  Ges. W. vol. XVI, p. 383; CM vol. 13, p. 492.
104  See the pioneering research subsequently carried out by Freud on the consciousness of repression.

repression or as the archetypal concept of evil – represents an individual mystery that can only be sketched in broad terms. Failing conscious awareness of its outward manifestations and their effects, failing any sort of suffering from the conflict between what until now has been 'good' and an obtrusive 'evil,' and finally, lacking any kind of ethical basis to which one might appeal, all attempts to handle evil would be bound to misfire.[105] These were all requisites Nietzsche neglected and renounced, in spite of his insistence on overcoming oneself and on founding a 'new morality.'

Having come to the end of this excursus, let us now return to the text of the *Genealogy of Morals*.

## Second Essay: 'Guilt,' 'Bad Conscience' and the Like

In the second essay, Nietzsche tried to come closer to a definition of the psychology of resentment. He recognized – a fact already indicated in the introduction – that *the connection between the failure to discharge affects on the outside and these turning inward* was fundamental to it. It was one of his greatest accomplishments that he should have discovered in these very "postponed, unforgotten, hidden" affects the cause of unconscious reactions waiting to 'ambush' the individual. He thereby pointed to the infectious center within the soul that Freud took up in his theory of repression, and the traumatic effect of repressed memories.

We cannot agree with Nietzsche's additional attempt to derive moral impulses, *ideals* in particular, from the same hidden affects of vengeance and hatred. It sounds grotesque to attribute the Jewish ideals of justice and obedience to resentment resulting from personal feelings of impotence, and even worse to make an analogy with

105  L. Frey-Rohn, *Das Böse,* p. 203ff. Insofar as Nietzsche's *own* relation to evil was a questionable one, it must be said that he possessed a fine ethical sense, even though he did occasionally let himself be goaded into emotional outbreaks by his sister Elisabeth.

211

Christian ideals of love as embodied by the redeemer, who is likewise reduced to a mere sense of impotence. The height of grotesqueness is reached when Nietzsche interprets the symbol of God's self-crucifixion and His attempt to save mankind as a "mystery of the inconceivable final cruelty of the spirit." By leading all ideals back to resentment, he remains very one-sided, overlooking the possibility that humane, spiritual or religious motivations and drives could be at work. Nietzsche believed he recognized not only the root of all created ideals in resentment, but also the origin of *feelings of guilt and bad conscience*[106] and, ultimately, of mankind's decadence in general. He found a paradigm for this situation in the example of a broken contractual agreement between a creditor and a debtor,[107] i.e., when the debtor cannot fulfill his obligations. Whilst the creditor is in the stronger position and so has the right to punish and cause suffering, the debtor is weighed down by the plight of impotence: he has to pay off his debt and has no chance of defending himself. The inevitable result of the debtor's position was, in Nietzsche's view, the emergence of a torturous resentment, followed by an inner nurturing of feelings of vengeance and hatred, a radical change in emotions. The culminating point of his suffering, as Nietzsche conceived it, was reached in the violent suppression of the instinct of freedom, which unavoidably led to a bad conscience and to feelings of guilt.[108]

As far as Nietzsche was concerned, the deepest source of "bad conscience" was the destructive effect of what had happened at the very beginning of mankind's history: the violent segregation of wild and primitive man from his animal past forced upon him by cultivated man. He regarded the torture domesticated man felt at the limitation of his liberty, and so from his own bad conscience, as having been initiated by the cruel act of tearing away his animalistic

106  Ges. W. vol. VII/2b, p. 350; CM vol. 5/2b, p. 297, § 4.
107  Ges. W. vol. VII/2b, p. 360; CM vol. 5/2b, p. 305, 307, § 8, 9.
108  Ges. W. vol. VII/2a, p. 375, 379; CM vol. 5/2a, p. 318, 321, §14, 16.

roots. In his opinion, this represented the beginning of humanity's decadence:

> "*This instinct* of freedom forcibly made latent – we have seen it already – this instinct of freedom pushed back and repressed, incarcerated within and finally able to discharge and vent itself only on itself: that, and that alone, is what the bad conscience is in its beginnings."[109]

In Nietzsche's eyes, such a *repression of undischarged instincts* stood as the greatest and most uncanny disease to which humanity had been subject since losing its barbarity. This illness attained its summit in the pain experienced by the individual as a result of the violation of his drives, which from then on he could only discharge themselves in the form of guilty feelings and self-directed aggression.[110] It goes without saying that Nietzsche's free spirit and consistent love of the heroic should have prompted him to interpret this manifestation of "man's suffering of *man, of himself* "[111] as the ultimate expression of self-violation. It signified nothing less than a declaration of war by the individual on his former instincts. Nietzsche's enthusiasm was such that he even believed "bad conscience," that is, the pang of conscience, to be the origin of the "self-violating ideals" of selflessness, self-denial and self-sacrifice, amongst which he grotesquely included the sacrifice of Christ on behalf of mankind. To a certain extent, this interpretation was a contradictory one: when one really examines this example of self-sacrifice, it actually appears to come very close to the quality of self-overcoming that Nietzsche valued so highly, and which he similarly deemed sacrificial – a sacrifice in the service of creative self-development.

109  Ges. W. vol. VII/2b, p. 383; CM vol. 5/2b, p. 325, § 17.
110  We encounter a similar interpretation in Freud's work on *Civilization and its Discontents*.
111  Ges. W. vol. VII/2b, p. 380; CM vol. 5/2b, p. 323, § 16.

Though the expansion of his argument was controversially based on the exclusively *personalistic psychology* that characterized the *Genealogy of Morals* overall, he nevertheless enjoyed the honor of being the first to discover the psychological link between resentment, the repression of aggressive impulses and feelings of guilt, even if he did neglect the role of the archaic in preparing for moral problems. It is thus only right that he should go down in the history of psycho-pathology as one of the *forerunners of Freud's teachings on neurosis,* as Ellenberger[112] and Assoun,[113] among others, have stated.

*Third Essay:* 'What is the Meaning of Ascetic Ideals?'

His discussion of the ascetic ideal was Nietzsche's third treatment of the problem of resentment. Starting with the psychology of the priest who flees into an ideal of asceticism, Nietzsche succeeded in coming to what he regarded as far-reaching conclusions about how frail every form of ideal was. Nietzsche's representation of the ascetic ideal concluded with his presupposing a fundamental contradiction within the priest's self[114] in the form of a conflict between *an affirmation* and an *equally strong rejection of worldly existence.* The only possibility of bridging this gulf

112  Henri F. Ellenberger's studies on the relationship between the psychological concepts of Freud and Nietzsche are noteworthy, but he goes too far in assuming that Nietzsche's ideas "permeate all of psychoanalysis" ('The Discovery of the Unconscious,' p. 754).

113  Assoun's work on *Freud and Nietzsche* is thorough and subtle. Although he, too, is impressed by the coincidences of the conceptions of both men, he also stresses the important differences between them, in particular, with regard to their respective views on the *meaning* of guilt and feelings of guilt. Whereas Freud traces the causal nexus of these symptoms back to prior sexual development, Assoun sees Nietzsche as emphasizing the factual, original existence of the moral problems of bad conscience. Freud underlined the etiological significance of narcissism, while Nietzsche stressed the etiology of nihilism and the loss of value. For one, it was the problem of neurosis that was the main concern, for the other, that of the development of culture.

114  Ges. W. vol. VII/2c, p.426, 429; CM vol. 5/2c, p.363, 365, §11, 13

within the priest's own will to live lay in this 'sick animal' escaping into the ascetic ideal. The ideal thus acquired, in Nietzsche's opinion, the function of artificially staving off the slow degeneration of the priest's life. The sentences below have a drastic ring:

> "... life wrestles in it and through it with death and *against* death; the ascetic ideal is an artifice for the preservation of life."[115]

The discrepancy within the priest's attitude to life was to Nietzsche's mind also echoed in the exercise of his office. As the savior, 'shepherd and defender' of a sick herd suffering from resentment, it was up to him to try and "become master of the suffering," something that could only be achieved by highly ambivalent means. On the one hand, he endeavored to distract and lull his flock by working towards neighborly love, on the other, it was his job to deflect the *resentment inwards*. In both cases, he revealed himself to be what Nietzsche came to regard as a cruel physician, since he both interpreted the suffering as punishment for the individual's sinfulness and, in addition, made him the guilty party as far as the individual's own inner plight was concerned.[116] This was because it was essential for the priest to make outward-directed resentment an inwardly directed one, a trick Nietzsche condemned as the most dangerous and fatal that the religious interpretation of the world could perform.

In Nietzsche's overall scheme, the exposure of the

115 Ges. W. vol. VII/2c, p. 430; CM vol. 5/2c, p. 366, § 13.
116 "Broadly speaking, the ascetic ideal and its sublimely moral cult, this most ingenious, unscrupulous, and dangerous systematization of all the means for producing orgies of feeling under the cover of holy intentions, has inscribed itself in a fearful and unforgettable way in the entire history of man – and unfortunately *not only* in his history. I know of hardly anything else that has had so destructive an effect upon the *health* and racial strength of Europeans as this ideal; one may without any exaggeration call it *the true calamity* in the history of European health." Ges. W. vol. VII/2c, p. 460; CM vol. 5/2c, p. 392, § 21.

priest's self-contradiction served as a pretext for examining something of much greater importance to him. In the ascetic ideal, he believed he had discovered an inherent dichotomy peculiar to all ideals, namely, that adherence to any ideal unveiled an underlying conflict between the affirmation and negation of the world and its values. According to Nietzsche, it was characteristic of all the idealists, the "hectic in spirit," the "pale atheists, the antichrists, the immoralists and nihilists" that they should attempt to find refuge in metaphysical belief – belief in another world. With the help of their ideals, they tried to escape a conflict with an earthly existence they found unbearable. Yet, in doing so, the peace they hoped to discover proved nothing more than a painful delusion.

This situation profoundly fascinated Nietzsche because it demonstrated that this discrepancy was not only typical of spiritual ideals in general, but that it also applied in particular to the ideal of truth, with which he had always been especially preoccupied.[117] Like the related ideal of scientific knowledge, this ideal was founded on faith in a metaphysical, purely spiritual world and, similarly, the consequence of adhering to the ascetic ideal. Thus it, too, was characterized by the assumption that truth existed as a value "in itself,"[118] hidden behind the empirical world which Nietzsche had already objected to in Schopenhauer.

> "That which *constrains* these men, however, this unconditional will to truth, is *faith in the ascetic ideal itself,* even if as an unconscious imperative ... it is the faith in a *metaphysical* value, the absolute value of *truth,* sanctioned and guaranteed by this ideal alone.... Strictly speaking, there is no such thing as science 'without any presuppositions'; this thought does not bear thinking through, it is paralogical: a

117  For Nietzsche, truth meant knowledge of the sense and purpose of man and the cosmos, and insight into the ultimate and most profound value of existence, although he never expressed himself clearly on the matter.
118  See p. 39.

philosophy, a 'faith,' must always be there first of all, so that science can acquire from it a direction, a meaning, a limit, a method, a *right* to exist."[119]

It seemed disastrous to Nietzsche to believe in a metaphysical value and hold on tightly to a world of things in themselves since, at the same time, it meant a *devaluation of the worldly world,* in other words, that it would then be impossible ever to attribute deeper value to empirical reality. By combatting the ideal of truth for being inimical to life, Nietzsche may well be said to have finally rejected the Western metaphysical tradition stretching back to Plato and sustained by Christianity. He thereby brought to a close the dispute he had been conducting with the idealistic principles of contemporary philosophy since *The Dawn.*

The emphatic attack on the ideal of truth, however, seems rather disproportionate and inappropriate in view of the way he had previously stressed the relativity of truth and the perspectivism of knowledge. The inevitable conclusion is that Nietzsche was not only once more troubled by his perceptions of how fatal the effects of nihilism could be, but had also become much more aware of his own bond with the idealistic spirit of his ancestors. Whatever the case may be, he underlined with all possible insistence the fact that life and its individualism would go into an impoverished decline[120] as a result of holding fast to the ideal of truth. "Did not man thus become smaller? Did not existence, the spirit, even, lose all its value," the uniqueness of its emotional content, by sacrificing its warm tones in the general colorlessness of ideals, and being driven to nihilism by the sobering realization of having been grossly deceived and lied to? Nietzsche's reply betokened his frighteningly radical unwillingness to compromise: every presupposition that an ideal existed in itself – even the ideal of truth – appeared to him to be a mendacious distortion of the

119  Ges. W. vol. VII/2c, p. 469; CM vol. 5/2c, p. 400, § 24.
120  Ges. W. vol. VII/2c, p. 473; CM vol. 5/2c, p. 403, § 25.

world.[121] It was, therefore, necessary that each individual who wished to serve life and gain earthly knowledge should *see the lie for what it was* – a disillusioning process of realization for thinkers schooled in the Western tradition. Even Nietzsche himself, who, all his life, had been a passionate seeker of knowledge, received this insight as a deathblow. It meant that every attempt to fathom existence necessarily had to fail: "the total character of the world is in all eternity chaos," in the sense that order and structure were missing.[122]

Was it not so – Nietzsche went on to ask – that this discovery hid a still more disastrous factor? Was it not possible that life in general was directed towards error, dissimulation and self-delusion? Could it be that the highly lauded "will to truth," at its deepest level, was merely "a concealed will to death"[123] leading to the destruction of the individual?

In spite of the pain he felt at such destructive possibilities, Nietzsche was not so easily discouraged: well versed as he was in the art of self-overcoming and the surrender of cherished notions, it was two insights in particular that helped him over any depression he might have experienced.

The first encouragement was that he had made room for a *new evaluation of art*. In the *Birth of Tragedy* he had already established as the great attribute of arts its ability to portray the world in image and symbol.[124] Now he went a step further, according the aesthetic imagination an initially surprising significance, that of the only *legitimate* creative form based on "delusion and lies" to play a role in the life of man. That role was unique since it successfully counteracted the negation of life inasmuch as in art "the lie is

---

121 CM vol. 13, p. 193: "... there is only one world, and this is false, cruel, contradictory, seductive, without meaning.... A world thus constituted is the true world... *We need lies* to enable us to triumph over this reality, this 'truth,' i.e. to *live*...."
122 Ges. W. vol. VI, p. 148; CM vol. 3/3, p. 469, § 109.
123 Ges. W. vol. VI, p. 275; CM vol. 3/3, p. 576, § 344.
124 See p. 27.

sanctified,"[125] or, to put it another way, the beauty of illusion is actively pursued. In other words, art was, in essence, "the adoration of existence." As the expression of an affirmative will to give form, it promised those who know and those who suffer from life alike salvation from their misery and their torment. The spirit once again celebrated its resurrection in art, but this time it was a spirit irrational to the core.[126]

The other important insight concerned the question of how justified the search for truth was in the first place. What value could such a search still possess if truth unveiled itself as something illusory, a deceptive collage of lies and delusion – that same truth that since antiquity had belonged to the noblest of man's preoccupations and been identical in meaning to spiritual existence and even God Himself?

Nietzsche performed a *saltus mortale* in order to rescue the search for truth. Although he was not in a position to deny the fact that truth had renounced itself, he nevertheless placed his seal of approval upon the search for truth because it contained a value he did not want to do without: namely, the significance attached to *humanity's growing awareness of the extraordinary complex of problems surrounding the truth.*

> "... What meaning would *our* whole being possess if it were not this, that in us the will to truth becomes conscious of itself as a *problem* ?"[127]

In discovering the psychological meaning behind the search for truth, Nietzsche was able to clarify two points. On the one hand, he could confirm how justified his despairing dispute with the truth had been, on the other, anchor his intuitive understanding of the nullity of absolute

125 Ges. W. vol. VII/2c, p. 472; CM vol. 5/2c, p. 402, § 25.
126 To Nietzsche, art was "essentially the affirmation, blessing, adoration of existence..." CM vol. 13, p. 241.
127 Ges. W. vol. VII/2c, p. 482; CM vol. 5/2c, p. 410f, § 27.

values, which had plagued him since the early eighties. The insight gained into the problems thrown up by the will to truth exposed the hollowness of morality, or, to be more precise: morality lost its significance.

"As the will to truth thus gains self-consciousness – morality will gradually *perish* now: this is the great spectacle in a hundred acts reserved for the next two centuries in Europe – the most terrible, most questionable, and perhaps also the most hopeful of all spectacles."[128]

Nietzsche's proclamation that morality was empty may seem catastrophic to us, but his elimination of every prejudice and value in the history of Western culture still left one value that was not to be taken lightly: the immensely important factor of the human will. Like a man clutching at straws in order not to lose everything, Nietzsche held on to the notion that, irrespective of sense or purpose, human willing at least retained a fundamental significance. He wrote:

"But all this notwithstanding – man was *saved* thereby, he possessed a meaning, he was henceforth no longer like a leaf in the wind, a plaything of nonsense – the 'sense-less' – he could now *will* something; no matter at first to what end, why, with what he willed: the *will itself was saved*."[129]

Seen from the angle of the ideal of truth and the defeat of nihilism, the fact that man was able to will appeared to be Nietzsche's sole and ultimate value, a value capable of instilling the seeker of meaning with a belief in life that transcended the death of God and the invalidity of truth. Mankind could build a new future on this will, "this rem-

128  *Ibid.*
129  Ges. W. vol. VII/2c, p. 483; CM vol. 5/2c, p. 411f, § 28.

nant of an ideal."[130] However, Nietzsche omitted to say how this would still be possible when all values had been sacrificed.

Not being a philosopher myself, I will keep to my resolution of the introduction and avoid giving a philosophical assessment of Nietzsche's remarks. This is particularly pertinent in view of the exceedingly complex concept of truth Nietzsche employed, which, for him, meant far more than just the concordance of thought and reality. I would refer the reader to the excellent works by Jaspers and Loewith. It seems to me to be of psychological importance that Nietzsche's repeated interest in thinking his way all around the concept of truth was never restricted to traditional, rational methods, already noticeable in his opposition to 'great reason' (with its expansive meaning) and 'small reason' (intelligence).[131]

His incessant search for truth was principally motivated by a drive to reach "more than reason," at a *religious worth* and meaning for truth that lay in the darkness beyond considerations of "true and false" (Jaspers). The latter we may describe as the logically inaccessible secret at the heart of the world's Dionysian foundation. Although the denial of the existence of truth excluded any possible knowledge of the primary source, Nietzsche nevertheless left room for a conventional 'metaphysical relationship' between man and God.

Nietzsche was not in a position to bring his philosophy to a satisfactory conclusion on the question of religion, which was branded deep on his soul. His *logos* was too strong. It was rather left to the mystical revelations to unveil this side of matters. Insofar as he relied on his consciousness, he stuck to the idea that, in spite of the death of God and fragility of the highest values, there was no possible way to create the overman, the "man of the future." We read:

130 Ges. W. vol. VII/2c, p. 480; CM vol. 5/2c, p. 409, § 27.
131 See p. 94.

"This man of the future, who will redeem us not only from the hitherto reigning ideal but also from that which was bound to grow out of it, the great nausea, the will to nothingness, nihilism; this bell-stroke of noon and of the great decision that liberates the will again and restores its goal to the earth and his hope to man; this antichrist and antinihilist, this victor over God and nothingness – *he must come one day.*"[132]

Nietzsche's hope of overcoming nihilism comes close to the mystical idea of world-redemption in that it involves the equally mystical concept of the figure of the overman triumphing over God and the void. In this vision of the future, destiny and the heroism of decision were combined – beyond good and evil.[133]

Nietzsche sounded less certain of victory when, in the following year, he readdressed the same thought in *Twilight of the Idols:*

"One is necessary, one is a piece of fatefulness, one belongs to the whole, one is the whole; there is nothing which could judge, measure, compare, or sentence our being, for that would mean judging, measuring, comparing, or sentencing the whole. But there is nothing besides the whole. That nobody is held responsible any longer, that the mode of being may not be traced back to a *causa prima,* that the world does not form a unity either as a sensorium or as 'spirit' – that alone is the innocence of becoming restored. The concept of 'God' was until now the greatest objection to to existence. We deny God, we deny the responsibility in God: only thereby do we redeem the world."[134]

---

132  Ges. W. vol. VII/2b, p. 396; CM vol. 5/2b, p. 336, § 24.
133  See also Nietzsche's comments on *'amor fati,'* p. 185f.
134  Ges. W. vol. VIII, p. 101; CM vol. 6/2, p. 96f.

The fact that Nietzsche was reproached for atheism on the basis of this and similar remarks seems singularly inappropriate. The above-mentioned polemic against "God" was primarily directed at the "old" Judaeo-Christian God, who exclusively represented goodness and rational values. Nietzsche never gave up *hoping for a new god,* for a god who could promise a *transfiguration of creative life.* It was rather the case that he was disappointed by those peoples that had emerged in the course of the last two millennia neglecting to form such a god, a god to proclaim Dionysian creativity. "Two millennia together, and not a single new god."[135] In the final year before his collapse, we read the following statement on the making of new gods:

> "And how many new gods are still possible! As for myself, in whom the religious, that is to say god-forming, instinct occasionally becomes active at impossible times – how differently, how variously, the divine has revealed itself to me each time! ... So many strange things have passed before me in those time-less moments that fall into one's life as if from the moon, when one no longer has any idea how old one is or how young one will yet be – I should not doubt that there are many kinds of gods – There are some one cannot imagine without a certain halcyon and frivolous quality in their make-up. Perhaps light feet are even an integral part of the concept 'god.' Is it necessary to elaborate that a god prefers to stay be-yond everything bourgeois and rational? And between ourselves, also beyond good and evil? His prospect is *free* – in Goethe's words. And to call upon the ines-timable authority of Zarathustra in this instance: Zarathustra goes so far as to confess: 'I would believe only in a God who could *dance.*' "[136]

135 CM vol. 13, p. 525.
136 Ges. W. vol. XVI, p. 380; CM vol. 13, p. 525f (my emphasis).

Nietzsche's imaginative representation of a God who is both rational and a dancer may seem eccentric, but, leaving aside the sarcastic tone in his comments, they unmistakably betray the religious tenor of his personality. The God he outlines is one unifying height and depth, the light-hearted and the grave, wisdom and humor, all of which clearly alludes to a new, but perhaps questionable, *concept of a God who exists beyond good and evil.*

The more apparent the cynicism and ambivalence of his work become, the clearer it is that he is diverging from the Christian view of God and *openly referring to the figure of Dionysus,* in Nietzsche's eyes the "great ambivalent one," "the most deceitful and terrible one" and the genius of the heart. Towards the end of the work, more and more allusions to characters like the jester and the fool emerge, sometimes to describe himself, sometimes to represent Socrates, and finally to stand for the "higher man." He even went as far as to talk of the proximity of "buffoon and God,"[137] "saint and *canaille* "[138] and God and the satyr.[139] In a letter to Georg Brandes, he ironized himself as the "embodiment of world-historical cynicism."[140] The same situation is repeated in his inability to surrender himself fully to any concept of God, despite his "god-forming instinct," and bind himself to it. The seriousness that resulted from his physical suffering was just as characteristic as his ironic scepticism. To the same extent, his passion for knowledge was balanced out by his cynicism. All his life, Nietzsche remained a searcher dominated by the longing for an unknown God. God was the unrecognizable numen operating from deep within his soul. Karl Loewith puts it

137  *Ibid.* p. 244.
138  *Ibid.*
139  Ges. W. vol. XV, p. 35. Here Nietzsche refers to Heinrich Heine's "divine malice." See also Karl Jaspers, *Nietzsche,* p. 404f. Further references on p. 409f of the chapter on Socrates in Walter Kaufmann's *Nietzsche.*
140  See the letter of 20 November 1888 to Georg Brandes. Brandes was a Swedish philosopher who was the first ever to hold lectures on Nietzsche, in Copenhagen.

effectively and briefly: "Nietzsche's atheism [is] the godlessness of a man who implored this God at the start and end of his career." Can *searching for God with such insistence* really be called *atheism*?

Nietzsche supplicated this God from earliest childhood. In the 'Hymn' to the 'Unknown God,' we possess one of the first testimonies to his search, the major motif of which was again taken up in similar fashion in the 'Magician's Song'. He experienced the transformation of tragedy brought about by Dionysus as the mystery of "becoming one with primordial being." In seeking the inner core of this source, he allowed the search for truth to emerge from the depths as his controlling motive. As Zarathustra, the presence of the divine companion became his most impressive experience. He was able to come much closer to God in the course of a mystical trance that took the form of a fusion with Dionysus. It was not just the experience as an initiate of this God that resulted from the trance, but, in addition, the revelation of the mystery of eternal life and immortality. However, these experiences were never fully conscious ones. Nietzsche's scepticism and cynicism blocked the way to this. Throughout the conflict between the ego and the unconscious it was the ego that was always on top. Although his soul was constantly determined by his inner experiences, his ego demanded more and more autonomy until it finally set itself up as God's replacement. Even if the Dionysian did overcome him from time to time, it is nevertheless true to say that this was never anything but a mystical experience for Nietzsche and, therefore, had no decisive effect on his work. Even his mystical vision of the 'eternal recurrence' only managed to retain the significance of a postulate from which he expected new impulses to give the earth new form, a situation similar to that occupied by the overman. In spite of his search for God and himself, Nietzsche was prevented from coming to a full reckoning with his experience of the concept of God. His ego remained stronger than the God.

## III. Twilight of the Idols,
### Or How One Philosophizes with the Hammer

The work, *Twilight of the Idols,* is described by Janz as having been completed in a few days in a "quick and easy hand." It is less distinguished by the novelty of its thoughts than by its aggressive, pugnacious and irreconcilable attitude. In *Ecce homo,* Nietzsche looked back on the spirit that had then animated him as a "demon that laughs."[1] No other work of his is more independent, more subversive, more malicious. The idol at which he swings his hammer is the old truth of God, truth and morality. It is against this truth that he directs the "great declaration of war"[2] which distinguishes the book from beginning to end. Nietzsche compared himself with an 'untimely one' whose excursions led over and through all the values of his age. And indeed, his demon did drive him well beyond the boundaries of reality. It is a fact that he criticized many aspects of the *décadence* of his time, such as the collapse of values, the corruption of man, the rejection of healthy instincts and of worldly existence – but it was still more important to him to discover the means of overcoming them. His ultimate response to the decay of values was derived from mystical inspiration rather intellectual reflection. What did Nietzsche mean by *décadence* or nihilism, a concept that, for the first time in history, had penetrated our full awareness?

> "What does nihilism mean? *That the highest values devaluate themselves.* The aim is lacking; 'Why' finds no answer."[3]

---

1 Ges. W. vol. XV, p. 105; CM vol. 6, p. 354.
2 Ges. W. vol. VIII, p. 60; CM vol. 6, p. 58.
3 Ges. W. vol. XV, p. 145. Similarly we read in vol. XV, p. 155 "Every purely *moral* value system ... *ends in nihilism:* this is to be expected for Europe."

The disintegration of values and meaning reached its climax in nihilism. The desperate realization of the "vanity" of values became all-important and was best formulated in the words: "the nothing (the meaningless), eternally!"[4] The pessimistic tone of this thought, Nietzsche stated, pointed towards the inevitable recurrence of an *existence without meaning, goal or purpose,* which, as far as he was concerned, was the most negative representation of the myth of the 'eternal recurrence.' As a movement of opposition to the Christian era, nihilism had directed its main efforts against the supreme Christian values of immortality, faith in a transcendent world, truth and morality. Nietzsche principally denied the presence of a "true world" beyond this one. The overall character of existence could no longer be seized in metaphysical terms, Nietzsche thought, neither through the concept of an all-embracing unity, nor through one of absolute truth.[5] Belief in the absolute ignored both the factuality of the existential "lie" and the situation of "wishing not to see" reality.[6] In the bequest, he posed the following questions in an attempt to hold up the nihilistic loss of values:

"... could the lie be something divine ...
could the value of all things be based on the fact that they are false ...
could despair be merely the consequence of a faith in the *divinity of truth* ?
could *lying and falsification* (faking), the importation of meaning, represent a value, a meaning, a purpose in themselves?
should one not believe in God, not because he is true, but because he is false?"[7]

---

4  Ges. W. vol. XV, p. 182; CM vol. 12, p. 213.
5  CM vol. 13, p. 139f.
6  See p. 250.
7  CM vol. 13, p. 139f.

As previously in the *Genealogy of Morals,* Nietzsche recognized the central cause of the nihilistic tendencies of the present time as the modern belief in categories of reason,[8] which, by promulgating the idea of a fictional, unreal world 'in itself,' a transcendental world, aroused false hopes in reality. The inevitable effect such fictions had was not only to paralyze achievement, but also of failure in the worldly sphere. It became evident that any beliefs in absolute values were an illusion – a disastrous conclusion! Nietzsche's battle from then on was with occidental reason and its highest values of truth and goodness: in it, he saw the deeper *causes of all error, falsification* and *deception.* He came to the bleak assertion that "everything is now thoroughly false...." His view of the world as a fiction anticipated the 'As if' philosophy of Hans Vaihinger.[9]

He designated Socrates the prototype of an attitude that lifted reason to a tyrannical position and regarded it as the precondition for every sort of virtue. Here was a figure whom Nietzsche initially openly admired for his wisdom, boldness and superior dialectic, only to change his opinion in the course of time and finally reject him outright. Socrates' denigration of instinct increasingly became the object of Nietzsche's criticism, who accused him of maliciousness and moral corruption, even perversity. The *Twilight of the Idols* gave way to the temptation of branding him the very embodiment of moral decline; he was a "misunderstanding"[10] who carried within himself the very seeds of *décadence.* Attacks of this sort have to be approached critically for what they were: the 'other side' of his admiration for *logos.*

Nietzsche's critique of the nihilistic tendency to create

---

8  "Conclusion: The faith in the categories of reason is the cause of nihilism. We have measured the value of the world according to categories *that refer to a purely fictitious world.*"
   Ges. W. vol. XV, p. 151; CM vol. 13, p. 49.
9  See the article on Nietzsche in Vaihinger: *Die Philosophie des 'Als ob,'* p. 771f.
10  Ges. W. vol. VIII, p. 74; CM vol. 6, p. 73.

ideals is similar to that articulated in the *Genealogy,* only much more biting and unrealistic. To him, these ideals were the greatest danger ever faced by a culture striving for elevation and freedom. Thus, he thought:

> "... that until now ideals were the proper force behind the slandering of man and the world, the blight of reality, the great *temptation into the void*...."[11]

The idealistic man lived in an imaginary world that distorted worldly reality.

Nietzsche's other target was very much in accordance with his viewpoint on life, namely, to undermine every kind of morality not sustained by the *instinct of life*. His primary concern in this respect was Christian morality. Insofar as it was characterized by an attitude that despised nature and the instinctual world, whilst trusting to the victory of good and the annihilation of evil, it was to a high degree responsible for advancement of nihilistic tendencies. This was the case with every morality that aimed at improvement or altruism and thus disregarded the 'selfishness' that Nietzsche held in such high esteem.

Even the state, democracy and socialism were incorporated into his assault on nihilism. As a symptom of nihilism Nietzsche condemned, above all, the democratic movement in Germany, which, like every other democratic institution, lacked both a strong will and an organizational strength. Flying in the face of the conventional view that democracy strengthened the spirit of the individual, Nietzsche tended rather to see in it the breeding ground of "herd animals," for which the word 'authority' was taboo. Seen from the perspective of Nietzsche's high estimation of the great man, the overman, democracy and its effect of leveling out the truth "for everyone" could be nothing but "a symptom of

---

11 CM vol. 13, p. 56. This aphorism is a particularly harsh one: "I searched for great human beings; I always found only the *apes* of their ideals." Ges. W. vol. VIII, p. 66; CM vol. 6, p. 65.

the decline of the state."[12] By encouraging the small state, it was irrevocably predestined for its own destruction.

In contrast to the German state, which, like Western culture in general, was soft and rotten at the core, he praised Russia as a country still in possession of the strength to desire and to organize will. Free men did not flourish in greenhouses and the atmosphere of *laissez aller,* but in situations of great danger requiring the highest possible degree of effort and forcing on the individual full responsibility for himself. When viewed in this light, it was inevitable that Nietzsche would regard democratic efforts at culture as a striking example of the degeneration of instincts and *décadence.*

In his view, socialism and all the various forms of humanitarianism belonged in the same category as the democratic tendency and its 'morality of the herd animal,' which he deprecated as the great misunderstanding of Christianity – an attitude we can hardly agree with today.

For this reason, it may be of little surprise to notice that Nietzsche was a decided proponent of war. In *Zarathustra* and *Beyond Good and Evil* he repeated in similar fashion his argument of the 1870's – namely that war was necessary to strengthen humanity despite the fact that it also barbarized,[13] or that 'war preserved culture,'[14] as he repeated

12  Ges. W. vol. VIII, p. 151; CM vol. 6, p. 141.
   Nietzsche's conception of the state went through the most varied of stages. Whereas, in *The Birth of Tragedy,* he praised the state for being an institution necessary for the preservation of culture, as early as in the period of *Zarathustra* he was dissociating himself from this view, describing the state – "this new idol" – as a "hypocritical hound" that wished "to be the most important beast on earth" (Ges. W. vol. VI, p. 194; CM vol. 4, p. 170).
   Similarly, the fact that it "tells lies in all tongues of good and evil" is also referred to (Ges. W. vol. VI, p. 70; CM vol. 4, p. 61).
   As his picture of the world grew ever more dark in the course of the 1880s, it was clear that the polemical side in him had gained the upper hand.
13  Ges. W. vol. II, p. 329; CM vol. 2/1, p. 289, § 444.
14  Ges. W. vol. II, p. 356; CM vol. 2/1, p. 312, § 477.

in *Zarathustra* [15] and *Beyond Good and Evil.* In *Twilight of the Idols,* war even attained the status of the very means by which values were revalued!

> "War has always been the great wisdom of all spirits who have become too inward, too profound; even in a wound there is the power to heal."[16]

War was for him the necessary prerequisite for preserving life and mankind, as well as for overcoming nihilism.

> "A society that definitely and *instinctively* gives up war and conquest is in decline: it is ripe for democracy and the rule of shopkeepers."[17]

War educated for freedom[18] and peace. The free man was a warrior.[19] With a view to the "great life" and "great politics," wars were needed.

> "They renounced the *great* life in renouncing war."[20]

Yet, it would be unjust to approach such comments as if they represented references to wars fought out physically. Although Nietzsche always held the training of the defensive and aggressive instincts in high esteem, he was just as interested in the *spiritual battle.* In his opinion, what was required were strong natures capable of conducting a war

15  Ges. W. vol. VI, p. 67; CM vol. 4, p. 59.
"You should love peace as a means to new wars – and the short peace more than the long...." And he proceeds: "... it is the good war that hallows any cause."
In the same chapter it says: "Thus live your life of obedience and war. What matters long life? What warrior wants to be spared?... Man is something that shall be overcome."
16  Ges. W. vol. VIII, p. 59; CM vol. 6, p. 57.
17  Ges. W. vol. XVI, p. 179
18  Ges. W. vol. VIII, p. 149; CM vol. 6, p. 140.
19  Ges. W. vol. VIII, p. 150; CM vol. 6, p. 140.
20  Ges. W. vol. VIII, p. 87; CM vol. 6, p. 84.

with spiritual weapons. *Beyond Good and Evil* demonstrates the extent to which he expected the philosopher to share this belligerent attitude. In *Ecce homo,* he writes:

> "A warlike philosopher challenges problems, too, to single combat."[21]

Helpful to me in exploring the role war played in rejuvenating the soul were the broad areas on which Jacob Burckhardt[22] and Nietzsche seemed to agree. In the *World-Historical Observations,* the published version of lectures held by Burckhardt in Basle between 1868 and 1870 and attended by Nietzsche, we find, among other things, his thoughts on crises and wars. I confess ignorance as to who the *spiritus rector* of these shared ideas was. In contrast to Burckhardt, who drew his conclusions largely on the basis of historical fact, Nietzsche's intuitive comments reflected much more of the archetypal spirit of the age.

Nietzsche found confirmation for his conviction that the world was moving towards chaos in his prophetic visions of the future. It seemed to him unavoidable, inexorable and a matter of destiny that nihilism would increase. His prophecies of great power-struggles and terrible wars came so tragically true in the course of the 20th century that we cannot but admire his ability to sense the nihilistic tendencies of his age. He was one of the first to have the courage to draw attention to the European sickness of nihilism and to indicate more threatening developments to come. Yet, unlike his predictive capacity, the practical suggestions he made to stem this danger were extremely poor, partly due to the hopes he attached to great men, and the overman in

21 Ges. W. vol. XV, p. 21; CM vol. 6, p. 274.
22 Jacob Burckhardt, born May 1818, from 1858 onwards Professor of History and the History of Art in Basle. In the *World-Historical Observations,* we read, amongst other things: "War is a necessary factor in higher development," or: "A people only truly learns its full strength as a nation in war." He goes on to say that only through war "can the true renewal of life take place." See his chapter on 'The Historical Crises.'

particular, and partly also to a faith that had a decidedly mystical ring.

Though he was worried by the uncertainties held by the future, the final months of his sanity were colored by a notable optimism that the chaos would ultimately be averted. Both his experience of repeated illness and the *amor fati* connected with it pointed in the same direction: he was convinced that times of decline contained signs of new, restorative powers,[23] indeed *signs of self-curing.* These were much less the result of human intervention than possibilities of irrational transformation held within the epochs themselves. He therefore maintained the opinion that periods of nihilistic gloom should be lived through, and the positive impulses they revealed assimilated. He even suggested provoking crises and conflicts in order to release new creative urges for change. In *Zarathustra,* he had already, as we have seen, accorded the creative process the important role of producing new values from those condemned as evil by the collective.[24]

> "Principle: There is an element of decay in everything that characterizes modern man: but close beside this sickness stand signs of an untested force and powerfulness of the soul. *The same reasons that produce the increasing smallness of man* drive the *stronger and rarer individuals up to greatness.*"[25]

Nietzsche had demonstrated in *Beyond Good and Evil* that *the affirmation of suffering and illness* were vital to attaining such greatness.[26] The power of the soul was

---

23  Thus we read the following words at the beginning of *Ecce homo:* "Looking from the perspective of the sick toward *healthier* concepts and values and, conversely, looking again from the fullness and self-assurance of a *rich* life down into the secret work of the instinct of decadence – in this I have the longest training, my truest experience...." Ges. W. vol. XV, p. 11; CM vol. 6, p. 266.

24  See p. 122f.

25  Ges. W. vol. XV, p. 221f.

26  See p. 113 and 196.

confronted by the ability to suffer and sacrifice, assigning primary importance to the ethos of self-overcoming.[27]

> "Nothing avails: one *must* go forward – step by step further into decadence.... One can *check* this development and thus dam up degeneration, gather it and make it more vehement and *sudden:* one can do no more."[28]

But he was more pessimistic in a passage written down a year before his breakdown and dated November, 1887:

> "... I believe we have one of the greatest crises, a moment of the *very deepest* reflection of man on himself: it is a question of man's strength as to whether he will recover from and master this crisis: it is possible...."[29]

The guiding principle of Nietzsche's faith in the possibility of overcoming oneself was, apart from any personal experience or intuition, the *myth of the strong man,* the overman: it was this that helped him leave his doubts behind and reinforced his hopes for a new future. Renewers of the spirit could, at any time, emerge to give the world – the earth – a new turn: 'great men' were like 'explosives' in that they contained an immense power, and when detonated by chance, could "summon the great destiny."[30] Great men could even be, Nietzsche continued, criminal types; that is, strong men who, as a consequence of unfavorable circumstances, had become ill. What made them strong was their naturalness and their primitivity, in other words, the residue of a barbarity still preserved in them.[31]

The height of greatness was genius, which was distin-

27 See p. 120.
28 Ges. W. vol. VIII, p. 155; CM vol. 6, p. 144.
29 CM vol. 13, p. 56.
30 Ges. W. vol. VIII, p. 155; CM vol. 6, p. 145.
31 Ges. W. vol. VIII, p. 157; CM vol. 6, p. 146.

guished by an abundance of strength that expended itself without reserve. Napoleon was just such a genius, Goethe another European phenomenon.[32] The power of genius lay in the fact that the spirit was rooted in the most ancient of times and represented the culminating synthesis of the accumulated achievements of many races, Nietzsche surprisingly added. They were the inheritors of a long period of civilization. Inasmuch as such an atavistic trait indicated a process of 'once more recognizing and remembering,' and with it, of rejuvenating the 'entire ancient household of the soul' and its wisdom, genius, as Nietzsche saw it, was particularly suited to preparing the ground for overcoming nihilism. In view of this *return to an archaic substratum* as the actual birthplace of the new and futuristic, one cannot help thinking that, although Nietzsche seems to have had something very important in mind, he expressed it in a far too general way.[33] His basic idea was that genius should direct its thoughts backwards to the primeval structure it had inherited, a structure that was the spring of all new creativity and was in essence comparable with Jung's psychological notion of the 'collective unconscious.'

Concerning Nietzsche's own person, the above-mentioned regressive tendency may well also indicate a connection with his spiritual forefathers and point to the constellation of his own Dionysian personality, which becomes much clearer in his later conversion to the antique doctrine of mysteries. In *Twilight of the Idols,* as once before in the *Birth of Tragedy,* the mythical figure of Dionysus became an inner divine power.

But, in contrast to the aesthetic emphasis placed on the

32 Ges. W. vol. VIII, p. 162; CM vol. 6, p. 151.
33 It would be more accurate in psychological terms to interpret the regressive tendency as a reactivation of archaic, or, better still, archetypal pathways of the soul. C.G. Jung writes on resorting to the source of the collective unconscious: "Goethe brings in the Blocksberg and the Greek underworld; Wagner needs the whole corpus of Nordic myth, including the Parsifal saga; Nietzsche resorts to the hieratic style of the bard and legendary seer...."
C.G. Jung: Ges. W. vol. XV, p. 111 (C.W. vol. 15, p. 97).

experience of God at that time, he now experienced the Godhead in terms of a divine presence penetrating the whole of his spirit. His soul was enflamed by a 'Yes' to life that triumphed over all tragedy and bore his spirit up to a vision of eternal rebirth that transcended all iniquity. It could be regarded as a Dionysian Epiphany to the great personality concealed within, and, although that personality had always been there and gained powerful form in Zarathustra's visions, it now manifested itself again with renewed vigor under the pressure of Nietzsche's frightening intuitions of the future. In *Twilight of the Idols,* he wrote on the Dionysian mysteries:

> "What was it that the Hellene guaranteed himself by means of these mysteries? *Eternal life,* the eternal return of life; the future promised and hallowed in the past; the triumphant Yes to life beyond all death and change; *true* life as the overall continuation of life through procreation, through the mysteries of sexuality.... That there may be the eternal joy of creating, that the will to life may eternally affirm itself, the agony of the woman giving birth *must* also be there eternally."[34]

In surrendering to the god Dionysus and becoming one with him, Nietzsche gained access to the mystery not only of eternal life and immortality, but also to the deepest instinct for life – especially in moments of ecstasy. For the first time, he penetrated the secret of procreation and sexuality. He was deeply moved at inwardly participating in the living process of becoming and dying, and thus also in *the oneness of destruction and rebirth,* sacrifice and being sacrificed. In a state of high intoxication of the soul, he – the 'godless one' – was granted the most rapturous experience of God one could have, even if it was not in the traditional Christian sense. A Dionysian attitude signified for him:

34  Ges. W. vol. VIII, p. 172; CM vol. 6, p. 159.

"Saying Yes to life even in its strangest and hardest problems, the will to life rejoicing over its own inexhaustibility even in the very sacrifice of its highest types – .... Not in order to be liberated from terror and pity, not in order to purge oneself of a dangerous affect by its vehement discharge – Aristotle understood it that way – but in order to be *oneself* the eternal joy of becoming, beyond all terror and pity – that joy which included even joy in destroying.... And herewith I again touch that point from which I once went forth: The *Birth of Tragedy* was my first revaluation of all values. Herewith I again stand on the soil of which my intention, my *ability* grows – I, the last disciple of the philosopher Dionysus – I, the teacher of the eternal recurrence."[35]

In spite of the grandiose nature of this very picturesque vision, it is unsatisfactory as a suggestion for overcoming nihilism. Instead of directly approaching the highly realistic problem of the nihilistic loss of values from a worldly standpoint, Nietzsche fled into a visionary world. He *transferred the future into the past*[36] and expected the Greek mysteries to provide a solution to the burning problem of nihilism in the present.

The degree of his untimeliness and alienation from reality is considerable and confirms the impression that *his conscious personality was becoming overshadowed by a second, unconscious one.* The increasing expressions of self-confidence and his delusions of grandeur also come from the uncontrolled effects the other side of his personality was having on his consciousness. Lou von Salomé draws attention to his concealed inner life, his "suppressed loneliness." She knew Nietzsche better than virtually any-

35 Ges. W. vol. VIII, p. 173f; CM vol. 6, p. 160.
36 See also Albert Camus: *L'homme révolté,* especially the chapter on 'Nietzsche et le Nihilisme.'

one else and recorded what she knew in her memoirs.[37] The overwhelming impression is of a man hiding behind a mask, whose innermost being sporadically announced its presence with mysteriously whispered words. A similar description has been left us by Resa von Schirnhofer in her essay, "On Nietzsche the Man" [*Vom Menschen Nietzsche*].[38]

The gradual takeover by the second, mystical personality nevertheless left room for hoping that what was happening need not necessarily have ended in disaster; on the contrary, it might have represented the highest fulfillment Nietzsche's inner life could have had.[39]

## IV. The Case of Wagner

The work, *The Case of Wagner,* was written in the same spirit and at about the same time as *Twilight of the Idols.* It also carries the mark of a polemic and is full of biting irony. Although the title referred to Wagner, Nietzsche's

37 I quote from the documents edited by Ernst Pfeiffer concerning the meeting between Nietzsche, Rée and Salomé. Salomé got to know him "at a time when the overall impression of his being was already totally permeated by his deeply affected inner life and he himself was characterized by what he kept back and concealed. I would say that what he hid, the presentiment of a concealed loneliness, was the first strong impression that made Nietzsche so fascinating as a figure.... His eyes truly betrayed a lot, too. Even though they were half blind they still had nothing in them of the peering, blinking, unintentionally obtrusive manner of many near-sighted people: they much rather looked like custodians and guardians of their own treasures, of silent secrets no unauthorized gaze should wander over..."

From The Commentary, p. 422.

38 See Curt Janz, *Nietzsche,* vol. 2, p. 280.
At the same time, he writes of Nietzsche: "There he sat, motionless and in a tired posture, as if engrossed in experiencing his poetry all over again, wholly forgetting my presence, immersed in his own peculiar world, in that 'unknown,' 'insatiable' quantity Zarathustra talks of as being around him, in him" (in reference to the 'Night Song' and the 'Dancing Song').

39 See Ernst Bertram: *Nietzsche, Versuch einer Mythologie.*

attack was directed just as much at modern music in general, with which he was intensively and critically engaged. In both, he saw abuses and cultural decadence. When music was his target, he turned against the modern tendency to indulge in excessive romanticism, which he felt was spiritless, a 'physiological degeneration,' an 'impoverishment of life,' and finally, the expression of pessimism and nihilism as well. Instead, music should be the "affirmation, blessing, glorification of existence,"[40] as we read in the bequest. The composer Bizet and his 'Carmen,' in particular, seem to have come closest to fulfilling this inner demand for life to be affirmed. Insofar as his work, *The Case of Wagner,* represented a polemic – in Janz's words, an "open call to do battle" – it seems that it brought Nietzsche a certain relief.

> "To turn my back on Wagner was for me a fate; to like anything at all after that, a triumph. Perhaps nobody was more dangerously attached to – grown together with – Wagnerizing; nobody tried harder to resist it; nobody was happier to be rid of it."[41]

Seen from this angle, the work represented an act of liberation, perhaps even a *cure for something sick within himself;* that being his continued enchantment with the elemental power of Wagner's music. For, of Wagner he writes: *"Wagner est une névrose* ... he has made music sick."[42]

What until then had only been dimly hinted at now bursts forth from Nietzsche's soul: "Wagner was an actor-genius," who sought effects to overwhelm others. He was far less a musician than a theatrical person. Thus, he was most concerned with gesture, pathos and the magic of plot. As the "heir of Hegel,"[43] it was essential for him to express

40 CM vol. 13, p. 241.
41 Ges. W. vol. VIII, p. 1; CM vol. 6/1, p. 357.
42 Ges. W. vol. VIII/1, p. 18; CM vol. 6/1, p. 22.
43 Ges. W. vol. VIII, p. 33; CM vol. 6, p. 36.

an idea in his music. The secret of his influence on youth lay within the "puzzling realm of art" and its hide-and-seek game of a hundred symbols.

Through Wagner's music, Nietzsche became aware of what should be avoided in an opera. He summarized his expectations in the form of three requirements:

> "That the theater should not lord it over the arts.
> That the actor should not seduce those who are authentic.
> That music should not become an art of lying."[44]

The word "lying" is used here in its everyday sense, not just its philosophical one.

Nietzsche was also critical of German youth for allowing itself to be seduced by the magic of Wagnerian music, for banding together as its adherents and for creating a sort of 'theatrocracy.'

It was probably the disappointments of all the hopes he had invested in Wagner, supplemented by the misunderstanding and lack of attention accorded his own work, that caused Nietzsche to cry out against the German people and their culture a little later, in *Ecce homo* ('The Case of Wagner'). He used the basest of weapons when writing about the "indecency *in historicis*" of the Germans,[45] of their lack of vision for the values of culture and their cowardice when faced with truth and reality. The following outcry betrays the pain he had long held back:

> "I even consider it a duty to tell the Germans for once how many things they have on their conscience by now. All great crimes against culture for four centuries they have on their conscience...."[46]

---

44  Ges. W. vol. VIII, p. 37; CM vol. 6, p. 39.
45  Ges. W. vol. XV, p. 109; CM vol. 6, p. 358.
46  Ges. W. vol. XV, p. 110; CM vol. 6, p. 359.

He continued:

"... they have on their conscience all that followed, that is with us today – this most *anticultural* sickness and unreason there is, nationalism, this *névrose nationale* with which Europe is sick, this perpetuation of European particularism, of *petty* politics: They have deprived Europe itself of its meaning, of its reason – they have driven it into a dead-end street. – Does anyone besides me know the way out of this dead-end street? – A task that is great enough to *unite* nations again?"[47]

Despite his cynical abandon, at least Nietzsche did not disregard the resistance and fear shown by the German people towards the damaging and perhaps even dangerous influence of Wagner. He felt that the Germans were defending themselves against infection by something sick as they displayed their mistrust, suspicion and disgust.

It was understandable that Nietzsche's increasingly apparent change in attitude towards Wagner, so crassly different from the glorification of him contained in the *Birth of Tragedy,* should have elicited so much astonishment and displeasure. The criticism of this publication, however, came rather late, since contemporaries were hardly aware of the last works Nietzsche wrote before his breakdown.

---

47 Ges. W. vol. XV, p. 110f; CM vol. 6, p. 359f. The expression *névrose nationale* is interesting with regard to the dismissal of Nietzsche as a National Socialist, since it again highlights his deeply rooted rejection of all nationalistic ideologies.

## V. The Antichrist: Curse on Christianity

Like the previous work, *The Antichrist* is also the product of an explosion of long-suppressed aggressions.[48] It has the aura of the cry of a wounded soul. Nietzsche's attempt to free himself from his distaste for contemporary man with this inimical and hate-filled condemnation of Christianity is here less inhibited than ever. It embodies the same spirit as the *Case of Wagner* and its bitter polemic against Nietzsche's former idol, Richard Wagner.

What was the reason for this terrible hatred? *Who was the "other in him,"* whose mouthpiece he became? We can gather from the text that this 'other' was the Apostle Paul, the prototype of the ascetic priest that Nietzsche had already portrayed as both Paul and Saul in *Human All-Too-Human,* describing him as "the prosecutor of God."[49] The *Genealogy of Morals* had likewise contained sharp words for the ascetic priest as the embodiment of power and self-contradiction.[50] Finally, in the *Antichrist,* Paul comes to stand for the opposite type of the "joyous ambassador" and "genius of hatred,"[51] all of these being traits that characterized Nietzsche's own passionate animosity. We can hardly be far off the mark if we see this figure as the archetype of the inner antagonist in Nietzsche himself; in other words, Zarathustra's opponent who, as the buffoon, jumped over the tightrope artist in the work of the same name. Viewed psychologically, Paul was the *dark brother of the shadow that overran Nietzsche* in *The Antichrist.*

At the very start of the work, Nietzsche confesses his

---

48  *The Antichrist* is a work that was published as part of Nietzsche's bequest. Although it was declared completed in November 1888, it still contained orthographical mistakes and inconsistencies that were then corrected by Nietzsche's friend Peter Gast. In the end, it was first published in 1895, after additional editing by Elisabeth Förster-Nietzsche.

49  Ges. W. vol. III/2, p. 248; CM vol. 2/II/2, p. 591, § 85.
    See C.G. Jung, vol. VII, p 37 (C.W. vol. 7, p. 34).

50  See p. 214.

51  Ges. W. vol. VIII/4, p. 270; CM vol. 6/3, p. 215, § 42.

contempt for Christianity, which "has waged deadly war against this higher type of man" (the strong and powerful) and placed "all the basic instincts of this type under a ban."[52] The criticism of the Christian denial of the values of life, that is, the instincts of power and growth, is the thread that unifies the whole work. Wherever such a 'will to power' (the enhancement of life) was missing, Nietzsche considered the decay of culture would follow on inevitably, with nihilistic values gaining the upper hand.

The 'denaturalization of values' became, so to speak, the programmatic center of the essay, from where he passed crushing judgment on each of the basic precepts of Christianity in turn. This not only included the Christian view of God and morals, the notion of the redeemer and the concept of the Church, but also the idea of 'being Christian' and having faith. The worrying thing about this work had less to do with the thought content than with the vindictiveness of its tone and the animosity with which it assessed revered values. It was as if Nietzsche had cast off the last of his inhibitions and declared war on the 'theologian instinct' he knew from Protestantism and German philosophy. In spite of the violence of his assaults, it may also be said that his criticism did open many eyes to no few weaknesses in the ecclesiastical interpretation of traditional values. He was, above all, responsible for debunking its hypocritical and mendacious aspects and, not least, the inclination to amass power, something he had already condemned in similar fashion with regard to the ascetic priest.

He criticized the Christian view of God in just as subjective and extreme a way, proclaiming the Christian God as the "declaration of war on life" itself:

> "The Christian conception of God – God as god of the sick, God as a spider, God as a spirit – is one of the most corrupt conceptions of the divine ever attained on earth.... God as the declaration of war

52 Ges. W. vol. VIII, p. 219; CM vol. 6, p. 171, § 5.

against life, against nature, against the will to live! God – the formula for every slander against 'this world,' for every lie about the 'beyond'! God – the deification of nothingness, the will to nothingness pronounced holy!"[53]

These and similar words can be regarded as expressing Nietzsche's obsession with the ideas and values of the worldly, and also as the reason for the later comment that the roots of the Christian God were to be found in the "hatred of the natural," which, in the end, resulted in Him turning into an emasculated arbiter of the good. Nietzsche's observation that such a castration was the equivalent of forfeiting all the possibilities associated with 'ascending life,' like strength, courage and pride, and replacing them with a "hybrid structure of naught, concept and contradiction," betrayed the same degree of aggression. "What would be the point of a god," Nietzsche exclaimed, "who knew nothing of wrath, revenge, envy, scorn, cunning and violence?"[54] He would be nothing other than the monstrous product of impotence and weakness, the very prototype of *décadence* !

Nietzsche may have hit the mark with some of his criticism of the Christian concept of God – such as its universal *repulse of nature and life* or the related *one-sided accentuation of goodness,* – but the viciousness of his absolute and uncompromising attacks had an alienating effect on his readers.

The Christian notion of associating a good God with their concept of God was, in Nietzsche's opinion, the perpetuation of a transformation that had already taken place in the early Jewish era: the pressure of Babylonian domination brought about what Nietzsche assumed to be a radical revaluation of religious ideas and of naturally generated, ethically founded concepts, whereby the natural order became completely deformed. Under the influence of the

53 Ges. W. vol. VIII/4, p. 235; CM vol. 6/3, p. 185, § 18.
54 Ges. W. vol. VIII/4, p. 232; CM vol. 6/3, p. 182, § 16.

Jewish priestly caste this order developed, Nietzsche went on, into a narrow-minded morality based on notions of justice and sin, which gradually extended its dominion to color the entire Christian view of the world.

> "*Morality* – no longer the expression of the conditions for the life and growth of a people, no longer its most basic instinct of life, but become abstract, become the antithesis of life – .... What is Jewish, what is Christian morality? Chance done out of its innocence; misfortune besmirched with the concept of 'sin': well-being as a danger, a 'temptation,' physiological indisposition poisoned with the worm of conscience...."[55]

Nietzsche's vindictive polemic continued by turning on the Christian Church, whose moral concepts, as he saw them, revealed a barbed intolerance of life and instinct as illustrated by the notions of the 'afterlife,' the 'Last Judgment,' the 'immortality of the soul,' the 'kingdom of God' and the 'filiation of God.'[56] His criticism included the Gospel of Christ, which instead of glad tidings of Jesus and His resurrection appeared much more to radiate a spirit of revenge and resentment.[57]

There was a certain incongruousness about Nietzsche's reservations regarding the ecclesiastical exegesis of the Redeemer, which he explained away as the negation of worldly existence. He interpreted not only the lessons of Christ's martyrdom and resurrection,[58] but also the doctrine of "personal immortality"[59] as fatal – both of these principles of faith established by the Apostle Paul and thus bound to awaken his hostility.

55  Ges. W. vol. VIII/4, p. 246; CM vol. 6/3, p. 194, § 25.
56  Ges. W. vol. VIII/4, p. 264; CM vol. 6/3, p. 210, § 38.
57  This passage is a reference to Paul 1, Cor. 1, 20ff.
58  Ges. W. vol. VIII/4, p. 269; CM vol. 6/3, p. 215, § 41.
59  Ges. W. vol. VIII/4, p. 271; CM vol. 6/3, p. 217, § 43.

"Paulus simply transposed the center of gravity of that whole existence *after* this existence – in the *lie* of the 'resurrected' Jesus. At bottom, he had no use at all for the life of the Redeemer – he needed the death on the cross *and* a little more...."[60]

All these Pauline teachings represented, as far as Nietzsche was concerned, evidence of an *attitude versus life, versus instinct, versus existence* in general.[61] By rejecting any life-enhancing outlook that aimed at vouchsafing the future, one was utterly renouncing the meaning of life; by transferring meaning into a world beyond, one must have been proceeding "inevitably *into nothingness.*" Or, put another way, the meaning of life is reduced to the formula: "To live so, that there is no longer any *sense* in living...."[62]

Nietzsche was careful to segregate from his criticism of Church doctrine his esteem for the personality of Jesus It was important for him to separate Jesus, the man, from the dogmatic view of Him. His words on the figure of Jesus are like an oasis in the desert when he praises Him as the revelation of a "new practice"[63] of living and of an advanced way of life. He regarded the meaning of the "glad tidings" in terms of *life lived from the inside,* which he primarily understood as a "state of the heart."[64]

"The faith which finds expression here is not a faith attained through struggle – it is there, it has been there from the beginning; it is, as it were, an infantilism that has receded into the spiritual.... Such a faith is not angry, does not reproach, does not resist: it does not bring the 'sword' – .... Nor does this faith formulate itself: it *lives,* it resists all formulas."[65]

60  Ges. W. vol. VIII/4, p. 271; CM vol. 6/3, p. 216, § 42.
61  Ges. W. vol. VIII/4, p. 271; CM vol. 6/3, p. 217, § 43.
62  *Ibid.*
63  Ges. W. vol. VIII/4, p. 258; CM vol. 6/3, p. 205, § 33.
64  Ges. W. vol. VIII/4, p. 260; CM vol. 6/3, p. 207, § 34.
65  Ges. W. vol. VIII/4, p. 256; CM vol. 6/3, p. 203, § 32.

He resisted Renan's efforts to make a heroic genius out of Jesus in his book on Jesus' life,[66] and stated that it was the sublimity, the sickness and the infantilism of Christ[67] that made Him so attractive a figure. In the bequest, we can read:

> "Jesus is the *counterpart of a genius:* he is an *idiot.* One feels his inability to comprehend a reality.... Jesus is unheroic in his deepest instincts: he never fights: he who sees something like a hero in him, like Renan, has vulgarized the type to the point of unrecognizability."[68]

The word 'idiot' must not be misunderstood. What Nietzsche actually had in mind was a turn of phrase derived from Dostoyevski's book, *The Idiot,* a work with which he became familiar only after 1881. Nevertheless, the word 'idiot' disturbed Nietzsche's sister so much that she removed it from the first edition of *The Antichrist.*

As a consequence of a deeply inward attitude, Nietzsche explained, Jesus was completely unadapted to civilization and the state:

> "He speaks only of the innermost: 'life' or 'truth' or 'light' is his word for the innermost...."[69]

And in the bequest, Nietzsche made it even more clear:

> "If there is one thing I understand about this great symbolist, it is that he only saw and acknowledged *inner realities,* that he understood the *rest* (everything natural, historical, political) merely as signs and an

---

66 Joseph Ernst Renan (1832-1892), known for the book on the life of Jesus Nietzsche mentioned (1864).
67 Ges. W. vol. VIII/4, p. 256; CM vol. 6/3, p. 203, § 32.
68 CM vol. 13, p. 237 (1888). The Greek for 'idiot' is *the special one.*
69 Ges. W. vol. VIII/4, p. 257; CM vol. 6/3, p. 204, § 32.

opportunity to draw parallels, *not* as reality, not as a 'true world'...."[70]

Nietzsche's extreme opposition to seeing in Jesus the type of the redeemer is expressed in the following passage from the *Antichrist:*

> "This 'bringer of glad tidings' dies as he had lived, as he had taught – *not* to 'redeem men' but to show how one must live."[71]

In contrast to the "one Christ who died on the cross," Nietzsche branded the whole of Christianity as the *embodiment of mendacity,* of "monstrousness and falsehood." In view of such a state of affairs, it seemed to him "indecent" to still "be a Christian" today. He was highly contemptuous of the Christian person of "today," whose impure breath, he said, was stifling him to death. It was the Christian's choice to keep to the Christian Gospel and reject the abysses of existence, fleeing into a mode of thought insistent on the good and the fact "that the good should renounce and oppose the evil down to its ultimate roots"[72] – to Nietzsche's mind, a perilous outlook. As he most forcefully stressed, by thus *ignoring the discordance of life,* "which has in its instincts both Yes and No,"[73] one was courting endless miscalculations and errors. Whenever the "Christian person" believed he was doing good, he was doing precisely the opposite, evil. The results of equating the individual with the light side of morality were most aptly captured in the next aphorism:

---

70 CM vol. 13, p. 155. Nietzsche went on: "Thus the son of man is not a concrete personage of history but an 'eternal factor,' a psychological symbol not trapped in time...." Here Nietzsche displays an astonishing grasp of symbol.
71 Ges. W. vol. VIII/4, p. 261; CM vol. 6/3, p. 207, § 35.
72 Ges. W. vol. XV, p. 397; CM vol. 13, p. 473.
73 *Ibid.*

248

"... the more radically one desires the one, the more radically one achieves precisely the other."[74]

Nietzsche was quick to realize that the concepts of good and evil were psychologically conditioned and constantly appeared as *polarities,* so that it was impossible to think 'Yes' without also thinking 'No' at the same time. It was just as unlikely to want to be 'good' without the parallel desire to 'act negatively.' Life as it is actually lived, shows that

> "... for every strong and natural species of man, love and hate, gratitude and revenge, good nature and anger, affirmative acts and negative acts, belong together. One is good on condition one also knows how to be evil; one is evil because otherwise one would not understand to be good...."[75]

And in the bequest, he continued just as impressively:

> "... what good is it to hold with all one's strength that war is evil, not to do harm, not to desire to negate! One wages war nonetheless! One cannot do otherwise!"[76]

This view, described by Nietzsche as "complementary value concepts,"[77] puts the relationship between good and evil in an utterly new light that illuminated the one-sidedness of an attitude reducing man "to this half-sided efficiency."[78] This assertion highlights a significant psychological phenomenon: namely, that the more one-sided a conscious attitude is, the more one-sided the opposite inclination will be.[79]

74  Ges. W. vol. XVI, p. 377; CM vol. 12, p. 426. See p. 207f.
75  Ges. W. vol. XV, p. 396; CM vol. 13, p. 471f.
76  Ges. W. vol. XV, p. 398; CM vol. 13, p. 473.
77  Ges. W. vol. XV, p. 397; CM vol. 13, p. 473.
78  Ges. W. vol. XV, p. 397; CM vol. 13, p. 472.
79  L. Frey-Rohn, *Das Böse,* p. 168.

Fear of what the collective sees as 'evil,' Nietzsche tells us, also stood behind Christian hostility to science[80]: the resistance to 'knowing' that Old Testament man felt when forbidden to eat from the tree of knowledge is still very much alive. Knowledge was forbidden as the "germ of all sin," it was original sin itself. In its very first verses, the Bible contained "the whole of the psychology of the priest, his rejection of science." Nietzsche's embittered soul even went as far as to depict the entire moral world order as an "invention" directed against science and culture. Though what he said may still be relevant to certain orthodox religious circles, it cannot be denied that it went far beyond the reality of things.

Nietzsche considered Christian faith to be a further obstacle to the objective identification of the truth and so related to the previously examined rejection of worldly reality. What he was alluding to was the "old moral problem of knowledge and faith" he had first recognized in Socrates. He did not hesitate to write:

"Faith as an imperative is the *veto* against science – in practice, the lie at any price."[81]

Faith demanded that the theologian "closed his eyes once and for all so as not to suffer at the sight of irredeemable falsity." Luther seemed to him to be a case in point who was "only a cloak, a pretext, a *screen* behind which the instincts played their game...."[82] Nietzsche saw in faith, above all, "not wanting to know what is true":[83]

"By lie I mean: wishing *not* to see something that one does see: wishing not to see something *as* one sees it."[84]

80  Ges. W. vol. VIII/4, p. 281; CM vol. 6/3, p. 225, § 47.
81  Ges. W. vol. VIII/4, p. 283; CM vol. 6/3, p. 227, § 48.
82  Ges. W. vol. VIII/4, p. 266; CM vol. 6/3, p. 212, § 39.
83  Ges. W. vol. VIII/4, p. 290; CM vol. 6/3, p. 233, § 52.
84  Ges. W. vol. VIII/4, p. 296; CM vol. 6/3, p. 238, § 55.

All the big phrases, such as 'the will of God' and the 'Holy Book,' could be put down to "the conditions *under* which the priest preserves his power."[85] His intention was to dupe mankind into believing he was the "mouthpiece of God,"[86] thereby keeping intact the "holy lie":

> "The priest, too, knows as well as anybody else that there is no longer any 'God,' any 'sinner,' any 'redeemer' – that 'free will' and 'moral world order' are *lies:* ... All the concepts of the church have been recognized for what they are, the most malignant counterfeits that exist, the aim of which is to devalue nature and natural values; the priest himself has been recognized for what he is: the most dangerous kind of parasite, the real poison-spider of life."[87]

This comment closes the cycle of Nietzsche's thought. What Nietzsche ascribed to the priest applied *eo ipso* to Paul:

> "His need was for power; in Paul the priest wanted power once again – he could use only concepts, doctrines, symbols with which one tyrannizes masses and forms herds...."[88]

Was this not also partly an allusion to Nietzsche, or rather *the shadow brother in himself?* Could not his condemnation of Pauline doctrine equally represent projections of his own fantasies of power? Was it not his secret goal to himself find resurrection and bring salvation in the form of the figure of Zarathustra, the Persian Saoshant? And what about his uncontrolled attack on the priestly lie? Had he not admonished the art of play-acting in the magician's poem,

85 Ges. W. vol. VIII/4, p. 297; CM vol. 6/3, p. 239, § 55.
86 *Ibid.*
87 Ges. W. vol. VIII/4, p. 264; CM vol. 6/3, p. 210, § 38.
88 Ges. W. vol. VIII/4, p. 271; CM vol. 6/3, p. 216, § 42.

and in so doing, launched a hidden assault on his own pretence of greatness?[89]

He himself had noted down in *Beyond Good and Evil:*

> "Every philosophy also *conceals* a philosophy; every opinion is also a hideout, every word also a mask."[90]

Just as, psychologically considered, every overstated assertion concealed a corresponding repressed element, so Nietzsche's emotional response to the treacherousness of Paul, that is to say, his turn away from Jewish law,[91] might also hide Nietzsche's own betrayal of his Christian heritage. His hate-filled rejection of what Paul did in raising Christianity to a world religion could, from this point of view, be judged as Nietzsche's own unfulfilled fantasies of power. Similarly, his fanatical hatred of the Christian God and Christianity overall represented a weak spot in in psychical make-up, connoting deep-rooted, gnawing suffering; namely, *suffering at the disproportion between the unfulfilled drive for greatness,* on the one hand, and an equally *insurmountable feeling of physical and mental impotence* on the other. We can recognize in this conflict the problem of a man on the brink of being overwhelmed by the shadow side of his personality.

The pathological eruption of repressed desire for greatness and power is amply demonstrated in the very last notes he wrote, directly before his collapse: "The empire itself is a lie, of course: no Hohenzollern, no Bismarck ever thought of Germany...." And later on, he writes: "... after the old God has been abolished, I will be prepared to rule the world...."[92] It is therefore with the utmost caution that we must approach these remarks.

The dimensions of his bitterness at the failure of all his

89 See p. 154.
90 Ges. W. vol. VII/1, p. 268; CM vol. 5/1, p. 234, § 289.
91 Ges. W. vol. IV, p. 67; CM vol. 3/1, p. 67, § 68.
92 CM vol. 13, p. 646. These statements, which already betray the onset of madness, were made in December 1888, just before his breakdown.

efforts to renew culture is openly shown in the lament at the end of the *Antichrist:*

> "*All in vain!* Overnight nothing but a memory."[93]

> "The whole meaning of the ancient world *in vain:* ... I have no word to express my feelings about something so tremendous ... the whole meaning of the ancient world in vain!"[94]

His disgust at the present made him miss all the more the classical values of "nobility of taste and instinct" and "the great Yes to all things" he admired so much.[95] In contrast to *Twilight of the Idols,* in which the memory of the Dionysian wisdom of the mysteries inspired him to new hope, in *The Antichrist* there was an undertone of dull despair. *Melancholic resignation* at the *loss of the values of antiquity, irreconcilable hatred of the Christian domination of the world* and *flight into an overvalued self* were combined in frightful outburst:

> "I call Christianity the one great curse, the one great corruption, the one great instinct of revenge, for which no means is poisonous, stealthy, subterranean, *small* enough – I call it the one immortal blemish of mankind."[96]

The clarity and sharpness of his line of thought and the fascinating brilliance of his style could do nothing to hold back the overpowering impression of extreme impotence and feebleness behind the unbridled and unrestrained vehemence. The degree of arrogance apparent in the concluding statements of *The Antichrist* strongly indicates the catastrophe to come:

93  Ges. W. vol. VIII/4, p. 308; CM vol. 6/3, p. 248, § 59.
94  Ges. W. vol. VIII/4, p. 307; CM vol. 6/3, p. 247, § 59.
95  Ges. W. vol. VIII/4, p. 308; CM vol. 6/3, p. 248.
96  Ges. W. vol. VIII/4, p. 313; CM vol. 6/3, p. 253, § 62.

"And time is reckoned from the *dies nefastus* with which this calamity began – after the *first* day of Christianity! *Why not rather after its last day? After today?* Revaluation of all values!"[97]

There can be no doubt about the pathological nature of the document added to the work bearing the name 'Antichrist.' However, since the exact date of writing cannot be placed, the connection between it and the book of the same name is a shaky one.

The document reads as follows:

"Law against Christianity: war to the death against vice: the vice is Christianity. Enforced on the day of salvation, on the first day of the Year One (on 30 September 1888 of the wrong calendar)."[98]

Nietzsche's hopes of establishing a new aeon had been smashed. His expectations of overcoming nihilism to found a new order of values guaranteed by the descent of the great man had come to nothing. He had no option but to withdraw his projections onto the world and *turn his interest backwards onto his own person.*

In a manner similar to that seen in his fascination for the wisdom of the mysteries, Nietzsche's absorption in himself and his greatness led to a *regression to archaic features of the personality.*[99] In psychopathological terms, this condition can be described as a relapse to an infantile stage of autoerotism.[100] Applying Jungian psychology, I would explain what happened as an *inflation of the self,* or, put another way, as a manifestation of the 'second' or greater

97  Ges. W. vol. VIII/4, p. 314; CM vol. 6/3, p. 253, § 62.
98  In the Kröner edition, this passage has been dropped, while Colli-Montinari have included it in the *Antichrist* writings. CM vol. 6/3, p. 254.
99  See C.G. Jung, *Symbole der Wandlung* [*Symbols of Transformation*], Ges. W. vol. V (C.W. vol. 5).
100 A psychoanalyst would refer to this as a regression to the level of primary narcissism (Freud, Ges. W. vol. VIII, p. 297; S.E. vol. 8).

unconscious personality that is always latently present. Both the pronounced lucidity of Nietzsche prior to his breakdown and his increasing *estrangement from reality,* which ended with a narcissistic glorification of himself wholly unrelated to the world of men, may well indicate just such an activation of his inner being.

That this process would abruptly finish with his mental breakdown was discernible both in his so-called 'insane jottings'[101] and in his bequest. The situation is also coincidental with the fact that, at the same time, a cerebral-pathological factor had emerged that in all probability speeded up the process.

## VI. *Ecce homo: Or How One Becomes What One Is*

The archetypal figure at the root of Nietzsche's final work, *Ecce homo,*[102] is the god Dionysus. At the very outset, Nietzsche describes himself as a "disciple of the philosopher Dionysus,"[103] and the work closes with Dionysus' declaration of war on the crucified Christ. Nietzsche's identification with the symbol of the self reaches its climax here: the entire piece is the expression of his self-enhancement, his untimeliness and his corresponding withdrawal from contemporary events. Loathing for humanity alternates with glorification of his own greatness and work. In a letter to Brandes, he writes:

---

101 After his breakdown Nietzsche wrote various letters to Cosima Wagner, Jacob Burckhardt and Peter Gast, which, though megalomaniac and unrealistic, were still intellectually coherent.
See p. 156.

102 The existing work was published posthumously and based on the original manuscript plus several later contributions and emendations, which detracts somewhat from its authenticity. It is, therefore, advisable to ask whether the individual references made are commensurate with those publications Nietzsche himself was responsible for.

103 First mentioned in *Beyond Good and Evil,* see p. 193f.

"I have told the story of myself with a cynicism that will become world-historical. The book is called *Ecce homo* and is an unscrupulous assassination of the crucified Christ; it ends in thunder and lightning strikes against everything Christian or infected with Christianity, which destroys one's hearing and sight. I am after all the first psychologist of Christianity and can, as the old artillery man I am, bring up heavy artillery no enemy of Christianity has ever supposed existed...."[104]

*Ecce homo* stirs ambivalent feelings in the reader: on the one hand, this passionately written confession, described by its author as the "highest superlative of dynamite," has an electrifying effect; on the other, its high-handed tone and totally unrealistic self-adoration only succeeds in repelling us.

He constantly finds new ways to accentuate his merits, attributing them to his "incomparable father"[105] and protracted sickness.[106] Both of these factors did indeed determine his life to a certain degree. His father seems to have remained an archetypal figure of intellectual greatness all Nietzsche's life, and was the impulse behind the important projections made by him onto such significant personalities as Schopenhauer, Wagner, Burckhardt and Rée.[107] To the

---

104 Letter to Georg Brandes of 20 November 1888. He was Professor of Literature in Copenhagen.

105 Ges. W. vol. XV, p. 15; CM vol. 6, p. 269.

106 Ges. W. vol. XV, p. 18; CM vol. 6, p. 272.

107 This is not inconsistent with what he mysteriously writes at the beginning of *Ecce homo:* "I am, to express it in the form of a riddle, already dead as my father, while as my mother I am still living and becoming old" Ges. W. vol. XV, p. 9; CM vol. 6, p. 264. He adds that his own life took a downward turn at the age of 36, in the same way as that of his father, who died at 36. Indeed at 36 (1879), Nietzsche did give up his Basle Professorship, and from then on led the life of a wanderer, at the same time beginning his assault on rationalism, reason and science. He increasingly cut himself off from public life (the world of his father) and allowed the unconscious, inner *daimon* (the mother's world) to take over.

256

same extent, it was his illnesses, and especially the suffering they caused him, which secured and fortified his instinct[108] – by which he meant the art of overcoming the self and being selfish[109] – an attitude which instilled a spirit of belligerence. The cleverness of his instinct, the "psychological wisdom," he put down to the intuitive grasp of what was the proper nourishment for strengthening the spirit. He even held an appropriate situation and climate[110] responsible for giving his spirit a subtle understanding of genuine culture and writing. Last, but not least, it was from his innermost instinct that his deep-rooted aversion to the cult of concepts sprang, a cult that neglected and despised the basic circumstances of life.

Alongside the panegyric to his infallible instinct, Nietzsche praised his originality as a writer. With a display of unparalleled arrogance, he extolled his writings for their serenity, their sophistication and their cynicism:[111]

> "… for I come from heights that no bird ever reached in its flight, I know abysses into which no foot ever strayed."[112]

He stressed that it was part of his uniqueness to possess in addition "the art of *great* rhythm, the *great* style of long periods."[113] He sought to assuage the nagging feeling that his works were misunderstood and ignored by mentioning how radically new his experiences were, and so, too, the language in which they were couched:

---

108 Ges. W. vol. XV, p. 18; CM vol. 6, p. 272.
109 Ges. W. vol. XV, p. 43f; CM vol. 6, p. 293f.
   Selfishness was, as he had already demonstrated in *Zarathustra,* a 'vice' essential to self-realization, while in self-overcoming, he saw a quality that was indispensable to the creative process.
110 Ges. W. vol. XV, p. 30f; CM vol. 6, p. 281f.
111 Ges. W. vol. XV, p. 54; CM vol. 6, p. 302.
112 *Ibid.*
113 Ges. W. vol. XV, p. 56; CM vol. 6, p. 304f.

"What one lacks access to from experience, one will have no ear for..."[114]

– a subtle psychological insight that simultaneously criticized the predilection of certain scholars for abstractions.

It appeared to him to be just as unique that his work should have been the first in contemporary philosophy about which its author could claim "that a psychologist without equal speaks from my writings."[115] Yet when he also maintained that he was the first psychologist of the "eternally feminine," he may justifiably be challenged; whilst allowing for the reverence with which he greeted the divine in woman (Ariadne), he was, nevertheless, constantly attracted to the fluttering "spangled skirts of the daughters of the desert," the "little beasts of prey."[116]

It was also an important factor that he possessed a sure *instinct for intellectual qualities* and for what was known as *greatness*. He venerated Heine for "that divine malice without which [he himself could] never contemplate perfection," and Shakespeare for his conception of Julius Caesar and the profundity of his understanding. He had already called Goethe a European phenomenon. The Parisian artists were equally close to his heart, for they "possessed *delicatesse* in all five of the artistic senses ... and the fingers for nuances." Although he had no great love for German art because it "ruined culture," he could still retrospectively state that he had breathed a sigh of relief on his first encounter with Richard Wagner: "Wagner had genuine greatness." Despite his repeated attacks on the latter's personality throughout the eighties, Nietzsche had to concede that Wagner was unique. Similarly, he expressed his deepest gratitude for the unforgettable days of their friendship. He wrote in *Ecce homo:*

114  Ges. W. vol. XV, p. 51; CM vol. 6, p. 300.
115  Ges. W. vol. XV, p. 57; CM vol. 6, p. 305.
116  Ges. W. vol. XV, p. 58; CM vol. 6, p. 306.

"I'd let go cheap the whole rest of my human relationships: I should not want to give away out of my life at any price the days of Tribschen – days of trust, of cheerfulness, of sublime accidents, of *profound* moments."[117]

He even admitted to himself that he could not have done without Wagner's music,[118] which sustained him in his youth and which, in contrast to 'the case of Wagner,' he designated the greatest antidote to everything German. Such a change of mood, that is to say, such a coexistence of opposite emotional states, was by no means unusual for Nietzsche. It was the essence of his innermost being to experience and suffer the *'Yes and the No' of his instinctual impulses.* The contradiction between passion for the philosophical idea and enthusiasm for art, like the conflict between *logos* and *eros,* also fit into this pattern.

Apart from the high profile accorded the cult of power, and leaving aside considerations of the authenticity of instinct and of the genius of the intellect, one wonders *what, in fact, constituted the actual essence of human greatness?* We find a hint of an answer in the early work, *Fate and History,* in which he emphasizes the cooperation of "strength of will and fatality" in association with the great man. An aphorism of the eighties shows us what he must have had in mind:

117 Ges. W. vol. XV, p. 37; CM vol. 6, p. 288.
118 In keeping with the optimistic spirit of *Ecce homo,* he mentioned: "From the moment when there was a piano score of *Tristan* ... I was a Wagnerian.... But to this day I am still looking for work that equals the dangerous fascination and the gruesome and sweet infinity of *Tristan....* The world is poor for anyone who has never been sick enough for this 'voluptuousness of hell.'... That in which we are related – that we have suffered more profoundly, also from each other, than men of this century are capable of suffering – will link our names again and again, eternally; and as certainly as Wagner is merely a misunderstanding among Germans, just as certainly I am and always shall be." Ges. W. vol. XV, p. 39; CM vol. 6, p. 289.

259

"Before destiny strikes us, one should treat it as a child and – give it the cane: but once it has struck us, one should try to love it."[119]

In *The Gay Science,* he had admitted that he would only say 'Yes' from then on, a confession made with joyful thanks for having recovered from his recent illness; in *Ecce homo,* it is the *mystical meaning* of his attitude that once more emerges, demanding for 'greatness' a mode of behavior capable of bringing together the incongruities of self-conscious willing, on the one hand, and the affirmation of existence on the other.

"My formula for greatness in a human being is *amor fati:* that one wants nothing to be different, not forward, not backward, not in all eternity. Not merely bear what is necessary, still less conceal it – all idealism is mendaciousness in the face of what is necessary – but *love* it."[120]

Since the overwhelming vision of the 'eternal recurrence' in 1881, such moments of inner rapture, when the second, deeper personality in Nietzsche seemed perceptible, had become rather rare occurrences. The vision of the recurrence was the first to expose to him the *numen* of an undivided affirmation of destiny and its binding nature. The dithyramb of Dionysus, entitled, 'Fame and Eternity,' in all probability composed a few months before his breakdown, might well describe a similar mental condition.[121]

119  Ges. W. vol. XIII, p. 323; CM vol. 10, p. 208.
120  Ges. W. vol. XV, p. 48; CM vol. 6, p. 297.
121  The *Dithyrambs of Dionysus* were, according to Colli and Montinari, partly written in the *Zarathustra* period and partly in the Turin period, i.e., in the autumn of 1888, three months before his collapse. They reveal the other side of Nietzsche, his poetic and artistic leanings. It may well be another indication of his fear of exposing his innermost self, one related to the extreme reticence he displayed to the very last, that these poems were only prepared for publication at the end of 1888.

...

260

"Soft!
Of great things – I *see* something great! –
one should keep silent
or speak greatly:
I look above me –
there seas of light are rolling:
oh night, oh silence, oh deathly silent uproar!....
I see a sign –
from the farthest distance
slowly glittering a constellation sinks towards me....
Highest star of being!
Eternal tablet of forms!
*You* come to me? –
. . . .
Shield of Necessity!
Highest star of being!
– what no longing attains
– no denial defiles,
eternally Yes of being:
eternally am I thy Yes:
*for I love thee, O eternity!* "[122]

In *Ecce homo,* Nietzsche's tendency to become absorbed with himself and exaggerate the importance of his own personality became all too obvious; yet, it is also true to say that the following summary glossing his basic conceptions also proved the exceptional clarity and lucidity of his mind. The analyses of his works are amongst the most significant things he has left us, and they shed a great deal of new light on his spiritual and intellectual progress. It is unnecessary to go any further into this, since I have already treated his main thoughts and motivations at the respective stages of his work.

As we can judge from his other writings, it was only in *The Case of Wagner* that Nietzsche shook off his reserve, with the consequence that he was then more violently prone to his pent-up aggressions.

122  Ges. W. vol. VIII, p. 435f ('Fame and Eternity,' 1888); CM vol. 6, p. 404f.

In the final section, 'Why I am a destiny,' Nietzsche refers to his *world-historical importance,* thus illustrating the fact that he had lost his grasp on reality and become completely immersed in himself. The excessive degree of his self-glorification and his extreme conviction that he had a mission to fulfil are both embarrassing and repulsive. Just as unrealistic is a statement in the bequest to the effect that the arrogance he was fully aware of possessing should not be interpreted negatively, but rather as positive proof of his greatness – in other words, because he stood by himself and his beliefs. In the last section of *Ecce homo,* we find his overvaluation of himself at its strongest:

"I know my fate. One day my name will be associated with the memory of something tremendous – a crisis without equal on earth, the most profound collision of conscience, a decision which was conjured up *against* everything that had been believed, demanded, hallowed so far. I am no man, I am dynamite. – Yet for all that, there is nothing in me of a founder of religion.... I have a terrible fear that one day I will be pronounced *holy:* ... I do not want to be a holy man: sooner even a buffoon. – ... But my truth is *terrible;* for so far one has called *lies* truth. *Revaluation of all values:* that is my formula for an act of supreme self-examination on the part of humanity, become flesh and genius in me.... I am a bringer of glad tidings like no one before me; I know tasks of such elevation that any notion of them has been lacking so far; only beginning with me are there hopes again. For all that, I am necessarily also the man of calamity. For when truth enters into a fight with the lies of millennia, we shall have upheavals, a convulsion of earthquakes, a moving of mountains and valleys, the like of which has never been dreamed of. The concept of politics will have merged entirely with a war of spirits; all power structures of the old society will have been exploded – all of them are based on lies: there will be wars the like of which have never yet been on earth. It is only beginning with me that the earth knows *great politics.* "[123]

Nietzsche prides himself in being the first *immoralist,* the "annihilator *par excellence.*" The expression 'immoralist' covers two sorts of negation: firstly, that of the hitherto pre-eminent type of the good man, and secondly, that of Christian morals.[124] Insofar as he deals with *the psychology of goodness,* Nietzsche stresses the lie as the necessary prerequisite of anything good; "not *wanting* to see at any price"[125] is the condition of its existence, and "good men never speak the truth, they are mendacious to the core." Unlike these, it was, according to Nietzsche, the type of man envisaged by Zarathustra that could conceive of reality as it essentially was: "all that is terrible and questionable in it – *only in that way can man attain greatness.*"[126]

Turning to the other of his negations, that of *Christian morals,* he counted it as one of his greatest achievements to have discovered "the antinature of morality."[127] Part and parcel of this was contempt for the instincts and the mendacious invention of a 'spirit' to ruin the body, to make sexuality unclean and to adore a morality of un-selfing that revealed a will to the end.[128] In the same way, traditional morality had come up with the concept of 'God' in order to oppose life, and likewise the concepts of the 'afterlife' and the 'true world,' with the intention of devaluing the existence of this one and only real world. He brought his desperate assault on Christian morals to a close with the following words:

123 Ges. W. vol. XV, p. 116, 117; CM vol. 6, p. 366.
124 Ges. W. vol. XV, p. 119; CM vol. 6, p. 367.
125 Ges. W. vol. XV, p. 119; CM vol. 6, p. 368.
126 Ges. W. vol. XV, p. 122; CM vol. 6, p. 370.
127 Ges. W. vol. XV, p. 124; CM vol. 6, p. 372.
128 Ges. W. vol. XV, p. 124.

"Finally – this is what is most terrible of all – the concept of the *good* man signifies that one sides with all that is weak, sick, failure, suffering of itself – all that ought to perish: the principle of selection is crossed – an ideal is fabricated from the contradiction against the proud and well-turned-out human being who says Yes, who is sure of the future, who guarantees the future – and he is now called *evil*. – And all this was believed, *as morality! – Écrasez l'infâme!*" [129]

This, the last document he wrote for publication, demonstrates both the *strongest possible claims to power* and the *most hopeless feeling of impotence:* on the one hand, the most extreme form of inner distress, on the other, an exaggerated sense of triumph. It was clearly the *suffering of an ego overpowered by the greater personality.* The unsatisfied longing for a well-bred hero to vouchsafe the future found its compensation in sullen revolt against everything weak and Christian (for him, the very embodiment of weakness).

His schizophrenic condition is unmistakable. The letter below leaves no further doubt in our minds as to the split in his personality. It is addressed to Peter Gast:

"*Ecce homo* so exceeds the term 'literature' that even Nature itself cannot provide an image: it veritably blasts the *history* of mankind into two pieces – the highest superlative of dynamite...."[130]

The work ended with a threat reminiscent of a battle cry:

"Have I been understood? – *Dionysus versus the Crucified....*" [131]

129  Ges. W. vol. XV, p. 126, 127.
130  Letter of 9 December 1888.
131  Ges. W. vol. XV, p. 127; CM vol. 6, p. 374.

This declaration of war shows the whole of Nietzsche's writing to be a *pugnacious and most painful confrontation between the Dionysian spark in his soul and the spiritual heritage of his Christian ancestry.* Participants in this religious drama of self-destruction are the Crucified, he whom destiny has sacrificed, and his opponent Dionysus, the god that proclaims the recurrence. Nietzsche regarded both types as martyrs, but with conflicting ambitions. Thus we read in the bequest:

"The god on the cross is a curse on life, a signpost to seek redemption from life: – Dionysus cut to pieces is a *promise* of life: it will be reborn and return from destruction."[132]

Nietzsche was, in essence, both: the eternally reborn, shredded Dionysus and the crucified servant of God. Both of these embraced the two *complementary aspects of the archetypal image of God and the archetype of the self.* In his work, Nietzsche struggled to shape a new image of God that would do justice to both sides of his personality, but he did not have sufficient inner strength to bear the strain. He could not find the power required to give form to his vision of the future, neither in the picture of the world drawn by his contemporaries, nor within himself. Over-stressed by the demonic demands imposed by the self, his ego was overcome by the concept of greatness. Nietzsche was incapable of withstanding the pressure from inside: his search for himself ended in insanity. His conscious fate was sealed by the notion that he himself was God.

The breakdown was triggered by the fateful event involving a cab horse in Turin. In Janz, we read that Nietzsche allegedly threw his arms around the neck of an old horse he thought was being mistreated by a coachman and embraced it in tears. After this event, which took place at the very start of 1889, his lapse into insanity was rapid.

132  Ges. W. vol. XVI, p. 392; CM vol. 13, p. 267.

The so-called 'insane jottings' originated at this time, some of them signed 'Dionysus,' some, 'the Crucified'; in each case, the signature is remarkably consistent with the tenor of the text. As Werner Ross writes, they are "mad and profound, uncanny and splendid."[133] In them, Nietzsche not only airs the secret of 'Ariadne,' but also the lasting impression Jacob Burckhardt made on his life. In a letter of 4 January 1889, he wrote:

"Now you are – my friend – our greatest great teacher: for I, together with Ariadne, only have to be the golden balance of all things, we have in each part those who are above us ... Dionysus."[134]

In a letter written on the 5th of January, Ariadne is practically identified with Cosima Wagner:

"The rest is for Frau Cosima ... Ariadne.... Now and then magic is performed – ...."[135]

The next letter is dated the 6th of January and addressed to Jacob Burckhardt. It reveals a most disturbed state of godlike delusion:

"Dear Professor, in the end I would much rather be a Basle professor than God; but I have not dared push my private egoism so far as to desist for its sake from the creation of the world. You see, one must make sacrifices, however and wherever one lives."[136]

The letter to Peter Gast of the 4th of January betrays inner transfiguration and a mystical blissfulness:

133 Werner Ross, *Der ängstliche Adler,* p. 781.
134 Curt Janz, *Nietzsche,* p. 28
135 *Ibid.*
136 Werner Ross, *Der ängstliche Adler,* p. 781.

"To my maestro Pietro. Sing me a new song: the world is transfigured and all the heavens are full of joy."[137]

Transfiguration had been characteristic of Nietzsche's mystical experiences, as we have seen. These had always revealed to him the happy side of his night and shadow personality. At the same time as *Zarathustra,* such experiences had primarily revolved around the unfathomability of the 'great noon.' The reader is reminded of the following passage in *Zarathustra:*

> "A drop of dew? A haze and fragrance of eternity? Do you not hear it? Do you not smell it? Just now my world became perfect; midnight too is noon...."[138]

On another occasion, he was inspired to stress the bewitching quiet of the midday hour, as well as the "cheerful, dreadful abyss of noon";[139] both the perfection of the "golden round ring" and, simultaneously, the sighs of a stung heart. His vision of the inner companion – Zarathustra – alludes to the mystical union of darkness and light and occurs during the 'Feast of feasts,' at which life and death are inextricably interwoven. In the years that ensued, it was the thought of becoming one with Dionysus that carried him with "the triumphant Yes to life beyond death and change" and his fear.[140] All of these mystical experiences can be seen in terms of Nietzsche's second personality breaking through: they were always impressively raptur-

---

137 Letter from Nietzsche to Peter Gast. The last existing handwritten statement by Nietzsche, dated 1890 – a period in which his mind was seldom lucid –, has a curious ring: "I am pleased, my dear, beloved lama, that according to your letter you are well, my little pet ... heartfelt – cordial – greetings from your confrère frère Friedrich Nietzsche, Naumburg/Saale, 13 August 1890."
138 Ges. W. vol. VI, p. 469; CM vol. 4, p. 402.
139 Ges. W. vol. VI, p. 404; CM vol. 4, p. 345.
140 Ges. W. vol. VIII, p. 172; CM vol. 6, p. 159. See Karl Loewith: *Nietzsches Philosophie der ewigen Wiederkehr,* p. 110, 112.

ous, but rarely reached the *level of full consciousness*. It was for this reason that Nietzsche could never bridge the *deep gulf in his existence between its conscious and unconscious dimensions*. Madness had the last word. The secret behind the ecstatic content of his last letter to Peter Gast remained inscrutable: could it be that his second, mystical personality had entered the 'well of eternity'? Had Nietzsche found his way beyond awareness and knowledge?

In conclusion, I would like to quote some verses from the dithyramb of Dionysius bearing the title, 'The Sun Sinks.' Revised shortly before *Ecce homo* was completed, it is a poem about death written from the depths of the soul, and, as such, a moving and timeless document:

> "You shall not thirst much longer,
> scorched heart!
> A promise is in the air,
> from mouths unknown it wafts to me
> – great coolness comes ...
> ....
> Stay strong, brave heart!
> Do not ask why.
> ....
> Gilded cheerfulness, come!
> sweetest, secretest
> foretaste of death!
> – Did I run my course too quickly?
> Only now, when my foot has grown weary,
> does your glance overtake me,
> does your *happiness* overtake me.
> Only playing if waves all around.
> Whatever was hard
> has sunk into blue oblivion –
> my boat now lies idle.
> Storm and voyaging – all forgotten now!
> Desire and hope have drowned,
> smooth lie soul and sea.

Seventh solitude!
Never such sweet
security, never such
sunlight warmth.
– Does the ice of my summit still glow?
Silver, light, a fish
my little craft now swims out...."[141]

141  Ges. W. vol. VIII, p. 426ff; CM vol. 4, p. 395ff.

# EPILOGUE

*A Concluding Assessment of Nietzsche's Life and Work*

Nietzsche's name conjures up two seemingly contradictory ideas in me: on the one hand, the image of someone inexorably in search of himself and God,[1] on the other, the impression of an explosive force that blew apart the spiritual and intellectual world. In proclaiming the death of God and in his anticipation of the overman, he openly announced his goal of creating a godlike being. And by challenging tradition and the principles of conventional authority to do battle, he emerged as a revolutionary spirit leading an assault upon the values of his age. His aim was to fashion a new image of the world embracing both its Dionysian source and the heights and depths of human existence. Setting aside all the patterns of thought hitherto applied, he followed his conviction that he had been chosen to perform a certain duty, – the renewal of the seat of the divine, which ecclesiastical doctrine had let fall into ruin. I do not see it as relevant whether we agree with Jaspers' view that this represented a substitute for the old image of God, or with Heidegger's contention that this was a new "principle of establishing value."

Without going too far into the unfathomable and inscrutable aspects of human destiny, we can still trace influ-

[1] See p. 147.

270

ences that worked upon his personality and world of ideas. In the personal sphere, it was indubitably the premature death of his father, which Nietzsche continued to depict as the most painful, albeit most beneficial, event of his life, even in the latter stages of his writing. Since the paternal image could not be nurtured in the strictly ethical and pious femininity of his home, it was repressed into the unconscious. At constant readiness to be projected onto suitable personalities, it lived on in him as an archetypal image of the 'great man,' the 'hero' and 'redeemer of mankind,' finally overpowering the human ego itself.

Since earliest childhood, Nietzsche's spirit had been accustomed to the values of dutiful obedience and self-discipline, which were further entrenched by the monastic regime Schulpforta imposed on his pursuit of knowledge and cultural values. Part of the indefinable quality of his behavior was determined by the influence of a Christian heritage distinguished by a succession of eminent and largely clerical personalities. An equally imponderable factor was the effect of the spirit of the age on his sensitive nature, and, in particular, the effect of archetypal prefigurations of the future, rendered more or less impenetrable by the fluctuations of the time.

What crystallized from these most varied of impressions was Nietzsche's unending quest to discover the secret of man and his existence. His work, *Fate and History,* was an early testament to his search for God, for the essence of being and of the world. It casts light on the depth and inevitability of his destiny. His unerring exploration of ever new approaches to the problem of being, his inexorable research into even the most embarrassing of discoveries, and his iron will were the elements that predestined him to become the most important psychologist and philosopher of his day. This tireless pursuit held the danger of placing too heavy a burden on him, a fact borne out when the *numinous* took possession of his personality.

He was not destined to savor his own fame. The end of his life was overshadowed by the incomprehension that

271

greeted his work and the torment of his own isolation. Only after his death, at the turn of the century, was interest displayed in his work and personality. After the first wave of enthusiasm had died down, the excitement passed on to further groups. There was hardly a literary or philosophical figure alive who did not fall under the spell of his thought and become forced to respond.

The radical manner in which he tore down spiritual values was not, however, sufficient to provide the necessary impetus for constructing a new world view. Nietzsche devoted all his energy to positing problems, but neither discovered their cause and basis, nor achieved a systematic presentation of his major concept of the 'will to power.' Yet, this does not detract from his invaluable contribution in stirring his contemporaries from their comatose state. His work represents an heroic accomplishment of the spirit that had to be atoned for: his Promethean theft of light was purchased at the cost of madness.

Equally creative as his questions about the roots of being and existence was Nietzsche's (prophetic) vision of the future. Thanks to his sensitive awareness of archetypal patterns in contemporary history, he not only anticipated important developments in the sciences – in particular, psychology, – but also political events of the ensuing hundred years. Although his political visions largely presaged what was soon to follow in National-Socialist Germany, existing evidence clearly shows that he had no direct influence on the currents of this movement. Nietzsche's opposition to socialism and nationalism,[2] as well as to anti-Semitism, serve to weaken any assertion of this sort still more. It was hardly his fault that disaffected minds and political opportunists sometimes drank at the same archetypal sources.[3]

2 See p. 241.
3 See p. 89ff. Thomas Mann is absolutely correct when he writes that it was "the most crude of all misunderstandings to mistake the Nazi incursion for Nietzsche's dream of barbarian cultural renewal." Mann: op. cit. p. 257.

What were his basic ideas?

As one of the sharpest critics of the end of last century, he attacked, with an extreme and surprising intensity, the principles of the European world view, based as it was on Plato and Christianity. Even in his earliest works, he appealed for a *renewal of culture* that rested on *affirming the irrational roots* of existence. As a follower of Schopenhauer and Wagner, he found, in music and in myth, a sphere of art that opened up the "Dionysian womb of the world," and with it, the primordial desire for, and suffering from, the tragedy of life. As early as this, his polemic was directed against Socratic rationalism and its denial of instinct, while also containing sharp criticism of the Christian negation of life and its notion of redemption.

In the *Untimely Meditations*, Nietzsche's affirmation of life emerged even more clearly. The inclinations of his age towards historicism and intellectualism he confronted with the idea of the unity of life, thought and willpower as epitomized by the culturally significant individual, the genius. *All spiritual considerations derived from life itself.* This was the first time he assumed the mantle of the untimely critic admonishing the cultural shortcomings of his age – both the decline of educational and scientific institutions and the "malady of history" of his times. With great intensity, he exposed the striking gulf between knowledge and culture, history and life, an insight that would leave a decisive mark on his later investigations. Nevertheless, at this stage his faith in the values of his age remained intact. Schopenhauer, whom he admired for educating mankind in truthfulness, was still his great model.

All the more surprising, then, was the complete about-turn in Nietzsche's attitude: a worsening of his health, doubts about his profession in Basle and, finally, profound disillusionment with his idol, Richard Wagner, began to undermine the trust he had placed in the ideals of his times. In direct contradiction to his previous reliance on great models and idols, he was now seized by a spirit of independence that 'compelled' him to shake off his emotional fetters. Not yet thirty-three, he made it his mission to criticize the bourgeois world-order in its entirety. A fanatical devotion to the truth overtook him and forced him to reconsider conventional value-systems. Supported by his friend, Paul Rée, whose experiments in freethinking he followed up, Nietzsche began to subject the ideals of his age to rigorous criticism. It became his most urgent concern to uncover the mendacious and false spirit of ideal constructs,[4] as well as the moral prejudices of his times.[5] He started by tracing the motivations unconsciously concealed behind the ideals, discovering first vanity and then the need for power as the essential drives. His struggle with bourgeois values and the *bourgeoisie* in general amounted to an assault upon the Christian moral attitude. One of Nietzsche's most useful achievements was to draw attention to the self-deceptions that lay behind guiding moral principles. His discovery that values were actually and decisively motivated by emotions and affects was revolutionary. He ascertained that it was life values that were of primary importance: not Christian ideals, but drives and instincts – an 'instinctive morality' – were what steered both ethical judgments and the recognition of the truth. This was a total reversal of the traditional way of looking at things. Nietzsche had gradually evolved from a moral philosopher into more than just a life psychologist; he had become a depth psychologist and replaced the contemporary rational world view with one that focused on vital, emotional and affective elements. Last, but not least, dreams and the imagination received new significance as a result of his realization that they contained a great deal of meaning for mankind as a whole. Nietzsche's epoch-making accomplishment was to highlight the fundamental importance of the instinctual unconscious[6] in understanding the intellectual processes, for

4 See p. 41.
5 See p. 49f.
6 See p. 53.

which he can be accredited with having pioneered depth psychology.

The juggernaut could no longer be stopped. From discovering the motivations on which ideals were based, Nietzsche proceeded to investigate moral prejudice. The work, *Human All-Too-Human,* had upset his contemporaries, but now he went on to question the values of truth, goodness, justice and brotherly love, dissecting traditional moral bias in a far more trenchant fashion. The demands he placed on mankind for absolute honesty in valuation and self-knowledge were, perhaps, the most unreasonable requests possible, of which the reactions of his contemporaries made him most painfully aware.

Further psychological discoveries followed in quick succession. The first was the role of the dark side, the shadow of man, as the constant companion of the seeker of light. It was not only the small, everyday things that foiled high expectations, but, above all, the inclinations of the individual and the collective to base their values on considerations of security and power. That even love itself was dominated by the demon 'power' belonged to his most 'repugnant' assertions. His criticism of the ideals and moral prejudices of the time culminated in his insight that both the as yet unchallenged universality of Christian morals and the objectivity of truth rested on false premises. In view of the fact that mankind's every drive, moral and intellectual, was directed by unconscious, instinctive impulses, he was given no choice but to propose the *relativity of values.* At the time of *The Dawn,* his intuition was already telling him that there was *neither absolute morality nor absolute truth.*

For Nietzsche, discovering the instinctual roots of the human spirit was tantamount to acknowledging the basic *emotionality* of all valuing and knowing. It meant a release from the limitations imposed on the accessibility of truth by prevailing theories of knowledge: truth, in Nietzsche's eyes, was not strict obedience to logical rules, but something involving the whole human being as part of the mystery of the living. Such an insight levelled the path towards a transformation of the classical theory of knowledge derived from Kant.

All of these disclosures stand together as a well-aimed blast at the positivistic theories of knowledge of his epoch. His observation that *life* is the main condition of the spiritual was a pioneering achievement with decisive ramifications for the future direction depth psychology was to take. Despite this fact, it still does not form an acknowledged part of today's pedagogies.

It is no surprise that Nietzsche fell seriously ill as a result of his exhausting intellectual activity. Once he had recovered from his physical collapse, he was, more than ever, an affirmer of life, praising it as a good that transformed everything into light and flame.[7] Life became for him a "means of knowledge," and he was overpowered by a "love of fate," the saying "to live and laugh gaily" being his motto from then on.

The time that followed was one of the most fateful phases of his life. It is from this that we have the historical picture of Nietzsche: Nietzsche as the proclaimer of the death of God and the 'eternal recurrence' of the earthly. The consequence of these two visions, in which Zarathustra announced his presence, was a remarkable upturn in Nietzsche's creativity.

With the activation of Zarathustra – an ancient symbol of spiritual creative power within Nietzsche – in the form of an inner companion, a deep source of inspiration was opened up. The new spirit, obvious from the start of the work, would never release its hold on Nietzsche. For the first time, he surrendered to a consciousness of his mission and the belief that fate had provided him with a duty to fulfill. The effect on the condition of his soul was also partly a consequence of his short but intense relationship with Lou von Salomé, and partly of the death of his long-term idol, Richard Wagner. Creative powers were set free in him, and he was demonically captivated by the need to harness them.

7 See p. 65f.

Zarathustra's merciless proclamation that God was dead[8] made clear the breach with the view of the world held in the past. Since the French Revolution the belief in God and moral absolutes had been weakened, but now these and the notion of a universal truth were given the final deathblow. Although such ideas had been in the air, it was inevitable that Nietzsche's direct questioning of God's existence would strike very much at the heart of the self-satisfied spirit of an age whose ideas of culture revolved around stale Christian ideals. Nietzsche also feared the reception his gospel of a new, law-giving overman and his message of the 'eternal recurrence' would get from his fellow men. Did they have the strength to withstand the lost promise of a redemptive afterlife, in other words, a world without God?

*Thus Spoke Zarathustra* is remarkable in many respects. In the form of spontaneous images and metaphors, it reveals a sequence of events that not only portrays the problems of the 19th century, but also anticipates the various processes of change and self-transformation Nietzsche himself would undergo. As such, it is, at the same time, the spiritual foundation on which the revolutionary complex of the "revaluation of values" – later addressed in the philosophical questioning of *Beyond Good and Evil* – was constructed. Three problem areas were sketched out: the questionability of morality, the reality of evil and the omnipresence of the 'will to power.' With each individual question, Nietzsche touched on pressing complexes of his age. It goes without saying that the radical and pointed nature of his analysis of these problems considerably alienated his contemporaries.

In relativizing traditional moral values, Nietzsche was principally attacking the Christian emphasis on the afterworld, the kingdom of God and absolute ideals. He opposed these with the reality of the body and the secular world, and especially with the integrity of the individual.

8 See p. 84.

His unswerving search for the meaning and goal of a human existence devalued by ecclesiastical Christianity led him to realize both the significance of self-fulfillment and the indispensability of the godlike gift of creativity.[9] By *advancing the creative process,* attaining new cultural values and creating the overman, he expected nothing less than to renew occidental culture and enter a new aeon. His point of departure was the human body: as the creative "belly of being" and embodiment of worldly values it not only contained reason and will, but also embraced every living function. By taking it seriously, an essential step towards the overman is made.

Nietzsche saw the Dionysian spark as inspiring creative formation; that same spark he had already celebrated in *The Birth of Tragedy.* The key to the enhancement of life and creativity was the Dionysian mystery of reproduction and transformation. Immersed in the light of Dionysus – in contrast to the contemporary cult of the intellect, – he first became aware of the overwhelming experience of the living spirit. And, indeed, it was through the deep distress of the creative human being that he discovered the two faces of the 'spirit': both its enchanting beauty and its icy coldness. This plight also exposed to him the clash between creating and being created within oneself. Insofar as the spirit acts as the creative hammer, it is experienced as the triumphant giver of form; when it is the anvil, the individual becomes the sacrificial animal of fate.

Through his examination of creative shaping, Nietzsche also recognized the need to *revalue the values of good and evil hitherto held.*[10] What he had in mind was to free the dark shadow side of the human soul from the prison that separated it from consciousness. The creative process, that is to say, the progressive voyage of exploration into the secret of being human, therefore included not only the values of good, but those of darkness and evil as well. Being a process that embraced propagation and annihilation, it was

9 See p. 120.
10 See p. 122f.

constantly both good and evil. Totally revolutionary was Nietzsche's conviction that such a process of development, towards both the individual self and the overman, meant that *what the collective condemned as 'evil' was actually the force of renewal.* As with his questioning of the old concept of morality, here Nietzsche was standing on thin ice. His thesis, whereby what had been good was now evil, and evil now new and good, was one that, when unthinkingly applied, could be dangerous. The Second World War has provided us with sufficient evidence of what can happen when 'evil' is seen as a fundamentally progressive impulse and men surrender themselves blindly to violence.

Although Nietzsche was right in recognizing the corrective influence self-overcoming could have when instinctual impulses encroached on one another, he gave too little consideration to the uncontrollable force those impulses possessed once unleashed. His point of departure concerned the idea of willing and creating and, as such, promised much; and yet, it was inevitable that the *motive of power* underlying all creative formation could become the cause of dangerous excesses. Whenever the motive of increasing power[11] and gaining superiority dominated human affairs, it fell under the sway of evil. Blinded by a myth of strength and power that compensated for his physical weakness, Nietzsche developed a psychology of power that was not only easy to misunderstand, but also, given its associations with evil, highly disturbing. Fascinated by those characteristics of greed, envy and the desire to dominate tarnished as vices by the collective, Nietzsche overlooked how threatening an attitude could be that interpreted the power motive as absolute and autonomous. In such cases, the individual abandoned his capacity for reflection and control and surrendered fully to the despotism of the instinctual sphere. Nietzsche's increasingly dark view of mankind allowed him to ignore this danger, though perhaps not willfully.

11 See p. 185.

279

Neither did his metaphysical extension of the concept of power to cover all things that existed, or that were engaged in the process of becoming, change anything. His now famous saying: "This world is the world of power and nothing besides,"[12] was a generalization that not only lacked ethical content, but was also misleading.

Moreover, the problem of the hierarchy of mankind was itself seriously intensified[13] by the appeal for increased power and violence. Nietzsche's *perspective of power and impotence* inevitably led, in social terms, to the glorification of a dominant class comprising the strong and powerful. In representing this attitude, he established the means for politically influential personalities to exploit his work for destructive propaganda purposes. It is, therefore, less than surprising that Nietzsche's cult of the strong man should have attracted many unsavory elements.

The greatest misunderstandings centered around Nietzsche's unfortunate fascination for the "blond beast." What he had actually intended in his Dionysian enthusiasm was – apart from a dig at German aggression – to glorify the primitive, original barbarity inherent in man.[14] By reactivating this he represented the utopian hope of rejuvenating the human species, a premise on his part that can only be explained, and hardly justified, by Nietzsche's hermit-like existence of total isolation from the world.

Nietzsche's psychological analysis of the confrontation with evil likewise belongs to his more dubious doctrines, especially his call to realize the reverse of what is judged by the collective to be good.[15] His conviction that the aspects of existence rejected by the collective were always the truest features of the human being was particularly strange when one thinks of how considerate and responsible he was to his friends. He demanded, above all else, that the evil he saw as the best part of man should be incorporated without

12  See p. 189.
13  See p. 202f.
14  See p. 205.
15  See p. 113.

further ado into reality. Such a demand was not only open to misinterpretation, it also represented a divergence from his normally ethical standards of behavior which would have grave consequences. Even if evil does have a certain importance in situations where it presents the only possibility the individual has of *reassimilating expended powers,* any dealings with it must be pursued with the utmost caution. But *extracted as an absolute from the psychic whole* without regard to the given circumstances, and applied to them *unconsciously and uncritically,* such a blind realization of evil could only end up destroying human society. Errors of this sort make obvious what little conception Nietzsche had of the reality of day-to-day life. The extent of his divorce from the real world made him unaware of the fact that realizing the evil drives must also entail the involvement of the 'good powers' within the soul. This would facilitate *the conscious separation of good and evil, reinforcing them within the greater whole.* Nietzsche's blind spot regarding the necessary existence of good not only made it impossible for him to experience good and evil objectively, it also barred any recognition of *the indispensability of an ethical basis to self-development.*[16] In his fundamentally narcissistic attitude, he inexcusably forgot that man also has a responsibility to others and not just to himself. On the strength of such an unrealistic outlook, even the positive aspects of his nascent psychology of evil have to be considered misleading.

In spite of our reservations, we must acknowledge Nietzsche's unfailing intuition of how *important it was to examine the unconscious and its evil* at a time when psychology was still the poor relation of science. Amongst the most valuable of his achievements was to recognize that any one-sidedness in the conscious mind – whether in reference to what is good or to what is perfect – always involved impulses from the reverse side. He knew that love and hatred, gratitude and vengeance, the 'Yes' and the 'No'

16  See p. 210f.

were determined in relation to one another. It is, therefore, all the more incomprehensible that he chose to ignore such insights as, for example, the constant presence of good in dealings with evil, in his psychology of evil.

Despite the embarrassment and widespread silence that greeted Nietzsche's radical formulations, the catastrophic experiences of the First and Second World Wars forced the issue of the psychology of evil. Thus Freud felt compelled to inquire into the question of the destructive instinct in man and his inborn inclination towards evil at the start of the 1930's.[17] C.G. Jung's investigations of individuation also led him to devote increased attention to evil and its role in the process of development.[18]

Quite apart from his criticism of morality, Nietzsche had a lifelong fascination for the problem of truth, a problem central to the occidental conception of the world. His concept of truth began with the definition of it as a metaphysical entity in itself, subsequently passing through various stages of negation until the very concept itself was denied. The first stage resulted from Nietzsche's opposition to the positing of absolutes and involved the *relative* and subjective nature of truth. As a consequence of making knowledge dependent on instinctive impulses, and because of the lack of a world-order and its value-system, any judgments that were made often proved to be false. However, he could not completely deny their effectiveness in preserving mankind. Though at first disappointing, gradually a positive side to this insight emerged in the shape of Nietzsche's pioneering discovery of the *perspectivism of knowledge,*[19] which would eventually lead to an extensive reconsideration of the conventional assessment of being. What previously had been regarded as an objectively valid statement, Nietzsche now saw in terms

17  See Freud: *Das Unbehagen in der Kultur,* Ges. W. vol. XIV (S.E. vol. 21).
18  C.G. Jung: *Psychologie und Alchemie,* Ges. W. vol. 12 (C.W. vol. 12).
19  See p. 176.

of *an individual interpretation of meaning* determined by the current state of an individual's instincts. It thus had all the qualities of a projection. For Nietzsche, the great value of this new outlook lay in the added depth and variety it acquired from including human feelings and experiences. In short: 'the more eyes, the more complete the view'! The perspectivistic viewpoint would later prove fruitful to psychology and psycho-pathology, since it permitted a greater understanding of the individual situation of the patient, his memory failures, his motivations and his complexes.[20]

Rather than content himself with the recognition that truth was relative, Nietzsche urged himself on to question the possibility of knowing anything of truth at all. His testing of the idealistic foundations of truth took him so far that he ended up unmasking it as an erroneous and illusory concept. This initially radical-sounding assertion rested on his conviction that every statement of truth concerning empirical reality must entail a more or less conscious belief in a metaphysical quantity 'in itself' existing as a timeless and universally valid ideal. Such a belief necessarily impaired the objective contemplation of a world in constant flux. As a result, judgments were so gravely impeded that they could be nothing more than the expression of lies and fictions[21] – a reckless generalization on Nietzsche's part. Even granted that Nietzsche correctly foresaw the progressive tendency to relativize truth – since confirmed by the discovery of acausal links between physical phenomena and the development of probability theory, – his claim that this totally invalidated the authority of truth is inconclusive. His statements are eminently contestable in that they are *irresponsible* enough to lend credence to the meaninglessness and purposelessness of life, thereby focusing on the nihilistic tendencies in mankind's existence. This declaration of the nullity of truth, when approached in terms of the core complex that generated it, signified the

20 See p. 180f.
21 See p. 217f.

ultimate consequence of the death of God and the loss of related universal truths. It ended with him disavowing occidental faith in the prerogative of the spirit in particular, and the dignity of man in general. The conclusion he drew neither delineated the problem of truth nor made any inner distinctions.

This anarchic, urgent inclination to abolish the truth was only one side of Nietzsche's profound personality. For another, mystical side of his being, *truth remained an unfathomable secret,* identical with the Dionysian source of existence.[22] He only aired this secret in the course of his mystical experiences. Otherwise, he continued to apply the philosophical concept of truth to 'the world.'

Although Nietzsche's philosophical statements on truth run deep, the net sum of his research is rather disappointing. Apart from the actual striving for truthfulness itself, the question remains as to what meaning was left to human existence once all of mankind's ideals, morals and truths had been declared void. The final conclusion has a certain grotesqueness, since the only justificatory meaning of life that Nietzsche acknowledges is the bare fact of human willing. This factor is further restricted to the notion of willing one's own future,[23] a premise – as Nietzsche himself emphasized – that ultimately revealed the meaning of the celebrated will to truth as a "concealed will to death."[24] From a logical point of view, one might also ask whether Nietzsche's belief in having proved the invalidity of truth through his striving for the truth was not itself a circular argument. The Sophists had been only too aware of how deceptive such a conclusion was.

Even the pain he felt at the destructive consequences of abolishing any claim to truth did not divert him from his own path. His iron will to overcome himself enabled him to reach a new evaluation of art.[25] Insofar as the artist in him

22 See p. 221.
23 See p. 220.
24 See p. 218.
25 See p. 218.

had a say, he acknowledged both the healing and blessing that art brought to man. What he particularly appreciated in art was its directness and spontaneity, its "singing of the soul." Its very capacity to devote itself fully to deception and illusion in a most unscientific way predestined it for the role of the legitimate guardian of lies and appearances. Without the slightest claims to truth, art represented a genuine manifestation of the will to form, albeit a deeply irrational one. Was this confession of Nietzsche's a sign of that very power to transform he had depicted as part of the Dionysian mysteries in *The Birth of Tragedy?* It is a fact that, as his writing progressed, the mystical side gradually gained in importance. Yet, at the same time, it also left behind an embarrassing impression of barrenness in his work, the outward indication of his slow withdrawal into himself. On the one hand, Nietzsche repeated his rebellion against the nihilistic decay of values, suggesting wholly unrealistic solutions to overcome the imminent crisis; on the other, he fled into his inner world.

Thus, in *Twilight of the Idols,* he undertook a desperate *spiritual battle against the lie* in human existence that devalued the worldly in favor of ideals, a lie that originated in the dominance of the old idols, "God, truth and morality." Nietzsche's words had something of a 'declaration of war' about them, including their overstrained want of concreteness. His one practical suggestion – that of attaining a reversal of nihilistic tendencies by willfully intensifying them, thereby initiating a new aeon – was totally unrealistic. He transferred what had frequently been his own experience of illness – sudden recovery at the very point of utter hopelessness – to the collective situation of man in such a way as to demonstrate that he was no longer cognizant of reality. In his fascination for the strong man he expected the arrival of the godlike human being[26] of the future to instigate a miracle that would overcome the crisis, freeing mankind from the impending collapse of values. This man

26  See p. 234.

of the future, as he had already stressed, was bound to come and return both hope to man and a goal to the world, thus proving himself "the victor over God and nothingness."[27] In his enthusiasm for the idea that such 'great men' received their wisdom by reverting to mythic prehistory, Nietzsche became ecstatically immersed in himself. In this state of trance, the pressure imposed by his fears for the future allowed him to experience as an overpowering vision the presence of the god, Dionysus, and the regenerative power of the mystery of eternal life.[28]

The feeling of joyous union with Dionysus and the fullness of power associated with it is, however, only one part of his personality. Another side of this happy religious experience was an inconsolable sensation of the void in himself whenever his relationship with the external world of men came into question. The contrast between his lack of contact with outer reality and his untimely thoughts, on the one hand, and the mystical attraction of the Dionysian, on the other, led to the increasing emergence of his inner duality.

It, therefore, comes as no surprise that the direct reaction to this feeling expressed in his works should be of a profoundly dualistic nature. Moods of defiant self-assertion and pretentious claims to greatness and glory tended to alternate with states of the most dismal despondency.

Thus, in *The Antichrist,* he gathered himself for his most vehement blow against the Christianity of Paul,[29] giving free rein both to his uncontrolled rage at Paul himself – a projection of his shadow power – and his bottomless bitterness about Christians in general. Free of all inhibition, he gave full vent to his loathing for Paul, whom he described as the "genius of hatred," to his contempt for the Christian hypocrite, and finally, to his grieving lament over the destruction of classical culture. *The Antichrist* ends with

27 See p. 222.
28 See p. 236.
29 See p. 242.

286

a terrible curse on Christianity.[30]

Equally unrealistic was Nietzsche's conviction that his work and existence were unique, which we read in *Ecce homo*. It culminated in him declaring the greatness and glory of his being, which he attributed to his "initiation by the god of mysteries," Dionysus. Both of his final writings are documents of his ultimate failure. The greatest possible happiness and the deepest mental distress were two aspects of one and the same center, his *suffering at the hands of mankind, the spirit of the age, and himself*. The task he seemed inwardly destined to perform, in a collection of works he imagined would cover all the basic principles of his worldview, was finally too much for him, as well as being beyond the capacities of his time. Neither his spiritual power to create, nor the objective state of contemporary science and research were sufficient to fulfill his considerable philosophical demands.

His declaration of *amor fati* was an attempt to overcome his desperate position,[31] that is, the unconditional acceptance of fate, both in the form of a painful suffering of destiny and of a painful mastery of it. It combined as one the logically incompatible opposites of the sacrificial animal and the triumphant hero, albeit only for a few moments and always in a state of mystical absorption.

These trances enabled him to experience as inner reality what he had intuitively anticipated in Zarathustra's speeches, in which the symbol of the child appeared as holy affirmation.[32] It revealed itself to him as the mystical goal of the search for God and the self. *He was never granted the sight of God as a conscious experience and was thus denied the opportunity of bridging his duality.* Madness brought his search to a premature close.

His failure was evident in the gradual way in which his conscious personality was overpowered by a second, unconscious one within his soul.

30  See p. 253.
31  See p. 260.
32  See p. 93.

Given Nietzsche's shocking fate, it seems superfluous to ask whether his mental breakdown was the product of a narcissistic disorder, hubris, an obsession with power or the first signs of an organic, cerebral sickness (progressive paralysis). In all probability, it resulted from a combination of the diseased psychical and physiological components of his existence. His conscious life undoubtedly ended when his personality rejected external reality and sank gradually back into his inner world, or in other words: when his ego became overshadowed by a second, unconscious personality. His visions, his prophetic presentiments and the accumulation (after *Zarathustra*) of his mystical possession all bear witness to the inner activation of this second personality within. The fate of his soul, already prefigured in *Zarathustra* (by the image of the buffoon – Zarathustra's mysterious opponent – jumping over the tightrope walker), was to turn into reality. The dark, hidden side of his being gained the upper hand. The breakdown manifested itself in the fateful episode with the Turin cab horse.[33] Nietzsche's soul died before his body.[34]

If we ask ourselves, in retrospect, what Nietzsche's outstanding and pioneering contributions were to philosophy and psychology, then first consideration must go to the way he stung his contemporaries into reflection and awareness. As no other before him, he drew mankind's attention to the *imminent crisis of culture and demise of all values*. Yet it was principally the loss of the highest value until then, the death of God Himself (by which he always meant the death of the Old Testament God), that his contemporaries were made to feel most. For it had the additional effect of undermining the absolute claims made for the values of morality and truth, as well as pointing forward to a decline in the preponderance of consciousness and reason. By demonstrating that crises were looming, he hoped to set forces in motion that would defeat them. His clairvoyant predictions and prophecies about the struggles to dominate

33 See p. 265f.
34 See p. 91.

288

the earth and the terrible wars they would entail went in the same direction.

Yet Nietzsche was not able to provide mankind with an image of the world that could exorcise the threat of a cultural crisis. Indeed, he himself expected the change to come from a sudden reversal of a slow build-up of nihilism, instead of trusting to active intervention of any sort. He was waiting for a nadir to arrive that would necessitate transforming man into the overman. However, though the prospect of a man "beyond good and evil," a godlike redeemer, was one that promised much, it was nothing more than an unrealizable and utopian vision of a future legislator and powerful upholder of culture, whom Nietzsche thought would shape the world in the image of antiquity and unify the cosmos as one. It was essentially this notion of the 'great man' that prevented him from seeing the full consequences of his criticism of western rationalism.

Notwithstanding this, the image of Nietzsche remained inscribed on the memory of mankind. It is not his attempts to solve the problems of his age that are associated with his name, but the flashes of intuition with which he illuminated the complex of problems surrounding the modern era, and especially the twentieth century. In searching for himself and the essential core of his being, he experienced, as in a mirror, the reflection of the cultural troubles of his times, manifest in discontinuity and a loss of direction. It is characteristic of Nietzsche's personality that, in addition to being a martyr of his fanatical devotion to truth, he should also be the victim of the age in which he was living. His predictive capacity allowed him to foresee the catastrophic confusion resulting from mankind's bondage to the demon of power. The battles fought between western and eastern powers in the twentieth century bear open testimony to how close his visions came to reality.

Today, as in Nietzsche's day, the *problematical area of nihilism* and, above all, the question of how to defeat and overcome it, is still very much with us. Mankind is confronted to a greater degree than ever before with the tormenting challenge of whether, or how, the wheel of world history could be given a positive turn.[35]

As far as I can see, nihilistic disaster can only be avoided through a radical transformation of man as a whole. As long as the highest value is projected onto the outside and into the future, it loses its direct appeal to man, both in the way it takes effect, and in the way it is affected. To overcome the notion of 'nothingness,' a life-affirming 'something' is needed that the soul can grasp hold of and use to counter the dissipating forces of anarchy. This is even more important if the individual does not generally possess the strength to tolerate the declaration that values and ideals are void without something to stimulate his own vitality and energy. It is all too easy for him to be seduced by religious surrogates. Whenever he thinks he can resist the concept of nothingness, he is a victim of his own self-deception, since he is secretly being driven to an unconscious instinctual goal. In place of the concept of the God he has denied, he falls prey to another power, whether it be sexuality, money, success or drugs – all of them substitutes affording temporary satisfaction, but long-term disillusionment and emptiness of the soul.

*A new symbol is needed* [36] to compensate in a meaningful way for the image of God that the collective regarded as

35 Karl Loewith's description of the state of transition mankind is currently undergoing makes interesting reading. "Nobody believes in the articles of faith anymore ... however, everyone lets everything carry on as before.... It is true that one no longer expects a Christian salvation through a just God sitting in judgment, yet one nevertheless tries, in the same sense, to come up with an earthly and political solution by means of social justice. One no longer believes in a kingdom of God to come, but still holds onto it in the form of a worldly utopia. One rejects Christian self-denial but still does not encourage natural self-assertion. One no longer believes in Christian marriage and the Christian state, but nothing prevents one from surrounding birth, matrimony and death with the appearance of Christian sanctification...." Karl Loewith, *Nietzsches Vollendung des Atheismus*.

36 See also H.K. Fierz: Ch. on 'Das verlorene Symbol' ('The Lost symbol') in *Die Psychologie C.G. Jungs und die Psychatrie*, p. 120ff (English edition forthcoming in *Daimon Verlag*).

indispensable and absolute. Such a religious renewal can only occur as *a mystery within the soul,* captivating the soul with its ineffable secret, whilst filling it with fear and anxiety.[37] It is man's privilege to relate consciously to the super-personal center within,[38] and then to incorporate it into his existence. It is unlikely that the nihilistic attitude of the individual could ever be transformed without him *consciously relating to this unconscious and inexpressible center.* Such a perspective on the creative core within the soul would bring us closer to the unfathomable *secret of being oneself.* It assumes the ability to subtly distinguish the impulses of the mind, not only in the form of brilliant insights or intuitive presentiments, but also through the sensations of the body. It is not important whether we establish such inner contact by means of imagination, meditative absorption, by dream or fantasy, or whether we achieve it through pain or well-being. The fact is that such contact with the creative source of being opens up a new dimension, a new grasp of meaning. In religious terms, it may be expressed as a "window onto eternity"[39] revealing a deeper, transcendental dimension that allows the individual to participate in a "higher world-order" and put an end to his restless searching. What applies to the individual applies equally to mankind as a whole. The question of overcoming nihilism and of the human race surviving hinges on how we respond to the problem, first brought to our attention by Nietzsche, posed by the impending collapse of values.

Nietzsche's quest for himself leaves us no practical solution for defeating and transforming nihilism. In killing the old God and declaring the nullity of morality and truth, and in pinning all his hopes on a godlike overman, Nietzsche exhausted all his powers. He himself had never been capable of devotion to an image of God. Even his projection

37 A reference to Sören Kierkegaard.
38 C.G. Jung designated this super-personal center the "self." For him, it had the significance of a unifying symbol, a *coincidentia oppositorum.*
39 C.G. Jung, Ges. W. vol. IV/2, p. 244 (C.W. vol. 15, p. 473).

onto the redemptive power of the overman was rooted in the past, despite being placed in the future. Although he experienced the greatest fulfillment during his mystical moments of Dionysian lucidity, he could never fully subordinate himself to this god. At the bottom of his soul, as is evident from the final words of *Ecce homo,* he was always fascinated by the counterpole of the Crucified, even if it primarily stood as something to challenge and struggle with. It appears that the extraordinary tension between the Christian and Dionysian view of the world, which he expressed in the battle cry:

"Dionysus versus the Crucified,"

overshadowed his life and work to the very end.[40] He granted neither image of God the dignity of an absolute and totally central position. The Christian view of God lacked the ability to say 'Yes' to worldly life and nature, while the conception of Dionysus was untimely and unrealistic in respect of Nietzsche's conscious world. Although Nietzsche described himself as a disciple of Dionysus, he limited this description to the notion of this god as a mystical object of absorption. Not even the 'self' aspired to the highest value, even though he had praised it as the center of inwardness and self-becoming. For his idea of the self lacked any reference to the super-personal.

Nietzsche's great error lay in seeking to gain, by external projection both onto a legislator and onto a man of the future, what could only be experienced through an inner mystery of God and man. What he 'knew' as a result of his mystical experiences – the presence of a divine being – could not be accepted by his conscious ego. He remained ultimately unaware of the depth and extent of his religious problem. His unconscious captivity within the *logos* and his unrestrained 'will to power' stood in the way of any subordination to an inner authority wholly unrelated to the

40 See p. 264.

292

ego. His ego reserved the right of assuming the function of a godlike center. *In the struggle with 'God,' the ego proved itself the stronger power.* As early as *Zarathustra,* we discover the significant words:

> "... if there were gods, how could I endure not to be a god...."[41]

Nietzsche elevated himself to a god and assumed the attribute of absolute creative power. It is typical of the tragedy of his life that, despite a desperate search for the numinous core which held together the innermost source of the world, he should have failed in the most urgent of his concerns, the search for himself and for God.

41 Ges. W. vol. VI, p. 124; CM vol. 4, p. 110.

# BIBLIOGRAPHY

ADLER, Alfred: Über den nervösen Charakter, Wiesbaden 1912
ANDREAS-SALOMÉ, Lou: Friedrich Nietzsche in seinen Werken, 1894
ANDREAS-SALOMÉ, Lou: Lebensrückblick, Insel-Verlag 1951, hg. von Ernst Pfeiffer
ANDREAS-SALOMÉ, Lou: In der Schule bei Freud, Hans Huber-Verlag, Bern, 1968
ANDREAS-SALOMÉ, Lou: Sigmund Freud/Lou Andreas-Salomé, Briefwechsel, Frankfurt am Main, S. Fischer, 1966
ASSOUN, Paul-Laurent: Freud et Nietzsche, philosophie d'aujourd'hui, 1980

BAEUMLER, Alfred: Bachofen und Nietzsche, Zürich, 1929
BERTRAM, Ernst: Versuch einer Mythologie, Berlin, 1918
BURCKHARDT, Jakob: Weltgeschichtliche Betrachtungen, Leipzig, 1925

CAMUS, Albert: L'homme révolté, Edition Gallimard 1951
CAPRA, Fritjof: Wendezeit, 4. Aufl., Scherz Verlag, Bern, München, Wien, 1983

DEUSSEN, Paul: Erinnerungen an Friedrich Nietzsche, F. A. Brockhaus, Leipzig 1901

ELLENBERGER, Henry, F.: Die Entdeckung des Unbewussten, Hans Huber Verlag Bern, Stuttgart, Wien, 1973

FIERZ, Heinrich Karl: Die Psychologie C. G. Jungs und die Psychiatrie, Daimon Verlag, Zürich, 1982
FOERSTER-NIETZSCHE, Elisabeth: Das Leben Friedrich Nietzsches, Leipzig, C. G. Naumann, 1895
FOERSTER-NIETZSCHE, Elisabeth: Der junge Nietzsche, Kröner Verlag, Leipzig
FREUD, Sigmund: Ges. W. Imago Publishing Co Ltd
Bd. II/III Traumdeutung, Bd. IV. Psychopathologie des Alltagslebens, Bd. XIV Selbstdarstellung
FREY-ROHN, Liliane: Das Böse in psychologischer Sicht, in: Studien aus dem C. G. Jung-Institut Zürich, Rascher-Verlag, 1961
FRIEDELL, Egon: Kulturgeschichte der Neuzeit, Bd. 1 und 2, Verlag dtv, 1976

HEIDEGGER, Martin: Nietzsche, Vorlesungen
Nietzsches Wort: Gott ist tot in: Holzwege, Klostermann, Frankfurt am Main, 1980
HEINEMANN, Fritz: Neue Wege der Philosophie, Quelle und Meyer, Leipzig, 1929
HILLEBRAND, Bruno: Nietzsche und die deutsche Literatur, Deutscher Taschenbuchverlag, 1978

JAMES, William: The varieties of religious experience, Longman, Green & Co, New York, London, Toronto, 1952
JANZ, Curt Paul: Nietzsche, Carl Hanser Verlag München, Wien, 1978
JASPERS, Carl: Nietzsche, W. de Gruyter & Co, 3. Aufl. 1950
JOEL, Karl: Nietzsche und die Romantik, Jena und Leipzig, 1905
JONES, Ernest: Das Leben und Werk von Sigmund Freud, The Hogarth Press, London 1956

Jung, Carl Gustav: Ges. W. Rascher Verlag Zürich, Bd. VI, VII, IX/2, X, XI, unveröffentlichtes Seminar über: Also sprach Zarathustra 1934–1939

Kaufmann, Walter: Nietzsches Einstellung gegenüber Sokrates (1950/68) in: Wege der Forschung, Bd. 521. Wissenschaftliche Buchgesellschaft, Darmstadt, 1980

Kaufmann, Walter: Nietzsche, Philosopher, Psychologist, Antichrist, Princeton University Press, 1974

Kerényi, Karl: Mythologie der Griechen, Rhein Verlag, Zürich, 1951

Klages, Ludwig: Der Geist als Widersacher der Seele, Leipzig, 1937. Die psychologischen Errungenschaften von Nietzsche, Ambrosius Barth Verlag, Leipzig, 1930

Lange-Eichbaum, Wilhelm: Genie, Irrtum und Ruhm, Ernst Reinhardt Verlag, München/Basel, 1956

Loewith, Karl: Kierkegaard und Nietzsche, Vittorio Klostermann Verlag, Frankfurt am Main, 1933

Loewith, Karl: Nietzsches Philosophie der ewigen Rückkehr des Gleichen, Felix Meiner, Hamburg, 3. Aufl., 1978

Loewith, Karl: Nietzsches Vollendung des Atheismus, in Steffen: Nietzsche, Werk und Wirkungen, Vandenhoek & Ruprecht, Göttingen, 1974

Mann, Thomas: Nietzsches Philosophie im Lichte unserer Erfahrungen, in: Thomas Mann: Essays, Bd. 3, No. 980

Montinari, Mazzino: Nietzsche lesen, Walter de Gruyter, Berlin, 1982

Nietzsche, Friedrich: Ges. W. Bd. I–Bd. XVI, Alfred Kröner Verlag, Leipzig
Bd. I:       Die Geburt der Tragödie, 1870
             Unzeitgemässe Betrachtungen, 1873–76
Bd. II:      Menschliches, Allzumenschliches, Bd. 1, 1876–1878
Bd. III:     Menschliches, Allzumenschliches, Bd. 2, 1877–1879
Bd. IV:      Morgenröte, 1880–81
Bd. V:       Die Fröhliche Wissenschaft, 1881–1882
Bd. VI:      Also sprach Zarathustra, 1883–1885
Bd. VII:     Jenseits von Gut und Böse, 1885–1886
             Zur Genealogie der Moral, 1887
Bd. VIII:    Der Fall Wagner, Götzendämmerung, Nietzsche contra Wagner,
             Umwertung aller Werte, (Antichrist) Dichtungen 1888
Bd. IX–Bd. XVI: Nachgelassene Werke aus den Jahren 1869–88
Bd. IX:      1872–76, Bd. X: 1872–76, Bd. XI: 1875–81
Bd. XII:     1881–86, Bd. XIII: 1882–88
Bd. XIV:     1883–88
Bd. XV:      Ecce homo, Wille zur Macht, 1888
Bd. XVI:     Wille zur Macht 1888
Nietzsche, Friedrich: Sämtliche Werke, Kritische Studienausgabe von Giorgio Colli und Mazzino Montinari, Bd. 1–15
Bd. 1:       Die Geburt der Tragödie
             Unzeitgemässe Betrachtungen I–IV
Bd. 2:       Menschliches, Allzumenschliches I und II
Bd. 3:       Morgenröte, Idyllen aus Messina, Die fröhliche Wissenschaft

Bd. 4:     Also sprach Zarathustra
Bd. 5:     Jenseits von Gut und Böse
Bd. 6:     Der Fall Wagner, Götzendämmerung. Der Antichrist. Ecce homo.
           Dionysos-Dithyramben. Nietzsche contra Wagner
Bd. 7–13: Nachgelassene Werke 1869–1889
           Bd. 7:   1869–1874, Bd. 8: 1875–1879. Bd. 9:1880–82
           Bd. 10: 1882–1884, Bd. 11: 1884–1885
           Bd. 12: 1885–1887, Bd. 13: 1887–1889
Bd. 14:   Einführung. Kommentar zu Bde. 1–13
Bd. 15:   Chronik zu Nietzsches Leben. Gesamtregister
NIETZSCHE, Friedrich: Der werdende Nietzsche, hg. von Elis. Förster-Nietzsche,
   Musarion Verlag, München, 1924
NIETZSCHE, Friedrich: Briefe, hg. von Richard Oehler, Inselverlag, Leipzig
NIETZSCHE, Friedrich: Briefe an Mutter und Schwester, Bd. I und II, hg. von
   Elis. Förster-Nietzsche
NIETZSCHE, Friedrich: Ges. Briefe, Schuster und Loeffler, Berlin und Leipzig
NIETZSCHE, Friedrich: Briefwechsel mit Peter Gast, Inselverlag, 1908
NIETZSCHE, Friedrich: Briefwechsel mit Franz Overbeck, Inselverlag, 1916
NIETZSCHE, Friedrich: Briefwechsel mit Erwin Rohde, Inselverlag, 1923
NIETZSCHE, Friedrich: Briefwechsel, Kritische Gesamtausgabe hg. von Giorgio
   Colli und Mazzino Montinari, W. de Gruyter, Berlin
NIGG, Walter: Friedrich Nietzsche in: Grosse Unheilige, Walter Verlag, Olten,
   1980
NINCK, Martin: Wodan und der germanische Schicksalsglaube
NOACK, Hermann: Friedrich Nietzsche, in: Die Philosophie Westeuropas. Benno
   Schwabe & Co, Basel–Stuttgart, 1962

OEHLER, Richard: Nietzsche-Register, Alfred Kröner Verlag, Stuttgart

PFEIFFER, Ernst: Briefwechsel zwischen Sigmund Freud und Lou Andreas-
   Salomé, S. Fischer Verlag, 1966
PFEIFFER, Ernst: Friedrich Nietzsche, Paul Rée und Lou v. Salomé, Dokumente
   ihrer Begegnung,
PODACH, Erich: Nietzsches Zusammenbruch, Kampmann Verlag, Heidelberg,
   1930
PODACH, Erich: Gestalten um Nietzsche, Erich Lichtenstein Verlag, Weimar,
   1932
PODACH, Erich: Notizbücher Nietzsches, Kampmann Verlag, Heidelberg, 1963
PUETZ, Peter: Thomas Mann und Nietzsche, in STEFFEN, Nietzsche, siehe dort

ROSS, Werner: Der ängstliche Nietzsche, Deutsche Verlagsanstalt, 1980
RUKSEN, Udo: Nietzsche in der Hispania, Francke Verlag, Bern und München,
   1962

SCHLECHTA, Karl: Friedrich Nietzsche in 6 Bänden, Carl Hanser Verlag, Mün-
   chen–Wien, 1980
SCHLECHTA, Karl: Der Fall Nietzsche: Aufsätze und Vorträge,
SCHOPENHAUER, Arthur: Die Welt als Wille und Vorstellung, Inselverlag, Leipzig
SEIDMANN, Peter: Die perspektivische Psychologie Nietzsches in: Die Psycholo-
   gie des 20. Jahrhunderts, Bd. I., p. 382

297

STEFFEN, Hans: Nietzsche, Werk und Wirkungen, Vandenhoek, Göttingen, 1974
Aufsätze von Karl Loewith, Peter Pütz und Hans Steffen
STEINER, Rudolf: Friedrich Nietzsche, Ein Kämpfer gegen seine Zeit, Dornach, 1926
Studien aus dem C. G. Jung-Institut Zürich, Bd. VII: Das Gewissen, Rascher Verlag

VAIHINGER, Die Philosophie des Als-Ob, Art: Der bewusst gewollte Schein bei Nietzsche, Verlag Felix Meiner, Leipzig, 1920
WOLFF, Hans: Friedrich Nietzsche, Der Weg zum Nichts, Francke Verlag, Bern, 1956

ZWEIG, Stefan: Der Kampf mit dem Dämon: Hölderlin, Kleist, Nietzsche, S. Fischer Verlag, 1951

# INDEX OF NAMES

# SUBJECT INDEX

**Meetings with Jung** is the first publication of personal diary entries made by British psychiatrist E. A. Bennet during his frequent visits in the household of Swiss analyst C. G. Jung during the last years of Jung's life, 1946–1961. The notes are at once deep, lively, serious and entertaining; an ideal introduction to Jung for the casual beginner, a warm and intimate addition to more scholarly works for advanced students of Jung.

ISBN 3-85630-501-7

**A Testament to the Wilderness** consists of ten international responses to a highly original paper by Swiss psychiatrist C. A. Meier. This colorful collection of authors views wilderness within and without, psychologically and ecologically, presenting a wealth of perspectives on an ancient – and at the same time eminently relevant – phenomenon.

Published with The Lapis Press.

ISBN 3-85630-503-3

# ENGLISH PUBLICATIONS BY **DAIMON**

*Meetings with Jung*, E.A. Bennet
*Life Paints its Span*, Susan Bach
*The Myth of Meaning*, Aniela Jaffé
*Was C.G. Jung a Mystic?* Aniela Jaffé
*From Freud to Jung*, Liliane Frey-Rohn
*Friedrich Nietzsche: A Psychological Study*, L. Frey-Rohn
*The Savage and Beautiful Country*, Alan McGlashan
*A Testament to the Wilderness*, Ed. by R. Hinshaw
*Talking with Angels*, (transcribed by Gitta Mallasz)
*Mourning: A Way to Renewal*, Verena Kast
*Imprints of the Future*, George Czuczka
*Healing Dream and Ritual*, C.A. Meier

Jungian Congress Papers:

Jerusalem 1983: *Symbolic and Clinical Approaches*
Ed. by Luigi Zoja, R. Hinshaw

Berlin 1986: *The Archetypal Shadow in a Split World*
Ed. by M.-A. Mattoon

---

*Available from your bookstore or from our distributors:*

*All territories*
Daimon Verlag
Am Klosterplatz
CH-8840 Einsiedeln
Switzerland
Tel. (55) 53 22 66

*Great Britain*
Element Books Ltd.
Longmead Shaftesbury
Dorset SP7 8PL
England
Tel. (0747) 51339

*Central USA*
Bookslinger
213 East Fourth St.
St. Paul, MN 55101
Tel. (612) 221 0429

*West Coast*
The Great Tradition
750 Adrian Way, Suite 111
San Rafael, CA 94903
Tel. (415) 492 9382